Stand in the Traffic

Stand in the Traffic

A Himalayan Adoption Story

Kate Saunders

Lake Dallas, Texas

Copyright © 2020 by Kate Saunders

All rights reserved. No part if this book may be reproduced, distributed, or transmitted in any form or by any means, including photocopying, recording, digital scanning, or other electronic or mechanical means, without prior written permission of the publisher. While all events of this memoir are true, individuals' names have been changed to protect their privacy.

FIRST EDITION
Printed in the United States of America

Requests for permission to reprint material from this work should be sent to:

> Permissions
> Madville Publishing
> P.O. Box 358
> Lake Dallas, TX 75065

Front Cover Photograph: Kathmandu, Shutterstock Royalty-Free License.
Cover Design: Jacqueline Davis
Photos courtesy of: Kate Saunders

ISBN: 978-1-948692-22-9 paperback, 978-1-948692-23-6 ebook
Library of Congress Control Number: 2019937659

For Dinesh and Leena

September

"Excuse me, madam . . . Excuse me."

I wake to a flight attendant leaning over my sleeping son with a handful of forms.

"Please fill these out before we arrive in Kathmandu," she says with smiling eyes and an Indian accent.

On the movie screen, a world map tracks the progress of our flight, only thirty miles to go. The plane drops and my stomach quivers as we descend into the Kathmandu Valley. Pressing my forehead against the porthole window, I expect to see saw-toothed ranges, but find billowing, cotton-ball clouds among rolling, velvet green mountains organized in a monsoonal waltz. The city is a hazy Legoland of ramshackle houses in yellows, blues, pinks and greens, hopscotched among traditional terracotta brick. I wonder how I'll ever manage to navigate the jigsaw lanes that run haphazardly through the jumbled dwellings. Images I've memorized from the *Lonely Planet* guidebook I've studied relentlessly melt away.

"Look, Jack, this is where we're going to live!" I grab my six-year-old son's arm.

"I see Mount Everest!" he squeals, pointing to a nondescript ripple of a foothill. The passengers around us chuckle as the plane turns, sweeping closer to the city. I look for the airport, anticipating the brilliance and magnitude of other capital cities we've passed through—Los Angeles, Osaka, and Bangkok. Instead, I spot a small, one-story muddy brown building, presumably the airport.

As we touch down, I'm stunned by the scene: a nation at war. When the U.S. State Department issued travelers warnings, citing political unrest and terrorist activity by the Maoist rebels, I'd perceived the risk to an American within Kathmandu to be trivial. The excitement of meeting my adoptive daughter overshadowed any fear, so I'd shrugged it off. Now, looking down the runway littered with military jeeps and helicopters, I'm smacked by the reality of the warning. Armed soldiers surround our plane and stand guard at the end of the rickety metal staircase unceremoniously rolled up to the cabin door. Without a familiar jetway, I'm suddenly nervous and surprised by my need for the comfort of first-world airport amenities. As we wobble down the stairs to the steaming tarmac, the soldiers gaze toward invisible points in the distance, taking no notice of me, Jack, or the big pink bunny strapped to his backpack. He'd purchased the bunny for a dollar at a yard sale (quite a bargain in his eyes), as a gift for his new little sister.

Like good sheep, we follow the other passengers to a dismal, near empty building. I'm disoriented without the usual airport landmarks: no bustling food court, no newspaper stand, no indoor-outdoor carpeting. The red-brown brick is feebly decorated with travel office posters of the region. Jack is elated when we pass a large brass effigy staring down from a pillar. He recognizes the Hindu elephant god Ganesh, Remover of Obstacles, like the one on my desk at home.

A small, grouchy man stuffed into a shrunken, paper-bag-brown uniform directs us to the appropriate line. We wait, though I'm not sure what for, and I quickly become irritated by the chaotic line, impatience rising inside me. I glance at the brass elephant god, and remember why I'm here, then take a deep breath and let the irritation melt away.

"Mommy, I need to go to the bathroom," Jack says.

"Well buddy, I think we have to get through this line first. Can you wait a little longer?" I look around for a restroom. "Is it number one or number two?" I whisper.

"I can wait. It's just number one." He sighs.

"This shouldn't take too long," I lie as I notice the sloth-like pace of the airport staff.

The queue inches forward until it's finally our turn. I'm puzzled by the rapid-fire questions from the men behind the counter, so I shake my head and offer a friendly smile as I hand over our forms and passports. The men chatter among themselves, apparently looking for something I'm missing. The Grouch returns, hands on hips, clearly disgusted, and motions for us to follow him. I scramble to gather our bags and summon Jack, too paranoid to let him out of my sight in this sea of strangers. We're led to a second counter where the Grouch snaps and snorts; his tone and gestures translate my shortcomings. As he turns to leave, the man behind counter number two smiles slightly and returns our passports. I ask him for a restroom, then bathroom, then toilet, and finally, he smiles brightly and directs us across the concrete building. As we turn to walk away, he says, "You very fortunate. You son is good luck." I thank him, smile, and shuffle on.

In the doorway of the bathroom, we find a woman in a dull beige sari on her hands and knees scrubbing the floor. Her hair is pulled back into a shiny knot at the nape of her neck. As I motion for Jack to enter the men's room, she glances up and I smile hesitantly. Her head drops back down as she continues to labor over the permanently stained tile. I think back to the chapter in my guidebook describing the caste system and try to wrap my mind around her status as an untouchable. Was this really her karmic lot in life? Or was it just bad luck? What cosmic circumstance had caused her to be down there and me to be up here?

Jack returns with a skip, visibly relieved, and we proceed down a flight of steps to collect our luggage. Unsure of what we would need for an undetermined amount of time in a foreign land, I'd continually added items to our luggage as I packed, so we are vastly overloaded. I search for where to collect our bags and spot some Buddhist monks from our flight. I assume they must know where to go, but then wonder, *Do monks even have any baggage to collect?*

I establish Jack in a safe location where I can see or presumably hear him scream as he is being carried off by the child bandits my over-cautious mother believes roam the airport. I spot our suitcases marching their way out on the conveyer belt. I'm almost done loading them onto a cart when a man appears out of nowhere, elbowing me aside to load the last few pieces. Then, palm out, he asks for something, but I don't understand. I hand him a few dollars, not really knowing why, and when he looks down at the bills, the look on his face tells me he doesn't find my offer to be as generous as I had and demands more. When I don't immediately comply, he loses his patience and begins violently pulling our bags off the cart. I hand him a couple more bills, and he stuffs them into his pocket, then gestures for us to follow. I stumble along, trying to keep up, calling over my shoulder to Jack as we step outside into the mob of waiting people.

"This is when we look for our name on a sign, right Mom?" Jack asks, clinging to my arm, a hint of panic in his tiny voice.

"Yeah, sweetie, you're right! I'm sure our ride is here to pick us up," I reply over-enthusiastically, but he frowns, seeing through my facade.

"Madam Saunders! Madam Saunders!" Out of the crowd comes a sparkling-clean, smiling, well-dressed man holding the coveted sign with our name on it. He hands me his Summit Hotel business card and explains that he has come to fetch us, then turns to Jack, and asks about our flight. I look around for the man with our bags, but he is nowhere to be seen. When we get to the van, our bags magically reappear and another man approaches demanding a tip. I look desperately to the gentleman from the hotel for guidance, but he casually glances the other way, deaf to my psychic plea.

"Hey, lady! You give tip! You give tip now!" The new porter yells, as he closes the space between us. Jack is already in the van, looking for a nonexistant seatbelt, so I acquiesce and offer up more cash, then quickly climb inside the van, ready to leave the chaos of the airport behind.

My romantic notions of resort-like beauty interspersed with temples and monks floating on enlightened clouds of bliss vanish as we drive through Kathmandu. We pass a shanty town of dirty shoeless children and mangy street dogs where vendors line the streets and seemingly abandoned construction abounds.

"Mommy! Look, there's a cow in the road! Look! There's another one!" Jack is nearly standing in his seat.

"Yeah, Jackie, the cows can go wherever they want here," I say, recognizing this is new and exciting for him, not frightening. "Here, cows are sacred, like Gods, so no one will harm them, or try to eat them. In Nepal, killing a cow is illegal."

"Wow! Cool!"

The hotel man chuckles while the driver dodges traffic, winding through endless roundabouts in a haphazard current of beeping taxis, motorbikes, and military trucks. I try not to watch as he turns directly into oncoming traffic to maneuver off the main thoroughfare. We drive up a winding corkscrew hill and pass another friendly plaster elephant, the doors of his cage open with marigolds blanketing his feet. The driver takes a sharp right turn into a tiny hidden drive where ferns peek out from between the cracks of moss-carpeted brick walls enclosing the puzzle-piece compound. I glance down at the *Wizard of Oz* charms dancing around my wrist and breathe a sigh of relief that this lush, emerald pocket is where our stay in Nepal will begin.

An entourage of charming staff appears to wrangle our voluminous luggage. Embarrassed by my unconscious extravagance, I stammer to explain we will be here for a long time as they strain to convert grimaces to kind smiles.

"*Namasté*, Madam Saunders, you are ready for your room?" a woman in a royal blue sari beams from behind the counter, placing her palms together in prayer position and bowing slightly. She points us in the right direction, and I'm amazed by the beauty of our surroundings.

I drink in the fragrance of the blooming gardens encircled by humble, two-story brick buildings. Slate footpaths meander from the lobby though the compound to the dining room, pool, gazebos, beauty parlor, and trinket shop. In our spacious room, we find twin beds with a small table between them, a dresser with a television perched on top, a sitting area with chairs and a table, a desk, and a bathroom. The men who brought our luggage already have the TV on and ask Jack if he likes cartoons. I thank them graciously, go to the phone, and pull a notebook out of my bag to find Annie's number.

Annie, an American, with two adopted Nepali children of her own, is the in-country facilitator for the stateside agency that is coordinating my international adoption. Her role is to guide adoptive parents through the paperwork process while in Nepal. My daughter-to-be, Devi, has been in foster care at Annie's home for the last few months along with several other children. Adoptions in Nepal are known to be exceptionally lengthy, requiring parents to make two trips to complete the adoption—one, at the beginning of the process to file paperwork, then another, months later, to sign documents after the file has been approved by the Ministry. Early on, I knew that once I met my daughter, I wouldn't be able to leave her, and I believed the sooner she was in my care, becoming part of our family, the better off she would be. I'd taken a chance and asked the agency if they would allow Devi to live with us if I stayed in the country to wait out the four-to-six-month process. I felt it was important for us to begin to bond before we all traveled back to America. Surprised by my commitment to my new daughter, they happily agreed. But then the phone call came:

"Hello, Ms. Saunders, unfortunately we have become aware of a problem with your application. Nepal will only allow a single woman to adopt if she is over 35 years of age," a woman from the adoption agency said in a slow, sober tone.

"Oh, I know. Since the process takes so long, by the time I'm through the queue, I'll be 35," I said confidently.

"Well, not exactly," she hesitated. "We have been informed that you cannot begin your application at the Central District Office until you are 35 or your file will be rejected," she paused, "Would you like to consider passing on the referral for this child and wait a bit longer until you are able to adopt?"

Pass on the referral? Able to adopt? My mind raced. "Well, this is all very surprising. I need to think about it," was all I could choke out.

She said she understood and would have Lauren, my caseworker, contact me as soon as possible.

Looking at the worn picture of Devi I'd carried with me since the referral, I was stunned that I could lose this little girl just because of my age. I'd sold my business, the house-sitters had moved in, our bags were packed, and our flight was set to leave within days. I wouldn't give up on her now.

Several frantic phone calls later, the trip was still on. Devi would still be permitted to live with us until the paperwork could be filed and the adoption processed, but with my birthday still five months away, our four-to-six-month stay had just doubled.

And now, we're here, and it's real. I'm about to meet my daughter.

I pick up the telephone and gingerly push the buttons. Although I've only spoken with Annie once on a conference call, her voice is familiar, and I feel comforted, like a baby bird being welcomed under a warm wing.

"Are you ready to meet your little girl?" She sings, excited for me. "I'll send Suraj right over. Ten minutes?"

I rustle around in our bags to find my camera and a couple of toys we brought. I'm jittery, unsure how to prepare for this epic meeting. I pull out a snack Jack's not interested in, but it satisfies my need to primp.

We scamper up the steps to wait outside the lobby until a funky blue wanna-be-Jeep turns down the drive. The well-dressed and polished Suraj opens a rusty door for us.

"Hello, Kate! Please, get in." He turns to Jack, "Are you excited to meet your little sister?"

"Yeah," Jack mutters. "Where's the seatbelt?"

"Oh, don't worry about it, Jackie, we're not going far. We can't wait to meet Devi," I say to Suraj. "We're tired, but excited . . ." I trail off, suddenly at a loss for words. Years of customer service small talk, and I have nothing to say. My senses are overwhelmed and I'm unsure how I will ever find my way through this maze of a city. Everything blends together with no discernible landmarks, street signs, or addresses. Kamikaze drivers muscle their way through the narrow streets, honking incessantly. There is so much to take in; it's impossible to grasp the big picture, like trying to make sense of a jigsaw puzzle when the pieces are first scattered from the box.

Too many twists and turns later, Suraj darts down a tiny lane and pulls up at a large blue metal gate. He honks, and a woman in a burgundy *kurta* with a jeweled *tika* on her forehead opens it and we drive through. Among the toys, bikes, and children, I spot Devi, sitting in a camp chair, clapping her hands with a grin so adorable I swallow hard, fighting to hold back the tears. Emotions bubble up from my heart like champagne to celebrate the occasion, and I fantasize that her glee is for me. The *didis*, Nepali for "big sister or nanny," have told her that her mommy is coming, but in reality, I know, the smile is for Suraj. Whatever her muse, the effect is the same. I am in love.

I try not to leap from the vehicle before it comes to a complete stop, the flight attendants' instructions still ring in my head. I grab my bag packed with party favors, take a deep breath and approach Devi. Before I know it, we are surrounded by children, *didis*, and now Annie as well, all encouraging Devi to come see her "mommy." I desperately want to be this person, but feel uncomfortable with the title; I've done nothing to earn either it or her trust. I want them all to stop and just let her come to me on her own, but it's already out of my hands.

"Devi, where's your Mommy?" a *didi* chirps in Nepali, carrying her to me.

"Hi, Devi," I say softly, smiling as I reach for her hand, but she quickly turns away, nuzzling her head into her caregiver's shoulder. The *didi* tries again to convince her to come to me, but she looks at me deep and long, and I can see her thinking, "Mommy? What Mommy? This isn't my Mommy..."

I'm reeling as my fairytale meeting with Devi crumbles around me. This isn't how it was supposed to be. I want to rewind and have another take. I don't want her to be afraid of me.

"It's okay," I say. "She can come to me when she's ready," I suggest, stung by the rejection, and take a seat in a nearby lawn chair, hoping not to look as desperate as I feel. Jack, however, is far less patient. He rushes to pick her up, kissing her and presenting her with the giant pink bunny she is almost scared of. She looks unsure about this new little boy but tolerates him until he's distracted by Annie's two children who are buzzing along a zip line through the tropical garden.

As I sit and wait, watching Devi toddle about, I ponder the brief history the adoption agency provided. She had been found abandoned on the street by a police officer six months earlier and taken to the orphanage. While she was there, authorities placed a notice in the newspaper with her picture and description in hopes of finding her family. After thirty days and no response, she was legally classified an orphan and moved to Annie's house to wait for a referral to an adoptive family. Because she had been abandoned, there was no information about her parents, siblings, medical history, birthday, or why she was left alone on the street. She had been assigned a birthday of March 5, one day after she was found by the police, but seeing her now, still so tiny, I have a hard time believing she's already two years old. I can't help but wonder about her mother.

The next few hours are a delicate dance of giving Devi her space while making myself as tempting as possible, taking calculated risks to engage with her. It isn't long before she crawls into my lap to investigate me. I give her a little sheep made of smooth, brightly colored wooden rings on a yellow, nylon cord. My head spins as I struggle to take slow even breaths and try not to fall over. I'm deliriously in awe of her—her chunky little legs, her soft mocha skin. I notice her ears have been pierced, though the holes are empty, another piece of her past stripped away and lost. When

I gaze into her onyx eyes, she has a deep knowingness about her, as if she can see my soul. She is a little girl who did not come from my body, but it's as if I've always known her. I feel my heart tug as if an intangible wispy web is weaving our lives together. Her tiny fingers turn the sheep around and around as she studies it. Then, abruptly, she wiggles off my lap to show Kamala, the head *didi*; her loyalty still intact.

Evening approaches, and with our last airline meal long gone, Annie offers to take us to Fire and Ice, a legendary pizza place in Thamel, the hip tourist hub of Nepal. Hesitantly, I ask if we can bring Devi along, and to my surprise, Annie says it's fine. We pile into the jeep, Devi on my lap, Jack and Annie's kids in the backseat. I say a silent prayer, and trust Annie to keep us safe through our seatbeltless drive in the chaotic traffic.

Devi seems content to sit in my lap and watch the sights flash by. As we cruise through the city, Annie gives a running commentary of various landmarks and shopping options. I'm skeptical that my jetlagged brain will retain any of the information, until she mentions that Kathmandu lies on a major fault line. She reports that construction is poor due to a lack of building codes. Even the airport runway is on the fault, so relief supplies won't be able to be flown in when the "big one" hits, and no expats will be able to fly out. I'm flooded with anxiety and question what I've done. As I take a deep breath, I feel Devi relax into me and am reminded why I'm here.

Annie sees the look of distress on my face. "Oh, don't worry about it. I mean, it could happen anywhere. Yosemite is going to blow and destroy North America, so you're no safer there than here!" I'm not comforted by this factoid.

I'm relieved when we arrive at the pizza place and we tumble out. After all of the potentially catastrophic culinary possibilities, our destination looks divine. I keep a tight grip on my handbag as we pass snake charmers, street vendors and questionable men with, at least in my mind, frightening intentions.

As we enter the restaurant, Annie is welcomed by name and the kids run off to choose a table. I leave Annie to order for us and excuse myself to clean up, toting Devi on my hip. It's been a while since I've had to negotiate a bathroom while juggling a small child, but the skills come right back. Devi allows me to wash her hands without a peep. As I dry my mine with the communal towel hanging on a rusty nail on the wall, her interest is piqued by my necklace—a flat, oval, purple and blue stone on a silver chain. With one grasp of her chubby little hand, it pops from my neck, and I'm reminded of other things about toddlers. I'm surprised by how easily she returns the remnants, and I hope her cooperation is due to her natural ease with me and our psychic connection, though my logical mind tells me otherwise. Her compliance is more likely due to the shock of being carried off from her familiar surroundings by yet another unknown caregiver. At least she is with Annie and her kids, I reassure myself. Whatever the reason for her behavior, when we're back at the table I take advantage of the opportunity to hold her in my lap and soak up her babyness.

I offer her tiny pieces of pizza and pasta, but she just picks at them and only a few bites actually make it to her mouth. She doesn't say a word, and I realize, I have yet to hear her voice. I can't see her face, so I ask Annie if she looks all right. Annie shrugs, saying she's fine, and returns to her infomercial of all things Kathmandu. By the end of the meal, Devi starts to try a few small pieces of crust, chewing hesitantly, but Annie's kids have become impatient and Jack is falling asleep on the bench beside me. I have no rupees, so Annie pays the bill, and we take off.

The *didis* are visibly relieved to have one of their flock safely home. I try to tell them what Devi ate, but they just smile and nod, reaching forward to catch her as she dives from my arms to theirs. While I've relished our first evening together, I feel guilty knowing the *didis* have a difficult night ahead with an overtired toddler who just had her first pizza. I wave anxiously as they carry her to bed, but she is back in her element and doesn't look back.

Morning comes around 3 a.m. for my overactive brain. I try to convince my monkey mind that I need rest, knowing the busy day will start soon enough. Devi isn't even up yet, anyway. Images of her click in and out of dreams, my lost little girl alone on the street. I float between worlds, waiting for my spirit to catch up with my body after being transported to the other side of the world at a wholly unnatural rate.

When the sun begins to rise, I'm satisfied that it's officially morning, and I slip out of bed. Jack is still sleeping, so I keep the curtains drawn and tiptoe to the bathroom for my first Nepali shower. After guidebook-induced visions of icy bathing in cement block stalls, I give thanks for the hot water and make every effort to keep it out of my mouth by holding my breath and rolling my lips inside. I turn off the tap, as requested by the plaque hanging on the wall among the traditional Nepali decor, conscious to conserve the precious water between soap, shampoo, and rinse, then emerge feeling refreshed. I slip back into the room where a bleary-eyed Jack rolls over mumbling, "Good morning Mommy, can we go see Devi now?"

"How about some breakfast first?"

I dig through our suitcases for something to wear, trying to remember the method to my packing madness. Which bag was for winter and which for summer? Which for Devi and which for Jack? Which one has the toys, books, and medicine? I fish out clothes for us both while Jack wriggles out of bed and opens the drapes to an abundant garden of flowers and ferns, trees heavy with bananas and bright-orange, trumpet-shaped blooms. The air is sweet with the perfume of exotic buds unfolding in the morning light. Dew clings to a plush carpet of grass; the terracotta snow lions growl with vines creeping from their mouths misted and fresh. A brilliant blue sky greets us as we step into our new world.

We follow the mossy brick steps to the dining room where we discover a bountiful array of breakfast options: cereal and granola with milk or yogurt, fresh fruit salad, four varieties of juice, sliced meats and cheeses, breads, rolls and pastries galore—tiny apple turnovers, fluffy croissant, and delicate Danish blooming with cream cheese and raspberry fillings. A smiling chef stands at a nearby table with a glorified camp stove, ready to make eggs to order with sautéed vegetables, potatoes, and sausages. I breathe a sigh of relief at our good fortune and start to load a plate, encouraging Jack to do the same, unsure of when our next meal would be. Only a few days ago I was treating Jack to a bagel at our favorite downtown breakfast spot. Now, it feels like a lifetime ago.

I stop by the front desk to drop off our key for the day. "Everything is absolutely lovely! It's going to be so hard to leave once we find a place to rent."

"It is good you are looking for a flat since your room is only booked through the eighth." The sari woman says, smiling serenely.

My mind swims to find the date. Is today already the third? I have less than a week?

"There must be some mistake," I stammer. "We just got here, we have nowhere else to go . . ." I fight to control the quake in my voice as panic climbs up my legs, through my chest and into my throat.

"I am sorry, Madam, but the entire hotel is booked. Madam Annie only made your reservation for the one week," she replies, still smiling while tapping at her keyboard, likely just for show.

"I guess we will be finding somewhere to live then," I say as I feel the ugly American creep into my tone. When the adoption agency assured me Annie would take care of booking the hotel for two weeks to give us time to adjust, I trusted it was taken care of.

Smiling Suraj ferries us to Annie's large brick home flanked by concrete servants' quarters. Jack is content to play with the other kids when Devi dismisses his brotherly advances, but she shows me a bit more attention, especially when I play aloof. I take out a wooden top, wind it up, and give it a spin. Intrigued, Devi ventures closer to watch me assemble the parts, wind the cord, and pull. She delightedly bumbles across the concrete pad that has served as her playground and hesitantly reaches out to touch the top. Feeling its soft buzz on her finger, she yanks her hand back in surprise and looks to me with giggles of delight. When the top slows and bobbles over, she snaps it up and brings it back for me to make more magic. I take advantage of her closeness and pull her into my lap to examine the new toy. Moments later, she wiggles to be put down, so I hand her the pieces to investigate. She struggles to assemble the parts, but her attempts are futile; only *I* hold the secret. She returns to me, enraptured, and I spin the top again and again.

When she starts to lose interest, I scoop her up and carry her to the nursery to change her soggy diaper. I'm enchanted by her tiny frame and cautiously examine the map of her body. The spotty circular blemishes on her side concern me; they appear to be recently healed wounds. There is a marble-sized sore on her thigh, a reddish-purple shade of angry. Her belly button is an "innie." She has a freckle near her right hip that will drive some college boy wild one day. She looks deeply into my eyes, studying my face, as I tell her what a pretty dress she has on, how nice and still she is lying, how good it feels to have on dry pants. I softly sing-song chatter, but she doesn't respond, lacking vocabulary to communicate with me, so she just stares, wide-eyed. I feel like a talk show host with an unwilling guest. Persevering, I resort to making babbling noises with my tongue pushing past my top lip and back again. *Bladerp.* Finally! The hint of a grin forms at the corners of her mouth. Encouraged, I *bladerp* again, and she smiles enough for me to see a few teeth. She *bladerps* back. I smile from so deep in my heart I can feel the tug of its roots. We are connecting.

I hear Annie coming down the steps, and the spell is broken. Shifting Devi onto my hip, I call out good morning greetings and scramble to catch her eye, anxious to ask her advice about our lodging crisis, as well as Devi's medical history. I follow her into the kitchen, feeling ridiculous vying for her attention like some groupie, but I'm desperate—a stranger in a strange land with a newly acquired strange child looking for a (hopefully!) not so strange apartment.

"I need a cup of coffee," Annie mumbles as she searches for a clean mug on the congested countertop. "What were you saying?"

I can't tell if she's spacey, annoyed, or just not a morning person. "I'm sorry to bother you, but our reservation at Summit was only made for a week, so I need to find a flat right away," I say, wishing for a miraculous solution.

"Well, why don't you just change rooms," she grumbles, clearly irritated by my drama. I try to calmly relay my conversation with the sari lady, but anxiety creeps into my voice. Annie breezes past me chuckling, "Oh well, there are plenty of places available . . . you just have to find one!"

I shuffle along behind her juggling Devi, who is now squirming. "Also, could I get Devi's medical records? I'm wondering about these scars on her trunk, and how about this sore on her leg?" I call out, pointing to the visible signs of my concern as she heads down the hall. "Do you know what it could be?" She is clearly disinterested, so I put Devi down to toddle back outside.

"The girls had some sort of rash over the summer," Annie answers vaguely. "I just don't have time to keep track of those things. Ask Kamala."

Kamala, the head *didi*, while compassionate and kind, speaks little English, so I'm confused about what she can tell me. I feel utterly deflated and on the verge of tears as Annie waves me away. "I'm taking my daughter to a friend's house," she concludes. "But stay as long as you like."

"Will Suraj take us home?" I call out pathetically as Annie scales the steps.

Obviously annoyed, she sighs. "You'll have to walk back. Here, I'll draw you a map." She scribbles on the back of an envelope, naming colorful landmarks as she goes: a produce vendor, a goat salesman, the blacksmith, a school that can't be missed.

I'm speechless.

Seeing my confusion, Annie pulls out a cartoonish map. "Here. This is the best one available," she says. "Really, you should pick one up." The map is a maze of twisting, squiggly lanes without names. Summit Hotel is clearly marked, but I have no idea where we are now.

"See? See how easy it is? Here, you can even borrow my map!" she says brightly, her gesture sealing the deal. "Have fun with your girl!"

I slink outside to find Devi having a snack with another toddler, Dawa, and Kamala. I ask about the scars, but her smiling bobbling nod and giggling, mumbling response tell me nothing. The only words I understand are "don't know," the only words that matter. I point to the sore on her leg but get the same response. Suraj, seeing my fading expression, asks if I'm okay, if I need anything. My head spins, and I start to ramble about the unexpected need to find a flat.

"I have friend help you. I call him." Suraj's smile brings the comfort I need. He asks what we are looking for, how big, where, how much I want to spend. I don't know the answers to these questions, and feel like I'm blindfolded throwing darts and hoping to hit the target.

Suraj's friend, Jaya, arrives by motorcycle within a couple of hours. "There is flat, down road," he advises. "You see now?"

We walk down the dusty, pot-holed street, dodging mysterious garbage and pathetic street puppies, until we reach a long drive with a sky-blue gate at the end. A scrawny man in a makeshift uniform escorts us into the compound then takes us to the landlord and his wife, who is peeking out from behind him suspiciously. The tall pink house is surrounded by concrete patios, and the available flat is on the bottom floor, one of my only requirements after hefting basalt-bodied Devi for less than twenty-four hours.

It's clean, with good light, and as I walk from one room to the next, I try to imagine us living here. The furniture is sparse and a little scary; the bathroom, a dank concrete closet, but at least there is a western-style toilet. I struggle to envision bathing the kids in the funky shower. When I enter the kitchen, I'm in shock. It's nothing but a small, square, concrete room. No oven, no range top, no refrigerator. Up against one wall is a rickety wooden table next to a tiny metal sink and a stray propane tank. Sparse cabinets dot the back wall, one door hanging cockeyed on a single hinge. I have absolutely no idea how I would prepare a meal in this room called "kitchen."

I try to hide my disappointment, not wanting to appear disrespectful. "I'll think about it . . . It's very nice, but I'd like to have a friend come see it with me before I decide."

"Yes, Madam. Many others look, someone today say they will take. You decide now or we give to other persons." The landlord replies respectfully, but I smell the oldest real estate trick in the book. Still, the pressure claws at me.

As we walk back to Annie's, Jaya tells me he knows of a few other places, so I suggest we meet in the morning. The sun dips in the sky, and I realize it's getting late. Then I remember, I still have to find our way back to Summit.

Jack and I wave goodbye to Devi, but she is already standing at the door of the outside kitchen, a *bapa* (cookie) in each hand, anxiously awaiting dinner. We slip out the gate with Annie's scribbled map. My heart thumps in my ears but I try to be brave, breathing deeply the exhaust-filled air, hoping to appear calm. Jack clings to my hand, overwhelmed by the sights and sounds that thus far, he had been protected from when traveling by car. We walk single file, tight against stone walls topped with rusty nails and broken glass, avoiding trash, street dogs, and the occasional, unidentifiable carcass while taxis squeeze by beep, beeping. Trepidation becomes excitement when I spot the goats, our first landmark, at the predicted corner. Jack, worn down by the day's events and jetlag, shows only slight interest. Slowly, I'm able to unravel stories of Annie's son, Tarak, playing the bully, excluding Jack from games and making fun of him. Jack had bravely endured the torment to be close to his new little sister. As I watch my exhausted and tattered little boy stumble down the dirt road, I second guess what I'm putting him through, wondering, *what have I done?* We pass a stoic Ganesh, and I point to the envelope map, reassuring Jack we are going the right way, but he is not impressed. Only one wrong turn later, we pass the monstrous, decrepit yet silent Gems Academy, which looks more like an abandoned warehouse than a school. Then, magically, we find ourselves at the back gate of Summit and enter the security of the Eden within.

In the dining room, while we wait for dinner, my ragdoll son begins to melt down, wailing his confession, "I want to go home!"

I try to cheer him up, laughing about him flying down the zip line in Annie's backyard while his friends were sleeping on the other side of the world. I slyly mention that none of his schoolmates had gotten to see a goat on the street corner today. Then, eventually playing on his sympathies, I remind him of Devi, who has been waiting for us to be her family.

"If we go home now, Jackie, we have to leave Devi here. She can't come with us yet." I lean over the table and look deep into his eyes. "You have wanted a little sister for so long, can you imagine your life without her?"

"Yes, I can," he replies with total resolve, and folding his arms for a pillow, puts his head down on the table.

What have I done?

Back in our room, I'm exhausted but restless and pace, as I listen to Jack's gentle sleep sounds. I tiptoe outside to the garden and feel the cool damp grass under my bare feet. I peek in on Jack, sure he is out for the night, and I make my way to the lounge for a cocktail to settle my nerves and slow my reeling mind. Flopping on the sofa, I flip through the *Shambala Sun*, comforted by the Dalai Lama smiling compassionately from the cover.

A tall, lean man with a curly ruff of silver blond hair and a deep tan saunters into the bar to friendly greetings. In worn jeans, a linen shirt, and flip flops, he's quite handsome, and I find it hard not to eavesdrop as he chats with the innkeeper about trekking, backcountry, porters, permits, and film. Then my mind clicks, and I realize, this must be Stephan Lane, the famed National Geographic filmmaker Annie mentioned was staying at Summit. She is friends with his ex-wife, and her version of the gossip was that he'd run off with his young and promiscuous assistant, leaving behind a wife and two teenage daughters who are nearly the age of his affair. The happy new couple went on to marry, and now have a daughter and son of their own, reportedly spoiled rotten. I'd briefly seen, and especially heard, the children a few doors down from us, but had yet to meet their parents.

"Mind if I join you?" The tangle of curly locks and electric blue eyes take me off guard.

"Oh, of course not!" I stammer and shift away from watching our room out the window as he puts down a beer and a bowl of *chivda*, a traditional trail mix, on the oversized coffee table in front of us. I instantly understand why his assistant fell for this confident, charismatic man. We chit chat about the beautiful weather, and I tell him this is my first time in Nepal, that I've just arrived to adopt an orphaned little girl. He tells me of his two children, very near Jack and Devi's ages.

"You're in for quite an experience. The revolution has been going on for some time now, about ten years. The Maoist rebels are fighting to change the corrupt government; they're intent on ending the monarchy. When *bandh* days are called, the shopkeepers are pressured to close up and taxis won't be running, so it's best to stay home," he explains, then takes a long swill of his beer.

I worry that maybe I should've listened to the State Department travel warnings instead of Annie's flippant remarks that the political instability was nothing to worry about.

"Nepal is like nowhere else in the world. It will change your soul forever," he continues. "You really must meet my wife, Christina. She'll show you all you need to know about life in Kathmandu. Look for her at breakfast. You'll be great company for her since I'm leaving for a shoot in Khombu in the morning. And good work with the little girl. Really, bravo!" He pats my knee.

And then he is off, drink in hand, gliding out the door, briefly greeting a party of climbers on their way into the bar: eight chiseled mountain men who look as if they've jumped right out of a North Face advertisement, just the distraction I needed.

After drifting in and out of sleep, I wake up early with a renewed sense of purpose. I'm nervous about apartment hunting with Jaya since everything is moving fast forward, but it's time to make our nest. I've accepted that I don't have time to settle in and explore neighborhoods, so I shift my focus to Devi and stay positive: the sooner I find a place to live, the sooner she can be with us full-time, and our new family can begin. I tiptoe around, hoping Jack will keep sleeping, but before I know it, he's up and ready to go. As I open the door, a squealing blond blur in a fairy dress flies past, pursued by an equally blond stout little brother wielding a sword with a crooked crown impairing his vision. A full-sized Mom version of the blond duo follows, juggling plates of food.

"Ugh! Well, it's easier than trying to get them to sit still in the dining room!" she sighs, shrugging as she smiles. "And who might you be?" she asks Jack, peeking out from behind me.

"This is Jack," I offer, nudging him to respond. "And I'm Kate."

"Oh, hi! I'm Christina, and those two are Jade and Iven. My husband mentioned meeting you last night, said you're here to fetch your little girl, eh? Kudos to you. There are plenty of kids in Nepal who could use some help. Well, I gotta run!" She motions toward the room the children have disappeared into, and from the sounds of it, are now dismantling. "Stop by later and the kids can play," she suggests, slipping into the doorway.

Jack stares at the closed door in a trance.

"Ooooh, a girl! Jackie likes a girl! Jackie likes a girl!" I tease as he turns as crimson as the orchid blossoms dripping from the trees.

We stuff ourselves at the breakfast buffet and set out to Annie's. Although I still feel compelled to cling to Jack's hand, he is ready to test his wings and runs ahead. He's keenly interested in the trash along the roadside, sure it can be transformed into a plane, race car, submarine, or spy gadget, but I remain vigilant, reminding him to leave found objects where they lay.

At Annie's, Devi comes to me almost immediately, curious about what magical object will emerge from my handbag. I've given up toting everything I can possibly imagine I might need like some displaced Mary Poppins, and now have only the bare necessities: my wallet, passport, a water bottle, and a new trinket. Today, it's a small, plastic, wind-up cat, and Devi is absorbed immediately. Tick, tick, tick. The yellow tabby squats down, then pops up in a backward somersault. Devi's eyes show her amazement. She loves the anticipation followed by the incredible feat. Clearly, neither she nor any of the other children, have ever seen a toy like this.

When Jaya arrives to take me apartment hunting, I kiss Jack goodbye (much to his dismay—embarassed in front the new kids), and I whisper that I hope his day with Tarak is better, then wave goodbye to Devi who is busy playing with Dawa.

I balk at the idea of buzzing around the city on the back of Jaya's motorbike, so we set off on foot. I assure him it isn't his driving skills that worry me, but, truthfully, I'm terrified of being smashed in a Third World crash and leaving my children motherless. Jaya's head bobbles from side to side, in neither a "yes" nor "no." It's a wobbling, bobbling noncommittal gesture that reminds me of the Princess Leia bobblehead doll that stood on the dashboard of my first car, tirelessly guiding late night adventures. This bobbling response seems to be the Nepali way of keeping everyone happy. By never saying "no," no one is disappointed, but no one ever gets a straight answer either.

As we set out, I'm nervous about what Jaya has lined up for me to see. I try to be clear about what I'm looking for, but don't know if my expectations are realistic. Annie says there are plenty of places available, but I shouldn't be too picky, so I stick to the basics: at least two bedrooms, an indoor bathroom, and no steps. I'm equally concerned about Devi falling or my back giving out from hauling her up and down. We meander through neighborhoods peppered with expats, following mazes of tiny footpaths bordered by teetering brick walls, velvety green and musky.

The first place we visit is a lovely sunny yellow concrete block home surrounded by beautiful gardens in full bloom and abundant lemon, guava, and avocado trees. On the main floor are the two available rooms and bathroom. We would share the kitchen and a well-stocked library with the owners for a few months until they go to India for the winter. The price is right, and the older couple is charming, but I have a hard time imagining living in such close quarters with them. While I'm eager to experience the full cultural flavor of Nepal, I feel we need at least a hint of personal space.

We move on, and Jaya gets a better sense of what I like—flowers and trees—and what I do not—vicious dogs on short chains. We tour a parade of flats with gaudy lighting, scary kitchens, and even scarier bathrooms. I have to be absolutely clear, *no* squat toilets.

Finally, after viewing half a dozen possibilities, a couple of which I refuse to even enter, Jaya's frustration with my seemingly simple requirements becomes palpable. Clearly, I have exhausted him.

"Madam, I have only one more to show you, but it has stairs," he says hesitantly, afraid of my response.

I look at him skeptically, frustrated that he can't just give me what I want.

"Is very near here, you just look?" he continues, practically begging.

I acquiesce and offer an affirmative nod. When we get there, I realize we have ended up across the lane from Summit. There, stacked up on a hill, the house is a concrete cluster of angles and odd-shaped windows with walls painted fire-engine red to look like brick. It is beyond gaudy, it is hideous. A guard in a bargain basement uniform opens the gate and ushers us inside to a wide circle of downwardly sloping, uneven concrete surrounded by twelve-foot-high concrete walls with intricately pressed concrete railings. It's a concrete jumble. The entrance to the house is up more than a dozen very steep concrete steps. There are no handrails, and since crawling isn't an option, I channel the Inca, imagining myself walking proudly up the steps of a great temple. As I reach the top, I realize how near to a temple this last house is.

Rising out of the concrete well of an entrance, we walk into a lovely garden bordered by a hot pink bougainvillea hedge with orange marigolds popping from the base and mounds of snow-white geraniums softening the entryway. Guava and persimmon trees hang heavy with fruit, and potted plants burst with color, dotting the wide railing. A smiling, well-dressed, and whistle-clean landlord uses a skeleton key to open the heavy glossy white front door while his wife, in a ruby red, jeweled *sari*, floats at a respectful distance behind him.

As I step inside, I look left to see two bedrooms separated by a bathroom. A dripping shower head unceremoniously sticks out of the rear wall, but it's well-lit and clean. A mahogany staircase sweeps up to my right, leading to a small loft, where I am told the master suite is located. Traditional woven bamboo chairs, a small sofa with colorful cushions, and a coffee table rests on a burgundy flowered carpet that gives warmth to the stark white walls. I glide across cool marble floors, through the sitting area, to the elevated dining space with a round table and four chairs of dark, heavy wood. To my left is the kitchen, minus first-world appliances, but the propane tank is neatly tucked behind a curtain under a camp stove-like cooktop, and there is a miniature sink with running water. Small, puzzle-piece cabinets, with tiny locking latches (*what would I need to lock up in the kitchen?*) line the walls. I peek inside to find them littered with dead bugs and mouse bait and take a deep breath. This is the best place I've seen so far.

The landlord and Jaya leave me to explore as I head up to the loft. I am delighted to find a cozy sitting area where the strange triangular windows are now artistic, framing a view of the Himalayas while cutting off the jumbled city below. I pad across the sable-brown, basket-weave wood floor and wind around the short hall to the master suite. The entry boasts beautiful built-in cabinets with a mirror and a hand-crafted armoire. It, too, is littered with miniature locks, and I wonder how I will ever keep up with all those tiny keys. On the opposite side is the bathroom, complete with sink, western toilet and even a *bathtub*. It's dream come true.

The rear wall of the bedroom is comprised of floor to ceiling windows with a glass door leading onto a large terrace with a breathtaking view of the Kathmandu Valley. In the distance, I spot Swayambhu, a Buddhist temple, with prayer flags fluttering in the breeze. The golden domes of lesser temples sparkle like hidden jewels, and water tanks pepper the city with winking silver solar panels. The picturesque backdrop of the snow-topped, sawtoothed ridges of the Himalayan range stretches as far as I can see in either direction, east or west. As I look out to the Roof of the World, I know this is home.

After another bountiful breakfast, Jack and I walk to Annie's to spend some time with Devi. She is becoming more comfortable with us and is increasingly interested. She knows we are hers; all the *didis* tell her so when we show up. "Devi, where's your Mommy?" they sing out to her. Taking this to be a game, Devi toddles over to me and whacks me on the leg, headbutting me and burying her face in the folds of my skirt. I laugh along, as it seems the script should go, but a cold ache twists in my gut, *Where is her real mommy?*

After plenty of playtime, we're all ready for lunch. Naps will be next, so Jack and I slip out for the afternoon. I need to start setting up the house, and Christina has offered to watch Jack for the day. I briefly question leaving him with such new friends, but decide a day at Summit playing in the pool will be heavenly for him, far better than a return to Annie's and being taunted by Tarak. As I prepare to leave, Christina shares that Jade has been waiting all morning for Jack to return, and she's hoping Jack's influence will bring an end to the sibling infighting. I chuckle and bid them farewell, setting off to accomplish my next task.

I sign the lease with the help of the landlord's brother, Hari, as translator. I'm thrilled to have the skeleton key in hand, but first I need to get, well, *everything*—dishes, cookware, appliances, linens. My head spins at the daunting chore. I have no idea where to even begin looking, so when Hari offers to take me shopping in his private car, assuring me that he knows where to find all the items on my list, and promises to make sure I get the best price, I can't refuse.

In small, concrete hole-in-the-wall shops, Hari helps me purchase a few wares, then, at the larger combination grocery/department store, Saleways, we find the rest. It's hard to keep track of everything I need in general, but other items are specific to my new homeland. There are no washing machines, so we buy huge stainless-steel bowls. Propane is expensive, and Hari insists an electric rice cooker is essential. Tea sets are a staple, as are cloth placemats and napkins—influences of colonial India. Still other items will have to be ordered, like custom sheets and heavy cotton blankets for the frigid winter months. I consider the need for an oven, the debate clearly dumbfounding Hari. His only comment is that "many expats find them useful." It's a big-ticket item, so I decide to wait and see if we really need it. I can't imagine baking anything any time soon, as I feel sweat roll down my back. Hours of shopping later, jetlag and exhaustion force me to downshift into the slow-paced Nepali world. My formerly frantic American mode becomes one of leisurely patience.

Back at the house, Hari kindly unloads my haul with assistance from the gate guard while I meet with the tailors Christina sent to help me. Nepali furniture is handmade, with no two beds the same size, so custom fitted sheets are a necessity. The tailors assure me they can make anything, and promise to be back the following day, then buzz off on their motorbike. While I shopped, Summit had delivered our mountain of luggage and piled it in one of the bedrooms. Looking around at all I have to unpack and organize, I'm overwhelmed and desperate for a break. I saunter across the lane to Summit where I find Jack lounging poolside and sharing chips (aka French fries) and mango *lassi*, a traditional yogurt and fruit shake, with his new best friend. He wants to stay and play, so I slip out to visit Devi.

At Annie's, I find the girls in the playroom beating drums with wooden spoons and tooting traditional flutes. Devi makes a beeline for me, her eyes crinkling shut with a giggling grin, and my heart melts. She's been on my mind almost constantly while I shopped, and I'd suppressed the urge to buy random items, unsure of what might make her happy. *Can she drink from a cup? Does she use a pillow? What is her favorite color?* Now, none of those questions matter. She doesn't need material items to fulfill her, she needs love. She needs a Mommy, and I am finally here.

As I sit on the floor, she brings me various toys, sure I have magical powers to bring to life those whose batteries have long since died. She wiggles into my lap, then hops off again, always on the go, looking for something else to share with me. I notice the light in the playroom fading and struggle to tear myself away from her, knowing it is getting close to dinner time and I need to get back to Jack. Hesitantly, I ask the *didis* if I can bring Devi with me, and they happily reply, "yes, yes!" and wave me out the gate. As we step into the alley, Devi looks back ever so briefly, then turns her gaze on me, winds her fingers in my hair and grasps a handful of my shirt, latching on like a monkey with her legs tight around my waist. Every step feels heavier but with more purpose as we move into our new life.

Once safely inside the Summit gate, I set Devi down and she takes my hand, glad to toddle along beside me, her eyes feasting on this new place and all it has to offer. We find Jack watching cartoons with Jade and Iven while Tara, their *didi*, sits nearby knitting. Christina peels them away from the television, and we trot across the lane for a tour of our new home. As the kids explore the house, disappointed the hard cotton mattresses are no good for bouncing, Christina tells me I have done well, but warns me to be wary of the landlord. He is a Brahmin, the highest caste of the largely Hindu social structure, who are infamous for their drive for material goods and social prestige with little regard for those around them. She explains that while within their own culture they are at the top of the totem pole, foreigners, especially Westerners, do not fit so nicely into their social hierarchy. With our lighter skin, we move up in the social rankings, something Brahmins are not fond of; however, not being Hindu, we are not of significance. Western women, especially, are difficult to accept due to the freedoms experienced outside this culture and the lack of submission within. Expectations of dress, mannerism, and, particularly, independence, do not cross cultural bounds, which can make for uncomfortable communications. A woman without a man is an easy target here, and Christina advises me to step carefully or I am sure to be taken advantage of.

After a pleasant Summit dinner, I leave Jack with Christina and her kids and hail a taxi for Devi and me. Proud of my ability to recognize the correct lane, I ask the driver to wait while I drop off Devi. She is happy to return to Kamala, and I try not to take it personally, even if I'm the one with the title "Mommy."

Upon returning to Summit, I collect Jack, exhausted yet still protesting, and we retire to our room for one last night. I'm finally able to *really* relax knowing I have met our housing deadline, and am looking forward to settling into our lovely new place. I drift off to sleep filled with dreams of my little girl with sticky sweet vice-grip hands.

On September 6, just four days after our arrival in Kathmandu, Devi has come home with Jack and me for good. She doesn't know it, but it's a Hindu women's Holy Day and festival, a very auspicious day for us to be joined, even if it is not yet legal, in mother and daughterhood. She seems comfortable and happy with toys of her own to toss about the playroom, walking with us to Summit, and polishing off her *dal bhat* without a fuss. When it is time for bed, we all get ready together, putting on pajamas, brushing teeth and reading bedtime stories. As I quietly explain each step of the evening to Devi, it is clear this is a new experience for her, and, once again, I think of her mother. I guess they didn't have books to read, and I wish I knew the songs she sang.

Jack and I carry his oddly long, narrow twin bed upstairs, placing it next to mine, since his downstairs bedroom feels very far away in our strange new house. Knowing Devi slept in a communal bed at Annie's, I am glad to share my almost double-sized bed with her. I hope this will help her transition and she climbs in next to me, unfazed. The lights go out, and so do I.

After breakfast at Summit, I stare into my new kitchen, wondering what I will do there. The novelty of my snack style lunches is wearing thin, and Jack is not-so-subtly questioning my ability to provide for my young. We have the rice cooker, but we really can't live on rice alone, and if I want to stick to my budget, fabulous Summit meals won't be an option much longer.

When I first began to consider adoption, my neighbors in the States had been sweetly supportive. Penny, a kindergarten teacher, and Rob, a religious studies professor, were my do-gooder support system. They'd spent a year in India with their two children, and when I decided to stay in Nepal to wait out the adoption process, they were all smiles and encouragement.

"What a wonderful life experience for Jack!" Penny cheered. "Of course, if you can afford it, get domestic help."

Domestic help? That seemed so archaic and colonialist.

Now, Penny's words are coming back. "Trust me, you'll need it."

Annie suggests an online neighborhood group to find a *didi*, and I quickly come upon a posting from a departing family recommending a couple who had served them well during their stay—he the cook, she the housekeeper and nanny. The ad is appealing, but I'm having trouble getting used to the idea of having one "servant" on my "staff." I know I don't need two.

Dinesh, a polite, smiling, soft-spoken man, comes over right after I call. He and his wife, Leena, live just down the lane with their three children. Although Jack takes to Dinesh immediately, Devi keeps her distance, clinging to my skirt and pressing her head into the back of my thigh, nearly pushing me over. With the local unemployment rate near 50%, Dinesh and Leena are desperate for work and more than willing to compromise. Since I only have enough work for one of them, we agree that Dinesh will start in the morning. As he leaves, I am fairly certain I can see a halo floating above his head.

Now that we're settled, getting Devi to a doctor is at the top of my to-do list. She has strange bumps and clear blisters, sometimes filled with puss, in patches on her hands and legs, and one has formed a boil on her thigh. I'm also curious about Devi's true age and hope the doctor where she was previously seen can make a more accurate assessment.

The doctor, a Nepali woman educated in the United States, is stunningly beautiful and politely refined. Devi clings to me like a tick on a street dog and is thoroughly uncooperative as the doctor tries to examine her. I struggle to point out the spots on her hands and legs as well as the scarring on her trunk, but the doctor seems disinterested, causing me to feel silly and overprotective. Then she asks if Devi is talking. I happily report that she babbles quite a bit, but I'm met by a look of suspicion and concern. Obviously, my answer is incorrect, so I nervously continue rambling. I tell her I'm looking into Nepali lessons, but, clearly, she's not impressed, and drops the line of questioning. She then asks more about me, why I chose to adopt from Nepal, and how I'm enjoying Kathmandu.

"Actually, I need to find some work," I confide. "My stay has been unexpectedly lengthened, and I'd prefer to generate some income, so I don't deplete my savings."

"What is your area of expertise?" she perks up, showing the most interest in our visit so far.

"I used to own a natural foods store and organic deli. I really enjoyed working with customers, and coming up with new recipes..." I trail off, thinking of my former life so very far away.

"I may know of something for you. Let me take your number." She hands me a pen and paper. "My husband has opened a small café, but really, it's just a hobby. He needs a manager."

The next morning, Daman, the doctor's husband, calls, laughing that his wife has played matchmaker, convinced she has tired of his project that is consuming all of his free time. We agree to meet later in the day at the café, conveniently located just down the road from our house.

"Really, I need a consultant more than a manager," he says. Although his staff is well trained, he's looking for someone to analyze his books and day-to-day operations and create a plan to bring in business from the lucrative expat community.

"*Dashain* is coming up next month. It's the biggest Hindu festival of the year, like your American Christmas," he explains. "It's the perfect time to bring in new customers."

I'm thrilled at the opportunity. I'll set my own schedule, spend time in the café to observe, then offer suggestions intended to improve business. While the salary is paltry, it will go a long way in Kathmandu. I need every rupee I can get. While I relish the idea of finally being a stay-at-home mom, I'm already beginning to feel the squeeze of too many hours alone with the kids, and this job will give my workaholic mind a venue.

During the next few days, as I watch the neighborhood children scamper happily down the street in their school uniforms, I know it's time for Jack to get back to school so he doesn't fall behind. Even Princess Jade has been forced out of the Summit gardens and back to the classroom at The British School, right down the lane within walking distance, but will only attend until her family returns to Paris in a month after Stephan finishes filming. We start our search there, but in the States, Jack had been in a free-flowing Montessori classroom that makes The British School feel stuffy and cold.

Lincoln School, the American school, is farther away, so we'll have to carpool with another family or take expensive taxi rides. The campus is beautiful, situated on a large, garden-filled compound with up-to-date, light-filled classrooms and happy, smiling teachers, as well as earthquake shelters. We're shown where the children eat lunch outside, as long there are no monkeys in the area. Jack and I look at each other and start to giggle, only to be immediately reprimanded, as clearly, monkeys are no laughing matter.

"Oh no, Ms. Saunders, this is a very serious issue. The monkeys have started infiltrating this part of the Valley and can be quite dangerous to the children, especially when food is involved," the Headmaster scolds. "The children know when the alarm sounds, to drop their lunches and come in immediately."

Really? A monkey alarm? I think. The search continues.

Finally, we come to the Children's House Montessori School located in a large, time-worn, three-story brick home, with one floor for each age group. The classes are small, the teachers kind, the children largely Nepali, though a more international mix I've yet to see. Small footpaths meander between the outdoor gym, playground, garden, and pens for small livestock. Jack finds his place and fits right in, so I arrange to have him start school the following Monday.

With a house, a job, and Jack in school, next on my to-do list is to open a bank account. I select a British-owned bank to eliminate the transfer fees when I need funds wired periodically. I enter the stark white bank office and am greeted warmly by a demure young woman in a hot pink and gold sari. Her matching fingernails are so long, I can't imagine how she's able to type. She offers me a seat at her cubicle, but once I state my business, she passes me on to a young man to help me open an account. When he presents me the application, I'm startled to find that I'm required to provide a signature from either my father, or my husband. The former being deceased, and the latter being fictional, I leave the space blank, but when I return the form, the young man makes it clear, this is not acceptable. I scan the page, looking for a loophole and find a space reserved for a recommendation from an employer. Unlike most women in Nepal who are not permitted to work outside the home, fortunately, I can fill in the blank. I phone Daman, and he speaks with the bank manager, a friend of his, and an exception is made. Daman quickly arrives and puts his signature on the all-important line.

Now, in addition, I have to provide a copy of my lease to verify not only my residency but designating the landlord as the man responsible for me since women are not permitted to own land. This interaction provides its own set of hassles, but eventually, Hari produces the necessary documents and I'm granted an account. Shocked by the experience, I realize the freedoms I've taken for granted in the Western world and become disturbingly aware of my limited power in Nepal.

Less than three weeks in, and the honeymoon is over. Sleep is elusive at best. Devi did so well at first, but now she wakes up screaming almost hourly after the near impossible feat of getting her to sleep to begin with. She wiggles and squirms, rolls about and shuffles her feet. She flaps her arms and incessantly makes noises—not loud, just a click of the tongue or a swish of a finger whispering over the sheet. *Whish, whish, whish, whish*, on and on and on and on . . . I try singing, but as soon as I stop, she starts fidgeting again. I drift in and out of slumber, exhausted to the bone. When she does finally sleep, I'm afraid to move, or even to breathe, terrified of waking her.

I look into her still face washed in the glow of the city lights sneaking through the space between the curtains. Her eyes aren't even completely closed. One eye stands guard at half mast, while the other floats restlessly, peeking under the sliver of a lid. The sight is eerie, like nothing I have seen before: zombie eyes, disturbingly vigilant, searching the dark for assailants. The scanning eye sees me and rolls to attention, but looks vacantly past. I speak to her gently and she starts to whimper, so I touch her softly, causing her to recoil violently and begin to wail. It's slow and rumbling at first, but the more I attempt to soothe, the worse it gets. I move to comfort her, but she frantically rolls away, trying to hide between the wall and the mattress.

"Mom, what is it? What's wrong?" Jack startles awake, ready for battle.

"Nothing, Jackie. Go back to sleep. Your sister is just having a bad dream," I whisper over my shoulder.

But her cries are like nothing I've heard before. Devi wails in pain, terror, and total despair. Her eyes are blank; she doesn't respond to her name. As I smooth the sweaty mat of hair from her forehead, she swats my hand away with a grunt and a yelp that borders on combative. She looks right through me.

I roll on my side, facing her hot breath, and hold her tight while she kicks at the wall and mattress. My back cramps and my shoulder aches on this pathetic excuse for a bed. I fantasize about what I would sacrifice from our abundant luggage to have filled an entire suitcase with a foam pad. Desperate for sleep, I sing, soft and slow, as much for Jack and myself as for Devi. "Don't worry, about a thing . . . cause every little thing, gonna be alright . . ."

She gasps and chokes as her energy winds down, and I hold her arms with my hand across her chest to keep her from hitting me in the face, pulling my hair or pinching me. She grinds her teeth like a caged animal and thrashes from side to side. Her spine tenses as I cradle her head in my hand to prevent her from whacking it against the wall and look into her rabid face with as much love as I can dig up, as tears run down my cheeks.

```
Hi Mom,
    Sorry to miss your call. The landlord cut
the international line without notifying me.
I'm told this is the Nepali way. Annoying is
what I call it!
    Jack started at the little Montessori
school. He is such a novelty, all the
kids love him! He is having a hard time
remembering everyone's names, they are all
so new and different. He is one of only
two American kids at the school, so he is
learning a lot about other cultures!
    Devi cries in the night but not for long.
As hard as it is, I know I'm doing the right
thing. There are enough sweet moments to
keep me going. We saw Annie at Summit a few
nights ago and she remarked how Devi's face
has changed, that she looks so much more
stable now.
    Give Mimi a hug for me!

Love,
Kate
```

I can't bring myself to tell anyone just how bad it is with Devi, secretly believing her difficulties are because of me and my shortcomings, unable to soothe or comfort her. I ask Annie what the *didis* did to get her to sleep, but her response is not helpful.

"Just put her in the room, tell her to go to bed, and shut the door."

Desperate for any clue to this sleep stealing mystery, I give it a try, and I'm met with disaster. I quickly realize it's a terrible idea to abandon an abandoned child. Thinking of her being left alone on the street is heart breaking, but at least it isn't as horrific as the accounts of children who've been trafficked and sold, a truly brutal scenario.

I try again to ask Annie's advice, after all, she's adopted two children from Nepal and helped countless other families to unite;

surely others have experienced these problems. She suggests patting her on the back or singing to her. Feeling deflated and utterly defeated, I return to my private hell of sleepless nights.

```
My Darling Daughter,
    I wish I could be there to give you a big
hug! You're doing a wonderful thing, and your
heart is so big, this new world is rough on
you!
    I have faith you will prevail!
Love,
Mom
```

At last, she sleeps! I've spent so long imagining what our family would be like, my visions of carrying her home in a lotus blossom are now now effectively shattered. She is everything I dreamed, and feared, and even more I didn't know that I didn't know. But like the fantasy at the beginning of any new relationship, loaded with expectations of love and intimacy, we wake up and find out that it is just what it is, *real*. All of the meditations and teachings on "releasing expectations" and "attachment to outcome" are lost in the reality of this 24/7 practice. I am solely responsible for creating this relationship. Devi is just a toddler with wants mixed up with needs, caught up in fits of pre-language frustration. I try to allow my ego to dissolve so I can be fully present with her, without desire for reciprocation, but I can't help wondering how many caregivers have come before me? Does she know this time it will be different? Or maybe that is just another myth we tell ourselves at the beginning of any new relationship: this one will be different.

October

"I don't wanna talk to you! Leave me alone!" Jack's muffled shout comes from beneath the bed as I peer underneath.

"Well, now you're trapped, and I'm not leaving, so you may as well come out and start talking," I say in the kindest voice I can muster. The day of tandem tantrums has me at the end of my rope. We all had such a lovely nap together, but obviously, someone woke up on the wrong side of Mommy.

"Oh yeah?!" He challenges as he wriggles and turns, attempting to break free of his self-inflicted trap. I see him start to giggle, but he's quick to cover it with a grumpy frown.

"Don't laugh! Don't *even* laugh . . .You're busy being mad at me, remember?" I tease and console in the same breath. "Really, Jackie, let's talk about it."

He squirms out to sit next to me. He's been grouchy and irritable for much of the day, so I've tried giving him space by taking Devi out on the terrace to play. I was hoping our songs and laughter would tempt him to join us, but it has only fueled his fire. I search his big brown eyes with their impossibly long, lady-killer lashes for some clue about the battle churning inside him. "Please tell me why you're so mad."

"I guess I just didn't know you loved her like that. I mean, I know you love her, but when you went outside and had fun, and left me all alone and angry I saw how you *really* love her." He looks at me with desperation and tears in his eyes, a look I have only seen once before, after the passing of our big black woofalump dog, Tommy.

"Jack," I say gently. "No one will ever take your place. Just because I love Devi doesn't change how much I love you. I can't imagine my life without you."

I search his face for some assurance that what I'm saying is getting through, "Jackie, I would lie down on the tracks for you!" He looks disturbingly confused. "That's a saying people use to show how much they care for someone," I clarify, but his face is still blank. "Okay, what I mean is, if some bad guy was after you, and was going to hurt you, I would lie down on the railroad tracks and let a train run me over if it would save you."

Shock floods his face and the tears start again. "But Mom, I would never want you to do that! Then our cord would be broken, and I would lose you forever!"

Where this "cord" talk is coming from, I have no idea, but am stunned by his enlightenment.

"You know, Jack, I loved my father very, very much. Some of my favorite memories are when I would sit on his lap while he read books to me, or when we went skiing or camping. When he died, I was so, so sad because I thought I would never be with him again, but you know what I found out? That cord? It's still there. I can still feel him sometimes."

I see him turning this over in his mind, considering it carefully. "How does that make you feel about the cord with your dad?" I ask hesitantly, afraid of what I may be stirring up. Jack's father had never been a consistent part of his life; his gypsy ways ran deep, prompting him to choose travel, adventure, and other women over family life. When I was six months pregnant, he left for Alaska to spend his summer fishing. I knew our relationship was in trouble, and soon discovered it was much less stressful without him. Not wanting our child to grow up watching us argue, at eight months pregnant, big and round, I moved his things to a storage unit, mailed him the key, and my life as a single mother began.

"My dad? Oh, it's just not there," Jack states matter-of-factly. "I think maybe, in the beginning, when I was a baby, the cord was just too short, and so when he went away, it just broke." Now he's reading my face, and it's his turn to provide reassurance. "But that's okay," he gently pats my hand, "because it just made the cord with you even stronger." He leans over and hugs me close. "But don't talk about being on the tracks. That makes my stomach feel sick." He's careful to explain these things to me simply and quietly—my amazing little teacher.

Later that night, as Devi cowers in the corner, hiding from her demons, I hear Jack rustle and feel cold little legs slide under the covers alongside me, his gangly arms twining around my neck, hugging me tight. His whisper brushes my ear, careful not to disturb the almost sleeping giant on the other side, "Just promise not to lay down in any railroad tracks."

"Oh, Jack, it's just an expression, like 'kill two birds with one stone.'" I search the darkness for his response.

Eventually, a tiny voice replies, "But Mom, I would never want to kill a bird either. Just promise, ok?"

"Ok, Jackie, I promise."

I'm startled awake by an unfamiliar noise and sleepy thoughts crawl through my brain as I try to get my bearings and remember which side of the world I'm on. I realize it's the phone and quickly roll out of bed to dash down the stairs and lunge for the receiver.

"Ah yes, good evening, this is Daman. Is your email address kbird@yahoo.com?"

"What?"

"I am sorry for calling so late. I have sent you very important email," he states, waiting for my response. "Okay?"

"Yeah, okay," I mumble, wondering what could possibly be important enough to call in what feels like the middle of the night.

"Okay, then, goodbye." He says in a cheerful voice.

As I stretch to hang up the phone, I hear wails of an angry toddler whose radar has detected my absence, and back up the steps I go.

In the morning, as soon as Devi is content at the table with a bowl of cereal, I check my email. I'd been waiting for feedback from Daman regarding my proposal to prepare Kidz Café for the coming *Dashain* holiday. Analyzing the business had been more difficult than I'd expected after my process was delayed several times. I'd been unable to access company accounts due to faulty passwords, then was given out-of-date sales figures and inventory reports. Several nights I sat discreetly reading a magazine behind my laptop, observing a vacant restaurant. The dismal menu of TV dinner-grade processed foods left me feeling sorry for Daman and his sad little café, so I didn't bill him for all the hours I'd spent trying to find a way to keep his business afloat. I knew no Westerner would pay a dime for a strawberry Duncan Hines cake with white icing, even if the box was prominently displayed as proof of the product's pedigree. Daman believed anything Western was superior, even if all you did to prepare it was add water and stir. The café needed an overhaul, so I composed a respectful proposal that detailed how to improve advertising, atmosphere, productivity and, especially, the menu.

```
Dear Kate,
   With few meetings I had with you, I have
realize you are not able to dedicate the
expected time at Kidz premise. As you have
mentioned your children to me several times
on our last meeting, this shows your priority
at this moment is your children whereas my
priority is to increase sales of Kidz. As
per our record, since you have received the
appointment letter (more than a fortnight has
gone by), you could hardly spend total of not
more than 8 hours (5 visits), and since our
```

```
priorities differ, it will best on both of
our interest not to continue with you as the
Manager of Kidz.
    Thanks for your valuable inputs.

Sincerely,
Daman Dangol
Director, Kidz Café The Food Station
```

Fired for talking too much about my children? Thanks for your valuable inputs? This is not the Nepal I want to be in, a Westernized, profit-hungry, disposable employee Nepal. I'm livid, but clearly Daman has considerable clout in the Valley, and it would be unwise to cross him. In addition, his wife is my daughter's doctor, a bridge I definitely don't want to burn. I feel trapped realizing that as a woman, I'm at a disadvantage, and I fear the trouble he is capable of creating for me. Could he close my bank account? Convince my landlord to evict me?

I send a carefully worded, polite response, that details the amount of time I devoted to the proposal and request fair compensation. His response is vicious. He insults my competency and questions my character, then finally states he will pay me no more than 1,200 Nepali rupees (NRS), less than $20.

Unable to hold back my hurt and anger, I tell him to keep his money; he will need every dime to save that sinking ship.

Thankfully, Dinesh interrupts me with breakfast. Custard rolls, persimmons, cinnamon-cardamom spiced pancakes, fresh squeezed juice, and home blended chai tea make the morning's battle fade. Our bird-call doorbell goes off braaack brack brack yacking and I look out the front windows to see Jade waving, her bouncy golden locks shining in the sun.

"Where's Jack?" hollers Iven as he tumbles in the door with a sword swinging from his belt. When Christina enters, the kids run off to the playroom, and we make ourselves comfortable in the wicker chairs by the huge arched window as Dinesh shifts the breakfast pastries and tea to the coffee table between us.

"I read that hideous email you forwarded from your former employer and I say, good riddance," Christina says, smiling over her tea. "You just can't cross an Asian male ego."

"It's ridiculous. He claims I couldn't run the computer program, but he never gave me administrative clearance."

"Oooohhh, I get it," she says, eyes flickering. "He lost face. This happened in front of his employees, yes?" I nod blankly. "Ooooo . . . doubly losing face! First, in you finding his flaws, then finding them in front of his employees. I get it now! Don't you see? He never wanted you to look at his books, or help train staff, or improve the menu, or any of the things that you offered. All he wanted was a hostess! A pretty expat face mingling with the customers and bringing charm to his pathetic little hole in the wall. He lost face, that's all there is to it. Dig no deeper."

"So, when he said he wanted a good mind on board, that was just talk?"

"Of course it was! He wants you to be smart, but not too smart—certainly not smart enough to find problems in his books or his business. He wanted you to be a naive yes-girl and ask no questions. Typical Asian man. His ego is so big, he can't possibly be schooled by a woman, and especially not a Westerner!" she concludes. "What you need is a good day of shopping. Let's go out for some cheap thrills and forget that miserable little man. We've got to get some things to spruce up this drab little place before I leave you to fend for yourself."

And off we go. Kids happy with *didis*, me happy with Nepal again.

Christina barks directions in Nepali to the driver as he dodges in and out of traffic.

"Don't show any sign of weakness, or they will take you for anything and everything," Christina instructs. "Always be confident, and they won't cross you; they have no idea what to do with confident women. Learn enough of the language to state your demands clearly, and they'll assume you know what's what. If they start yammering at you and you don't understand, just play aloof and ignore them. And always always always carry pictures of your children. Nepalis *love* children. That's a soft spot that can work to your advantage."

She relays a story of trekking far off the beaten path with Stephan and his crew on a photo expedition when they were picked up by a Maoist patrol. Their camera equipment was confiscated, and they were taken to an airfield to be questioned, but Christina was held apart from the rest of the group. As night fell, she began to feel fearful of one man who was quite drunk. To fend off his advances, she took out pictures of her children and was soon able to escape and find Stephan, who was busy negotiating the return of his hundreds of thousands of dollars of equipment. I'm shocked by her tales of dangerous adventure, but I am also an eager student in her crash course and appreciate her tough love instructions.

As we stop and go, stop and go along the narrow street lined with tall buildings, she points out various spots in the shopping district frequented by locals who have the best prices for quality knockoffs. She instructs me not to believe any label on anything from batteries (probably scavenged from a trash pile) to outdoor gear (a friend had a fleece jacket with a Northface label on one side and a Patagonia label on the other) to the biggest lemon of all, electronics. We pass a shopping mall of giant concrete pancakes balancing on popsicle-stick pillars; I can't imagine it will take much of a rumble for it to all fall down.

Christina commands the taxi driver *rook nus*, stop, and tosses him rupees as we hop out. We jet down a row of overcrowded shops toward the market, brushing past aggressive vendors, their wares spilling out onto the broken sidewalk. As the street disappears into a sea of humanness, the air is thick with incense and sweat. Christina darts this way and that, a veteran of this shopping battlefield. We pass through a maze of glittering rainbow seed beads and emerge at the infamous Freak Street where wandering Western hippies sought psychedelic enlightenment in the sixties and seventies. Then we move on to the textile stalls filled with vibrant material stacked from floor to ceiling and enter the one with the best quality fabric.

Upon seeing Christina, the men scamper to bring us padded

stools and steaming cups of tea as they fumble over themselves to present her with various selections. She doesn't see anything she likes, so we venture upstairs to a private stash of high-end options. After some prodding, the owner brings out the heavenly Egyptian cotton Christina has been holding out for, and she places an order. As we leave, she advises the men that I am a very dear friend, and they should help me with anything I need. They graciously agree, bobblehead nodding, smiling, bowing, palms together, *namasté*.

Back in the market, we drop spare change on cute colorful shoes, *tikas*, and bangles for our little girls. And that's when it hits me: I'm shopping for my little girl. The thought of her and the unbelievable blessing she is in my life quickly expands to recognizing the blessings all around me, here, in Kathmandu, Nepal. Christina sees the tears welling up in my eyes and smiles, hugging me close. She knows the significance of those little shoes.

"You are her mum now, and don't you forget it! You're the best thing that could happen to that little girl."

"Then why is it so hard?" I ask, choking back tears, and she starts to laugh.

"Oh, Kate. What in the world made you think this would be easy?"

Christina's departure leaves a sizable void, not just for me, but for Jack as well who misses his new love, Jade. We wave as they pull away from Summit, Jack a bit more vigorously, running down the lane as if trying to flag down a rescue ship. He sulks all the way home like a lost puppy-lover, but Dinesh comes to the rescue.

"Jackie, you go with me to get pastry?" Jack's eyes light up at the thought of sweets, and they are off to the farmers market, while Devi and I have a tea party with a zoo of stuffed animal guests.

I hear the kitchen door open and hear Jack's happy chatter, so go to see what goodies they've brought home, only to find him with a kitten in his arms.

"Look Mom! A *didi* had 'em in a basket and gave me one for free! Can you believe it? Free! F.R.E.E. That's FREE!" Suddenly, the misery of losing Jade has vanished, and Jack is sure he is the luckiest boy in the world. All I can think of is how I am going to fly a cat back to the States. I miss Christina already.

Lucky for me, another adoptive mother, Stephanie, soon arrives to pick up her toddler, Dawa, who is also living at Annie's. Dawa is the cool and gentle moon to Devi's fiery blazing sun. She's small and delicate, like a little fawn, with big, chocolate brown eyes and soft wispy hair. Shy and timid, she is also Devi's favorite target, at times forcefully taking anything Dawa has—toys, food, a chair—and little Dawa submits every time. The *didis* have their hands full with three other babies, so I'm happy to help by redirecting play and sparing sweet Dawa further torment by my little lotus blossom. Stephanie is here to complete the final paperwork for their adoption while her husband, at the peak of his guide season in the mountain West, is waiting anxiously at home. They'd traveled to Nepal for years, trekking in Khombu, and decided to give back to the community by becoming parents to one of the Sherpa children. With their deep-rooted connections and Nepali friends, they found a child in need on their own without a referral from a stateside agency. Annie, in conjunction with the orphanage where Devi had been, is facilitating the process, but this approach is creating its own set of challenges.

For a child to be legally classified as an orphan in Nepal, he or she must meet certain criteria. In a country where a back-door bribe can buy any number of morally unconscionable things, the U.S. State Department struggles to verify the orphan status of many children in an attempt to curb child trafficking. The result is a volatile and often exceptionally drawn out adoption process.

To complicate things, Nepalese law states that women are not permitted to relinquish a child without the father's permission. If the mother does not have this permission for whatever reason, the child is held in a government orphanage (yes, the scary kind) for up to twelve years to give the father ample opportunity to claim the child. In addition, no first-born child of either gender may be relinquished with or without the permission of the father because culturally, they are expected to care for their parents when they are elderly. It isn't hard to see why children are abandoned in the streets, since in many cases it's illegal to give them up. The U.S. Embassy is faced with determining whether or not a child is truly an orphan.

Although everything seems to be going along fine in Stephanie's process, I can feel her stress. Since she hadn't gotten a referral from an agency, she is under a different level of scrutiny. Still, she keeps her composure and never talks about just how overwhelming things are. I don't ask, and she doesn't tell; we just enjoy time with our girls, sharing outings around the Valley. She listens compassionately to my Devi issues, though Dawa, who is Stephanie's first child, doesn't seem to have any problems whatsoever. I'm the veteran parent here, but I feel clueless.

It's a bright, sun-filled morning, and Jack, Devi, and I trek over to Summit to meet Stephanie and Dawa for breakfast before an outing to Boudhanatha, the largest Buddhist *stupa* (temple) in Nepal. She needs to deliver a package to a Sherpa who is in the process of securing his visa to the Land of the Free to be with his American wife. She is looking forward to visiting some friends from Khombu, and we are happy to tag along.

Juggling plates and cups of juice, we move to the garden to sit at a big round table under an umbrella.

"How civilized for an American!" a lovely graying woman says sweetly, observing the girls digging at their egg cups as she passes by.

"Is it that obvious?" I say sighing, wondering how we've already managed to give off the obnoxious American vibe today.

"Oh, no! I just heard you speaking, that's how I knew. Is this your little girl?" she inquires while smiling down at Devi, who is stuffing as much egg into her mouth as possible.

"Yes, this is Devi, and this is my son, Jack," I offer as Jack peers, one eye closed, into the spout of the hot chocolate pot, hoping for one last drop.

"Oh! They are simply gorgeous!" she coos.

"Well, thank you!" I beam. "Are you staying here?" I ask, stretching the moment.

"Yes, I just got in yesterday. How long has your little girl been with you?"

"Only about a month now. We're living here while we wait out the adoption process."

"How long do you think you'll be here?" she asks, interested in our story.

"Unfortunately, the process is unpredictable, so it's hard to say. Usually it's four to six months, but there was a glitch in my paperwork, so we'll be here a bit longer. I hope we'll be home by spring."

"You must be a very dedicated mother. When I was living in Korea, back in the seventies, I helped escort babies to their adoptive parents in the United States. One time, a few other women and I had about ten babies, all crawling around the back of the plane, it was quite a trip! I remember when I got off with my little guy and went to hand him to his new family, I already felt so connected! I was so worried about whether they were the right family for him, if they would care for him, and really love him. But when I saw them at the end of jet way, and they were crying, that's when I knew it would all be fine. Somehow, I just knew they were the right family."

"That's how I felt when I saw Devi's picture for the first time. I tried to think it through logically when the agency called, before I saw her picture, but once her face popped up on my computer screen, I just knew she was the one, and I came as soon as I could." An equally lovely, younger woman with long black hair and a perfect porcelain complexion approaches us, looking very cosmopolitan in dark designer sunglasses.

"This is my daughter Nora. This is, oh, I've forgotten to ask your name!"

"I'm Kate, and there go Jack and Devi." I point to the kids, now busy exploring the gardens.

"I'm Louise," she says, and I think of my grandmother, Louise, from whom I got my middle name.

I walk with Nora and Louise to their table as a dashing man joins them, embracing Nora.

"Kate, this is my son Craig. He's been living here for a little over a year now," Louise says. Realizing the pair are not an item, I try to tamp down my interest in this handsome man, hoping not to be too obvious.

"Would you like to join us?" Craig offers with a charming smile, holding my gaze with his sea green eyes. He's tall, well built, and tanned with thick waves of honey-gold locks tumbling recklessly from beneath his bike helmet.

"I'd love to, but I need to keep up with my kids," I stutter like a schoolgirl, feeling my cheeks flush. I linger long enough to learn that Craig is a philosophy professor at Saint Xavier's College, and Nora has come to do volunteer work. It's Louise and Nora's first day here, and Craig has just come from his flat to meet them. We discuss the glorious weather, living arrangements, and the benefit of Nepali lessons.

"Give me your email and I'll connect you with my Nepali teacher; he's fantastic," Craig offers, and I dig into my bag for pen and paper. "We're headed to Tibet for a few days, but we should all get together for tea once we get back," he suggests, and my heart flutters. I'd rather stay and chat, but excuse myself to help Stephanie gather the kids for our outing.

We all squish into the backseat of a taxi with Jack in the middle and the girls half-sitting on the floorboard, eyeing each other. Now that each has her own sippy cup and her own Mommy, the competition has abated. I wonder if they know what's happening in their world. Do they have a psychic orphan connection? I know I feel a connection to Stephanie and hope our girls will always be friends.

As we near Boudha, street dogs dig through garbage piles next to goats tied to vendors' shacks waiting to be sold; produce sellers sit with blankets spread before them, their baskets emptying as the day wears on. The women here are dressed differently, no longer wearing *kurtas* or *saris* like those in our neighborhood. Their dresses look more like silk robes, high at the neck, neatly folded over with a contrasting color from the inside peeking out and belted with an apron of tiny striped, vibrantly colored, hand-woven cloth. They are breathtakingly beautiful as they float elegantly down the road. Shops flank giant concrete pillars that mark the gate of the *stupa*. As we enter, I'm handed a flyer announcing Boudha as a World Heritage Site, and I can see why.

Over scratchy loudspeakers monks grumble "*Om Mani Peme Hum*," filling the *stupa* proper. I'm washed over with serenity and a sense of dedication. I drop to my knees and bow my forehead to the filthy ground, like I had so many times when a spiritual teacher entered the room. After practicing Buddhism in small groups in the American West, I'm awed by the grandeur of the *stupa*, which looks like a giant wedding cake. Enormous slabs of glowing white concrete are stacked in ascending squares with a mountainous half scoop of snowy ice cream, topped by a block of gold with all-knowing eyes gazing down. Above, layer after layer of gold stairsteps climb to the sky, garnished with thousands of strings of prayer flags fluttering yellow, red, white, blue and green prayers. We walk around the *stupa*, circumambulating, while spinning the prayer wheels that line the base. My fingers touch the history of the worn softness created by millions of hands wishing prayers.

We meet Stephanie's friends from Khombu, and they lead us to their nearby apartment. They are proud of their new in-town accommodations. The space is small and cramped, but their hospitality joyously fills the space. They are intent on feeding us an endless supply of *momos* (Tibetan dumplings) and in spite of my "I'm stuffed" mantras, accompanied by hand and facial gestures, they continue to refill my plate, so I endeavor to choke down the yak meat that tests my vegetarian palate. Devi, however, eats everything in sight, so I use her as a human shield and pass off my *momos* while discreetly drinking as much of her bottomless room-temperature Coca Cola as possible in hopes of preventing her from exploding.

Eventually, even perfect, passive little Dawa grows bored and restless, so we say our goodbyes and catch a taxi home. Bumping and thumping along, the exhausted toddlers quickly fall asleep, and

Jack's view of the city improves without little girl interruptions. He is amazed by all the new and interesting modes of transportation.

"Mom, that guy has *bananas* on his bike! Look! Look! See *all those bananas?*" (To his credit, there are a lot of bananas.)

The driver chooses a different way home, and it feels a LOT longer. I've come to realize that any time I ask a driver if he knows the location of a particular destination, he will always say yes, but this "yes" has no bearing on the reality of actually finding the desired location. Without any street names or addresses, locations are found by description alone. "The blue gate just past the trash pile across from the vacant lot . . . if you get to the Ganesh statue, you've gone too far." At times, a driver has even insisted their chosen drop point is better than the one originally requested. Tonight is no exception and giving our driver the benefit of the doubt, I guess he is taking pseudo-shortcuts to avoid traffic, but every route is packed. We jostle back and forth as he zips down one lane, then crosses over to another, and then, HONK! HONK! HOOOONNK!!!! Epic traffic jam. To date, I've only seen two stop lights throughout the entire Valley, and in the absence of any system to maintain order, it's every taxi for itself. Traffic here has a life of its own, and with vehicles coming from every direction, all of the arteries are clogged; the intersection is in cardiac arrest. And there, in the middle of it all, is a partially clothed man, standing on a bucket, eating off of a piece of broken glass with grimy hands. "Crazy" is an international language.

```
Dear Mom,
    Jack's birthday was on Friday, so we
had his party in the Summit garden under
a gazebo. He is excited to have ten new
friends! In spite of the drizzle, they
had loads of fun wearing glitter hats and
masks playing goofy games Stephanie and I
concocted. Dinesh was a great help chasing
Devi while I played hostess.
```

Jack has been having big fun with Sarresh, the landlord's son, playing soccer in the alley with a ball of rags the local kids made. I wonder what they could do with an actual ball?

Over the weekend, we went to Phora Dubar, the American Club, with Annie, her kids, Stephanie and Dawa. I talked with Annie about what has been going on with Devi; I think Stephanie must have told her of my desperation. It's strange, she tells me horror stories of holding down her son in the bath like a wild animal when he came to her at three, but she can't hear my challenges with Devi. I told her I'm scared of making things worse. She laughed and said, "NO! I can't think of anything you could do to make it worse!" We talked about studies that show the more disruptions, moves and caregivers a child has, the greater their problems with attachment. Knowing that I am at least Devi's fourth stop (her mom, the orphanage, Annie's, now me), she resists attaching because she doesn't want to be left again. Annie said many adoptive families struggle with sleep issues that may take years to overcome. Devi probably feels vulnerable falling asleep, so she reacts to that fear, starts feeling anxious, then she gets more tired, then the feelings get more intense, she gets more anxious, it snowballs . . .

Thank you again for your love and support. It's reassuring to know that you are just a phone call away, albeit an expensive one!

Gotta run, I have to find the dog that lives on the compound. He got hit by a motorbike and is in sad shape. The vet is coming by to take a look. Good karma! :)

Lots of love,
Kate

Good Dog (I can't remember his Nepali name), lies at my feet while flies buzz around his oozing face. He whines low and soft as he slowly rotates his head from side to side, ears flopping, heavy with infection. When I ask about the dog's origin, Sarresh, the landlord's son, told me he was left behind by the previous tenants of our house, which explains his persistent, pathetic presence at our back door. When he comes to me limping and bloody, the road rash hinting that he was on the losing end of a dog versus motorbike encounter; I am unable to look the other way. Jack and I have been missing our canine companions back home, and while he can't perform any tricks and doesn't really fill the cuddle void, he's a fellow resident of the compound who stands guard on our front stoop, and I can't help feeling beholden to him.

Like vet superheroes, Dr. Devkota and his assistant zoom in on their motorbikes through the big metal gate and remove their shoes as they enter the house. They ask about the dog's history and are not surprised I know very little. Entering the playroom, we stumble over plastic ears of corn and tiny tea cups left astray after my earlier luncheon with Devi and her dollies. The vet and his assistant create a makeshift clinic out of the supplies in their Nike gym bag and our Little Tykes kitchenette. Good Dog isn't aggressive, but he is in pain, so taking no chances, the assistant tears a piece of gauze off a roll and swiftly wraps his muzzle. Good Dog protests mildly but is too weak to fight, and soon the exam is complete.

Dr. Devkota gives me instructions for medication and follow-up care while his assistant cleans up. Then, as he hands me the bill, I brace myself, not planning vet care into our budget. He explains each item line by line, written in an unfamiliar scripted code.

"1100NRS," he says, about $16. Wow! At these rates, I realize with some minor sacrifices that we can afford to help many more street dogs.

Devi chases the kitty, whacking him with a stick.

"Devi, please stop. *Bastadi* (gently)," I say, calmly taking the stick from her hand and offering her a shape sorter. She throws it down, grabs the stick, looks right at me, and thwacks the kitten again. I take a deep breath, snatch the stick once more, but this time when she grabs it she smacks me and I dodge to keep from being cracked over the head. I snap, yelling at her, but she just looks at me blankly. I scoop her up from the arsenal of potential weapons and deposit her on the playroom mat.

"That hurts the kitty! That hurts Mommy! No hitting!"

She is slightly shocked by the quick relocation and searches my face for the meaning behind my sharp words, then she gives me a creepy, vacant grin. The room starts to spin, and I know I need a break, so I get up and leave her on the mat. As I reach the door, she begins to howl, afraid of being alone, so I stop and sit down with my head in my hands. I need this incessant struggle to stop.

"Let's pick up the blocks," I suggest. As she toddles around the room, happy to understand what is expected of her and I see her for who she is: a confused little girl. I wonder how I have become such an angry, impatient person?

I fantasize about how I can get out of this. Disappear with Jack in the dead of night? Take Devi back to Annie and tell her I just can't do it? How can I love being here so much, and at the same time, so desperately want out? It seems like no matter what I do, how patient I am, how calmly I speak, Devi is just a mess. Every single day. All day long. And if I did give her back, what then? I'll be haunted for the rest of my life wondering what became of her.

In the morning, Stephanie calls to ask if I'd like to run errands with her. She and Dawa are set to leave soon, their adoption process nearly complete, so I jump at the opportunity for grown-up time with her. Annie's kids are having friends over, so I take Jack and Devi to join in the fun under the watchful eye of the *didis*. As we leave, Jack peeks over the wall, standing on the dog house, and relentlessly asks question after question: where we're going, what we're doing, when we'll be back. He usually prefers time with friends in the safe confines of a compound to bustling city life, so I don't realize he's anxious about another day with Tarak.

It takes a few hours to accomplish all the errands on Stephanie's list: passport photos, ATM, airline tickets, trinkets for nieces and nephews. I'm happy to be her copilot and relish the time listening to stories of magical adventures in the Himals with her husband. Her eyes brighten as she tells them, her commitment to the country of her daughter's birth palpable.

When we arrive back at Annie's, Devi is playing on the slide. I catch her at the bottom, then tote her back up as she giggles and squirms. I tickle her ribs, then let her slide down again. Kids are everywhere, swinging, riding bikes, zooming down the zip line, but I don't see Jack anywhere. Anxiety creeps up my spine, like when he was three and would leave the grocery store to visit his "friends" in the shop next door. In the back of my mind, I always knew he was okay, but a mini-heart attack still ensued. Leaving Devi with a ball, I go into the house, which feels unnaturally still in the fading evening light. As my heartbeat thumps in my ears, I quietly move about, afraid of disturbing Annie, and search the playroom, dining room, kitchen, and finally the nursery, where I find Jack alone, huddled in a shadowy corner.

"What's goin' on, buddy?" I ask as I kneel down next to him.

"Can we go now?" he whispers, refusing to meet my gaze.

"Umm, okay." I search his face for clues. "What's going on Jackie? Why are you in here all alone?"

"Can we *please* just go?" his voice squeaks, as tears fill his eyes. I hold him close, and feeling him tremble, I know now is not the time for questions.

"Let me tell the *didis* we're leaving." I find Devi with the other kids, anxiously awaiting the evening meal of *dal bhat*. I tell the *didis* that we're on our way out and not to feed her, and they bobblehead nod and smile. I hurry back inside to find Jack sitting at the bottom of the steps waiting for me, staring blankly ahead.

He looks exhausted, and I wish I could carry him, but don't dare mention the other small person needing to be carried, so I splurge and hail a taxi. He watches quietly out the window, ignoring Devi, who is intent on poking and pinching him into engaging with her. After dinner at Summit, Jack revives somewhat, though it's clear something is wrong.

With Devi distracted in the playroom, I sit with Jack while he watches Scooby Doo.

"Hey buddy, I wish you would tell me what happened at Annie's house today," I softly prod.

"It was nothing, Mom." He replies, trying not to miss any vital information Scooby and the gang are gathering to solve the mystery.

"It didn't seem like nothing," I say, shifting to place myself between him and the TV.

He finally gives in and sighs, "I thought we were playing hide and seek. Tarak said the best spot was in the rug, so he rolled me up in it." I know the one he's talking about, an old, heavy, jute rug used for afternoon picnics and outdoor playtime. In a perverse twist on the old game, Jack was now a "ghost," trapped in the rug while the other boys jumped on top, singing out, "Where's that new kid Jack? We can't hear him! Oh yeah, he's a ghost! Come on ghost! If you want us to find you, you'll have to scream louder!" I break out in a cold sweat as I listen to the account of Jack's near-smothering.

"So, what did you do? How'd you get out?" I ask, fighting to control my voice.

"I just got so tired, it all got real still."

I realize he passed out, and I feel like I'm going to vomit.

"When I woke up, they were gone and I could crawl out," he says matter-of-factly as he tries to look around me to see the cartoon caper.

"Then what happened?" I prompt, afraid of what could be next.

"The rest of the day they just wouldn't play with me. When I tried to play with them, they would say, 'Do you hear a ghost?' and then they'd start laughing and run off." Tears well up in his eyes and his voice quivers. It wasn't the fear of imminent death that had rattled him; it was being excluded in this brave new *Lord of the Flies* world.

I feel beyond helpless. "Why didn't you go to one of the *didis*?" I ask, trying to problem-solve after the fact.

"Mom, they don't speak English." He rolls his eyes.

"Oh, buddy, I'm so sorry I wasn't there to help when you needed me."

"That's ok, Mom." Jack is always quick to forgive my Mom mistakes and ease my feelings of failure. "But I don't really want to go over there and play anymore, okay?" he asks, timidly.

Now I get it. Jack had put up with the bullying to be close to his new little sister, taking his protective big brother role very seriously. I wish I'd paid closer attention to his interest in our outing. I'd missed his signals, and I'm sickened by the thought of what could have happened if the boys hadn't stopped when he passed out.

"Of course, sweetie!" I hug him close. "I just thought with the other kids there, you might make some new friends. Did you like any of the other boys?" I ask, hoping to find some light in the darkness of his day.

"Well, I was playing with this other kid, Chris, and we were having fun, but then Tarak started teasing him for talking to a ghost, so he left. They all do whatever Tarak says." He looks at the ground, embarrassed at being the odd man out. Then he glances up at me, with his big brown puppy dog eyes, "Can I sleep with you tonight if I get scared?"

"Of course, buddy. There's plenty of room in my bed for all of us." I smile to push back my tears, and I know it's me who needs him close to get past the mental image of his still, little body, rolled up in a rug.

s

A few days later, walking out of the Summit farmers market, two children dart past me toward the same delicious goodies I have in hand.

"Oh, I'm so sorry! Really, they pay no attention at all to where they're going, honestly!" A frazzled woman offers a smile as she pulls out her handbag and closes the door of a gleaming SUV.

"Oh, no problem. I have a couple of my own." I return her smile.

"Are they here?" she asks, looking around.

"No, they're at home with the *dai*, just across the way," I reply, gesturing toward our compound. "That's how I got out of here with only one bag of pastry!" We both laugh and introduce ourselves. Carol is a consultant for an NGO, and her husband, Alex, is with the World Bank. When I tell her about my pending adoption, we find that we both know Annie, and the degrees of separation among my Kathmandu expat social circle narrow. Then Carol looks at me with sudden recognition.

"Oh, my goodness! Did your little boy bring home a kitten a few weeks ago?" she asks a bit sheepishly.

"Actually, he did," I say, surprised.

"I am so sorry!" she gasps. "Your son was so sure it would be fine, and then when I looked around, he was gone." The kitten had come from her *didi*'s basket.

"Oh, don't worry about it, really. Our *Dai* refuses to utter the word 'no' to him. At least he wasn't on the roof with the kitten; that's his new favorite rule to break." I roll my eyes. "He loves the easy access from our terrace almost as much as he loves being a spoiled prince."

Carol's son comes looking for her, and I recognize him as Jack's one ally, Chris, from the ill-fated play date at Annie's. When Carol asks how Jack is adjusting to his new school and friends, I gingerly tiptoe around the topic of Tarak, and she confides that she had stopped letting Chris play with Tarak in the past due to bullying. She had hoped Tarak might have matured, but when I offer more details, she raises an eyebrow, suggesting things may not have changed after all. Comforted by this secret alliance, we exchange phone numbers and agree to get the boys together soon.

Devi is a puzzle and a force to be reckoned with. She is round and cute and cuddly (sometimes). She is funny and sweet and nearly empathetic. When Jack cries, she goes to him and pats him gently, knowing he is sad, though not aware that she is often the source of his pain. She plays peek-a-boo and is delighted when I find her in the folds of my flowing calico skirt. She giggles and smiles so big her eyes crinkle shut and disappear. She lies down on the floor next to me and pets the kitty, saying "maow maow", but then carries him by the neck and violently throws him down. She gets frustrated and whacks and bites and stomps her feet. She stands on the table screeching to get my attention. She wakes up in the night shrieking, hitting, and kicking, and when I try to comfort her, desperate to help her feel safe, she fights and pushes me away, still trying to hide between the wall and the bed. When we go new places, she grows increasingly anxious and nervously pinches me, while clinging to me with vice-grip legs. I often have to keep her in the baby backpack or she will try to eat anything resembling food off the ground. I feel like a hostage to her world.

When I do get away, however briefly, to try and gather the scattered remnants of my former self, to grasp at some degree of sanity, my penance is a return to her world fueled by anxiety that has now increased exponentially. Even the quiet of naptime is like a ticking bomb; the anticipation of her waking with screams of terror has me shell-shocked.

Days have slipped into weeks and now grow into months. Sleepless nights are taking a toll on all of us. Jack has developed survival skills to sleep through the nighttime frenzy by burying his head under piles of pillows. I stumble from one screaming bout to the next, holding her tight to protect us both from her erratic flailing as her cries reach epic levels of fear and desperation. My hands cramp from gripping her wrists to stop her from picking at her face or pulling out her hair. She outlasts me every time, and overtaken by exhaustion, I resort to restraint, my only ally in this battle against her demons of the past. I roll her up in a blanket, burrito style, and hope the swaddling will help her to feel safe. When she is finally still, I drop off, only to be awakened too soon by shrill screams from her latest night terror. Something has to give.

I Google "sleep disorders, adopted children," and scan the list of suggested techniques, then laugh out loud like the crazy person I've become. Most sources recommend leaving the child in the room with the door shut so that they learn to "self soothe." Aching for a solution, I give it a try, and she screams for nearly an hour while I hide downstairs, exhausted, afraid of how much worse it will be when I go back in. Maybe this is just a cosmic sign that I need little sleep and absolutely no alone time.

When I reach out to family and friends, I'm flooded with well-meaning suggestions: My mother encourages lullabies, but Devi can't hear me singing when she's out of her head screaming. "Rub her back" a well-meaning friend offers, unaware that my touch is like fire to her. "Just walk around the room with her," another mother counsels, condescendingly. I could walk all the way to Mount Everest, but she would scream the moment I put her down. "Ask a Rinpoche for a blessing," a Buddhist guides, although Christina has already taken us to one. "I think she has not enough to eat," says Dinesh, and I look at him sideways, unable to imagine how much more a child her size can consume. "She's just really scared," sweet Jackie concludes, and I think he's probably the only one who's right. Everyone seems to have the solution except me, and I wonder if we will ever be able to stay in a hotel room again without someone calling security? Will she ever be able to go to a slumber party? Will she ever go away to summer camp? Will I ever sleep for longer than an hour again?

As I sit on the terrace savoring the last sips of my afternoon tea, I hear pigeons cooing in the eaves and startle, afraid Devi is already waking, and I pray she's still asleep. Sand passes quickly through the hourglass, and I feel like Dorothy trapped in the witch's castle awaiting my imminent doom, so I savor the last few moments of silence before my tiny captor wakes. I look out to the Himals and try to breathe deeply.

When I decided to adopt, I was aware of the many older children in need, so I was willing to accept a child up to five years old. I passed the long winter nights waiting for a referral, reading anything and everything I could find on international adoption, particularly of older children because their potential issues could be very different from those of infants. I'd spoken at length with Lauren, the stateside facilitator, and she assured me that, according to Annie, Devi showed absolutely no signs of attachment disorder. Since I naively thought my daughter-to-be was well adjusted and the many troubling issues I'd read about were of no concern, I'd left my books at home.

But now I have to figure something out. I feel like an annoyance to Annie, always bugging her with my questions, begging for advice. It's clear she's out of answers and disinterested in my plight. She continues to tell me that Devi's behaviors are normal and that I've had it easy since Jack isn't a very complex kid. When I ask about Devi's past, she shrugs with a dismissive smile and says, "don't worry about it, just move on," then follows up with an anecdote about how hard it's been with her kids, but now they're fine. When I try to talk with her about Jack being rolled up in the rug, evidence that all is not fine she brushes me off, and attributes the whole incident to Jack not being used to playing with real boys. Eventually, to silence my squeaking wheel, she hands me a book, *Attaching in Adoption*, by Deborah Gray, and a much-needed light switches on. A laundry list of behaviors that Devi routinely exhibits makes me realize I'm not crazy; nothing about her behavior can be classified as normal. Though the book is written for parents adopting older children, it gives me a starting point for online research so I can begin to understand what I'm dealing with. I learn that infants attach to new parents with less difficulty since they have usually experienced fewer caregivers and disruptions. Older children have the advantage of language that enables them to communicate with the adults around them and aids them in their transition, but toddlers are caught in between. Developmentally, they are beginning to venture out to explore the world around them and learn new skills, but still need the safe home base of a primary caregiver. Without that center, a toddler is like a teenager with a new driver's license and the parents are out of town. There's no one to set boundaries or to retreat to and feel safe with after a big adventure. An abandoned toddler is like a tiny juvenile delinquent.

I decide to contact the agency directly, since Annie, I realize, has given all she can to my cause. I don't want to undermine her or complain to her employer, but I need help, and I need it now. I'm drowning in a sea of screaming, biting, hitting, and kicking. The endless nights of Devi's nerve jacking night terrors have left me raw, and I'm helplessly watching my relationship with Jack erode under the pressure.

Anxiously, I dial the number for the stateside agency. Lauren is thrilled to hear from me, which comes as a welcome relief since I imagine Annie has told them I'm an overly demanding mess. I hesitantly ask if she has time to speak at length. I'm sure she can hear the desperation in my voice, and she responds with kind concern. She listens patiently as I describe some of Devi's aggressive behaviors, the mysterious questions from the pediatrician regarding whether or not she would speak, and the agonizing sleepless nights. Lauren assures me that this isn't all in my head, I'm not overreacting, and, no, the behavior Devi is displaying is in no way normal. After an extensive conversation, I'm confident she will support me and feel reinvigorated that help is on the way for my little one. Lauren promises to contact Annie, as well as the orphanage, to find out as much as they can about Devi's past. I'm hopeful they hold the key to helping me understand what triggers her outbursts, like when I tried to wash her neck and elicited a violent response. It sounds like this is the first time Lauren has heard of my problems with Devi, which makes it painfully clear that Annie has never even discussed our issues with her.

Lauren explains that Devi's behaviors suggest attachment disorder at the least and most likely also indicate signs of abuse, neglect, and trauma. "Devi is compelled to evoke a negative response from you to create an environment similar to what she has likely experienced in the past. As strange as this may sound, in the care of a kind, loving and nurturing person, Devi doesn't know how to respond. She may have never experienced this dynamic, so it feels uncomfortable for her." Lauren explains in terms I'm able to understand, though it all sounds upside down and backward. "Provoking a negative reaction from you, no matter how heart-wrenching it is to recognize, is actually what feels normal to her."

I am crushed. No longer is this merely my arm-chair-internet-guided diagnosis; Lauren's confirmation makes Devi's problems real. They are no longer just scary monsters under the bed.

"This isn't your imagination," she says. "Jack is a well-adjusted, normal boy. Your baseline is realistic," she says, then adds soberly, "It's a hard reality, but some children are better off living in an institutional setting. We'll understand if you choose to disrupt the adoption."

I know this is the agency lingo for "give her back," and I thank Lauren for her time and support and tell her I need some time to think and I'll be in touch.

I'm reeling and realize a part of me wanted her to say, "Devi is just a strong-willed toddler, suck it up!" But she didn't. Instead, I heard, "Oh, Kate, I'm so sorry." As the severity of Devi's mental and emotional ailments set in, I feel myself begin to shut down. I ache to look away from what could have happened in her past to traumatize her. I've been unconsciously holding out every bit of hope that none of this was true, that nothing bad ever happened to her, but like the prayer flags fluttering from Swayambhu in the distance, it's impossible not to see all the flags Devi is flying are red.

```
Dear Kate,
    Maybe you should just come home and
get Jack in a decent school. You could get
some kind of job, anything, and then go
get Devi on your own in the spring when
all the paperwork is finished. But then, I
think about how much it would undo all the
good you've already done, and how much she
will have changed in another 6 months. And
really, she's just doing what all two-year-
olds do. She'll get over this stubborn stage.
Remember, you were very independent! You and
your friend Stevie were just like Devi and
Dawa. You took everything away from him, too!
She's probably at the height of her two-ness,
she'll come around soon. In the meantime, let
her sleep in her own room! And Jack, too!

Love,
Mom
```

Dear Mom,

    Thanks for the good thoughts. I hear you about the two-ness, and I certainly hope she's peaking right now. Unfortunately, the information I've found so far points in a different direction. I thought about your suggestion to leave, but then I'm just another person that has left, and six months is a very long time for a very scared little girl. That's what she is, just a scared little girl. Besides, I have the rest of my life to sleep!

    I spoke with Lauren from the agency this morning for quite some time and she believes Devi shows signs of attachment disorder, most likely due to abuse, neglect and trauma. I checked around the Valley, at Jack's school and CIWEK, the international clinic, looking for someone to do play therapy with her, but came up empty. Clearly, mental health is not a priority in the third world. I'm going to work on some things to build attachment during our waking hours so that maybe she will be more relaxed going into the scary sleep time. I appreciate your suggestion about her sleeping in her own room, but it's really not practical, I get so little sleep as it is, I can't be running up and down the stairs all night. I'll give it some more time, then look at the possibility of drugs. (Can you believe I even said that? Me, health food junkie?)

Lots of love,
Kate

Working out transportation to school for Jack is next on my to-do list. I've been taking him via taxi, an inconvenient and relatively expensive option. The school provides a bus for a fraction of the cost, and now that Jack has settled in, I think he is ready to take the next step and start riding with the other kids, I know I am. With no street names or addresses, the only way to ensure that Jack will be brought to the correct residence is to ride along after school to show the driver exactly where we live, down the lane from Summit, in the alley across from Laxmi Dairy.

I catch a taxi to school in time for the tidal wave of after-school bliss that floods the potholed alley outside the school gate. After the tide goes out, I find Jack and we pile into the minivan (aka school bus) with a dozen other exuberant kids. Since there are no seatbelts, everyone squishes in where they can. They all know the drop off order, so those who are off first station themselves on the floorboard close to the sliding door, ready to pop out of our clown car. We meander down lanes through neighborhoods I didn't know existed, and I'm stunned by the beautiful compound gardens, the ornate architecture, the clean and tidy alleyways. We're greeted again and again by a smiling social class of Nepalis I haven't yet encountered.

Clearly exhausted, the little girl next to me repeatedly drops off to sleep, her head eventually rolling to the side and thumping on the window. As the crowd in the bus thins, I slide over and put my arm around her baby bird shoulders to cushion the remainder of her ride home. As we bump along, I look down at her remarkably beautiful face and daydream about what color *sari* her undoubtedly lovely mother will be wearing and what her compound will look like. I struggle to remember enough Nepali to compliment her *Ama* on her divine daughter.

When I glance up, I notice the neighborhood has changed dramatically. We have left the charming residences along twisting lanes for a short alley leading to dilapidated multistory buildings. We come to a dead end in the ominous shadow of the structure beside us and stop at a double wide maroon gate. Over the nail-tipped wall, I can see that the compound contains a large, four-story brick residence. A uniformed guard yanks the handle of the minivan and slides the door open. He grabs the little girl's arm, shaking her awake. She sits up groggily to collect her oversized backpack from the floorboard and stumbles out the door of the bus, unaided. Incensed, I wonder if her mother knows her little girl is treated this way, but when the gate opens, all I see is concrete and a sea of dirty, shoeless children, then the gate swings shut. As we pull out, on the white cinderblock wall, among the hieroglyphic Nepali, in the same maroon as the gate, I see the words "Children's Home." This is an orphanage.

"*Dai, Dai!*" I call out to the driver. "The little girl," I stammer, pointing to the gate, sure there has been a mistake.

"Devi, Madam? She is orphan."

The hair stands up on the back of my neck, and I feel as if I've been given a peek into a parallel universe. In only a few short years, this is what *my* Devi's life could be.

```
Hi Mom,
    It's amazing just how "normal" things are
beginning to look. I still dream of home,
always going back to get something I've
forgotten or check on the dogs, but in waking
life, it's so far away! My groovy little
grocery store was another lifetime, may it
rest in peace!
    Stephanie and Dawa left last week. She
was incredibly stressed about the Embassy
interview, worrying she may know "too much"
about Dawa's past, creating cause for further
investigation. But, she got through it, so
now I have faith, it can be done! Devi and I
will miss them terribly, but we are looking
forward to a reunion stateside.
    Good Dog is still stinky but hilarious,
already back to roaming. I brought home a
couple of puppies that were living in a pile
of concrete mix, getting just big enough to
wander into the street and get squashed, not
a good sight for Jack on the way to school!
Thankfully, the vet said he will find homes
for them since they are both boys. I guess
they don't like girl dogs here, either.
I picked up the momma dog too (the taxi
```

drivers think I'm nuts) and got her spayed. She had been living at the chicken vendor's shack down the lane. Now that she's gotten a taste of the good life, she comes and goes as she pleases, squeezing under the gate and guarding the front stoop in Good Dog's absence.

   Jack is supplementing his Nepali schoolwork with the homework that Mr. Jacobs sent with us. It's incredibly easy for him, so I'm encouraging him to do more, then I won't worry about him being behind when we get back. Mr. Jacobs made a good point - Jack has so many new stresses on him right now, let the work they give him at school be easy, that way he can be a superstar and enjoy just being a kid. At night I have been reading him *The Hobbit*. I think he can relate to Bilbo Baggins, being so small and alone, far from home on some crazy adventure he got dragged along for. There's a great reward for dear Bilbo in the end, though I'm not sure Jack will agree that Devi is a treasure!

   Speaking of my little bundle of disaster... You know, after coming back from my morning trip to the Ganesh temple on our lane, I had a mini epiphany. I have to surrender to the situation and stop trying to fix her, just accept her for who she is, screaming and all. I can't take it personally! The best way I can help her is to be a kind, patient and stable person in her life. I'm doing my best to love her even when she's screaming!

Love you,
Kate

Dear Kate,
   I was talking to a woman in the office, Holly, who has been asking about your

progress. She said she had the same problems with her son when he was younger. She had a terrible time getting him to go down at night, and he also had problems with his temper and how to control it. But she's taught him acceptable ways to channel his feelings, or how to avoid the conflict in the first place. Holly says that he's just a very intense little boy. See, you're not the only one!

The important thing is that whether something terrible happened to her in the past (or it didn't!!) you're trying your best to do something, not ignore it or throw your hands up in defeat. I guess I just think like a psychologist: Okay, that happened to her (or not!!), it's over, it can't be changed. Just move on.

Hang in there!
Mom

While I know my mother is trying to be supportive, her recent communications sound questioning and dismissive. Clearly, she is in denial that anything dark could be in Devi's past. I know her need to paint all the ills of the world rosey, but, really, did she think I was just making this up?

I dream I'm in the garage with my father while he works on our old, yellow '78 International Scout. He's getting frustrated because he's a south paw trying to work with tools made for righties. "I have all these tools, but I can't find a way to use them," is the unspoken message. Waking up, I realize, I am my own worst critic, and I feel like I lack the tools needed to care for my little girl. This dream helps me to see a new reality: I have the tools I need—love, patience, and compassion; I'm just having a hard time using them right now.

As I walk from the market down a quiet lane with Devi on my back, my thoughts roll over the dream again and again, and I wish for my father's presence in more than a fleeting midnight message. Stopping to let Devi out of the backpack to stretch her legs, we come upon some women selling flowers, and Devi is entranced. She peeks out from behind my skirt to look longingly at the women. One comes close and kneels down to her level, speaking softly in Nepali, and reaches out to sweetly touch her cheek. Devi watches her intently, as if she might know her, searching her memory for a connection to this woman. Suddenly she withdraws and buries her head in the back of my thigh. I feel the frenetic energy that I've learned is the warning signal that she is about to blow, and I swing her up onto my hip. I offer a polite *"Namasté"* to the women and turn to go, then notice Devi looking over my shoulder, holding their gaze solemnly as I carry her away.

The rest of the frustration-filled, napless day, Devi is nothing resembling compliant. She pulls at me, demanding to be held, then violently arches her back, and nearly falls over with squeals and squawks. Once we finish dinner, I take her up to the loft and turn on quiet classical music while I give her a long slow bath, drying her off gently and combing her hair. She lies down obediently for a massage, her favorite part of the day, and as I rub lotion into her soft mocha skin, I feel her relax and soften; magically she's calm. I speak to her kindly, telling her I love her, and that I'm so happy she's my little girl. We are connecting, *really* connecting. She looks up at me, and her eyes comfort my exhausted spirit. "Mommy," she says as she reaches up to softly touch my face, and I melt. I fight not to cry, afraid of dissuading her with confusing nonverbal cues. I quickly wipe away my tears as I gather her up in a blanket for our bedtime story, the one with the mommy who always loves the little girl, no matter how naughty she is. She points with a chubby finger to the mommy in the book, "Mommy," then pauses and looks up to me, touching my chest, "Mommy," she repeats, eyes crinkling shut with giggles. And in this moment, I know, every second of this struggle is worth it.

I am *desperate* to get across the street, but there is never a long enough break in the steady stream of traffic to get all the way across. This is ridiculous. I can't spend the rest of my time in Nepal trapped by traffic! So far, I've managed to avoid the challenge by only frequenting merchants on our side of the busy road, but I need to figure this system out. The only option seems to be to do what I see the locals do, just walk out there and stand in the traffic, which would require defying my screaming mind and all my logical instincts, while hoping I don't get mowed down in the process. But where? The road curves up a hill, making it impossible to see in both directions for any distance. I pace back and forth, trying to pick the best starting point. Then I spot a monkey stuttering along the sidewalk, getting ready to make his move. He looks left, then right, then left again, then right, and slowly but deliberately, wades out into the traffic, crossing from one haphazard non-lined lane to the next. I watch his technique intently as he perfectly times each move, drifting with the ebb and flow of the vehicular current. I haven't seen any dead monkeys in the road, so I guess he knows what he's doing. I sneak up and start to follow him, careful not to startle him; I'm thankful for the guidance, and trust the zooming taxis will avoid me as they do him. Success!

My heart racing, amazed I made it across the road alive, I look up to see Nora and wonder sheepishly if she saw my monkey see, monkey do, moment.

"Kate, it's so good to see you!" she sings, giving me a hug. "We got back from Tibet a few days ago, but I'm still getting settled." She shares her list of things she's looking for to make her concrete box apartment a little homier. Then, pausing, she takes a closer look at my tired expression, "Are you okay? I'm sorry to say this, but you look terrible."

"I haven't been getting much sleep lately," I confess, then tell her the short version of Devi's sleepless nights, downplaying their severity in an attempt to ward off any more well-meaning advice.

"Wow, that sounds really rough," she empathizes, then brightens and suggests, "How about some grown-up girl time? I know of a fabulous little place we can get a foot massage and pedicure for only a couple of bucks. I get that you're not the foo-foo kind of gal, but even *you* deserve a little pampering!"

I appreciate the offer and gladly take her up on it. She promises to stop by for a cup of tea the next afternoon, and as we go our separate ways I suppress the urge to cling to her kindness and follow her home like a lonely street dog.

Thanks to my monkey friend, I've now doubled my shopping territory, and I slide in and out of various handicraft shops. They all seem to have the same wares for sale, but I drift through each storefront anyway feeling drunk from lack of sleep. I unconsciously handle textiles and pottery I have no intention of purchasing but go through the motions in an attempt at normalcy. I feel like everyone can see the hopelessness hanging off me like the grim reaper's cloak.

I wander past grubby men lingering on the sidewalk and stumble into a furniture shop. I saunter past the same wickerware tables, sofas, and coat racks I've seen in all the other shops, but then, in a dim corner, I see it—the one item I have come to believe is unknown in this part of the world. I've already asked every furniture maker I've met for one, but am always met with a look of confusion. But here it is, like the Holy Grail, glowing in a sliver of sunlight peeking through a crack in the wall, the twisted legs of a rocking chair. I trip through the crowded room to get to it, not yet believing my eyes. As I reach the object of my desire, I find myself shaking as tears of joy, relief, and utter exhaustion spill from my eyes, while my heart bangs in celebration. I quiet my breath, wipe away my tears, and pull myself together to locate the shopkeeper.

I find him outside, smoking a hand-rolled cigarette. "Please, please," I say and lead him to the crowded room. Despite his attempts to sell me other items along the way, I have no interest in anything else. Finally, he pulls out the coveted chair and carries it into the daylight for me to admire, then motions for me to sit. The golden bamboo is smooth and soft, the seat perfectly curves to cradle my tired back. I slide my hands along the arms, leaning so far back I nearly tip over. The shopkeeper laughs at my shocked expression and my white knuckles gripping the arms of the chair. I continue my test drive, with every rock feeling like I'm about to topple over, but I don't care; in this world, it's perfect. The shopkeeper can see how badly I want it and inflates the price, but with Christina's advice in mind, I haggle fluently, down to something I can live with, and finally, the chair is *mine*.

As the matchbox taxis buzz by, I realize that fitting my prize inside one of them is hopeless and question how I will get it home.

"You buy more," the shopkeeper offers, smiling long and wide, "*coolie* bring chair."

He has me and we both know it, so I relent; he's going to upgrade this sale one way or another. I select a bookcase I can't believe will actually support the weight of books, an armchair for the terrace, and a small table. We negotiate until he's satisfied and calls the coolie. I practically skip home to wait for my special delivery.

When I spot the coolie walking up the hill, my jaw drops. Slightly bent at the waist, he carries not only the rocking chair, but also the bookcase, armchair and table, all bound together in a massive cluster of bamboo and twine. He looks like a turtle with an oversized shell. His face is deeply grooved by time and sun, his eyes are cloudy with cataracts; his cracked and broken toes grip worn rubber flip-flops. I guess he must be at least 70 years old. He unloads the mountain of wares, and I offer him lunch. He refuses to come inside the house, preferring to squat by the kitchen door where Dinesh fills his plate with a generous helping of *dal bhat*.

Hoisting the chair over my head, I gravitate to the terrace, ready to rock my troubles away. Devi isn't too sure about the long rails running below the chair, but curiosity gets the better of her and she climbs up onto my lap. We start slowly with tiny rocks and she's delighted, leaning forward and pushing back to make the rocking bigger.

Suddenly, angry words rise up from below, and I peer over the railing to see what all the commotion is about. Dinesh is with the ranting *coolie*, who is holding up his flip flops, shaking them in disgust. Dinesh disappears inside, then reappears with his own shoes. By the time I gather Devi and dash downstairs to find out what's going on, the *coolie* is on his way out the gate, and Dinesh is standing barefoot in the garden.

"What happened?" I ask, slightly out of breath.

"Oh, is nothing Madam." Dinesh smiles in reassurance.

"What happened to your shoes?"

Dinesh twists and turns his toes in the grass, looking this way and that, like a child caught doing something naughty.

"The puppies eat his shoes, Madam." Dinesh admits, unable to tell a lie.

Oops.

```
Hi Kate!
    I just saw you an hour ago, but had to
write and let you know how touched I was to
see how your heart is caring not just for
your daughter, but for the forgotten puppies
struggling to survive in the streets. No
kidding, you may not appreciate your own
talents!
    Let's get together with Nora for tea soon.
I hope the Nepali lessons are going well,
what a beautiful gift to share with your
daughter to keep her culture alive. Devi
couldn't have a better Mom or brother. You
are her best karma!

Namasté,
Craig
```

I'm surprised by Craig's kind words and feel like I'm dreaming. Tea with a cute boy and a new girlfriend? Or maybe I should think of this as tea with a new girlfriend who happens to have a cute brother? I decide to go with the latter; after losing both Christina and Stephanie, I need a new girlfriend more than I need the complication of an intimate relationship.

I trot over to Summit to soak up some quiet time before meeting Nora and Craig. Rain and cool mist fog up the Valley, a sure sign that fall is in the air. As the drizzle turns to a late season monsoonal downpour, I accept that I'm probably going to be stood up. Then, like a scene from a chick flick, Craig steps in the door, and scans the room; when he sees me, his face brightens. He saunters over, shaking out his wet locks.

"What are you doing here?" I ask in disbelief.

"Well, I couldn't leave you here alone, now could I?" he replies, pulling off his soaking sweater. "Nora sends her apologies. She's staying home, warm and dry."

"Here, take this," I say, tossing him the bulky wool layer I'd peeled off earlier.

We order tea and talk easily, discovering our paths nearly crossed years before. We had attended rival high schools in the Washington D.C. area and had frequented many of the same haunts. He shares the story of his fallout from the seminary, how he came to his current job teaching philosophy in Kathmandu, and his future travel plans. "So now, the question I'm sure you're tired of answering, but I'm going to ask anyway: why did you decide to adopt?"

"Well, since I'm an only child, I wanted Jack to have a sibling. I'd been waiting and waiting and waiting for Mr. Fabulous to show up, but then one day I realized, what kind of independant woman am I postponing a family for some imaginary man? My mother wanted me to go the artificial insemination route, but I couldn't face telling a child their father was number 284F. Friends tried to convince me a night in Telluride would turn up a "donor," but that didn't feel right either. Then, when the Asian tsunami hit, I woke up to the reality of how many children there are in this world without families. After that, it was easy to let go of wanting to create another little human."

"Wow, I really admire that. So, why Nepal?"

"Since I'm single, I didn't have much chance of adopting domestically, so I looked into international adoption. The literature suggested looking for a country whose culture you would want to incorporate into your life. The message of the Buddhist teachings I'd been to really resonated with me, so Nepal seemed like a good fit."

"And what do you think now?" Craig leans closer to hear me over the growing crowd in the lounge.

"Now, I can't imagine having made any other choice."

After tea, Craig insists on walking me home and invites me to a surprise birthday party for Nora. At the door, he gives me a hug and holding my face in his cold hands, kisses both cheeks. He thanks me again for the loan of the dry sweater, and I wonder if he is genuinely interested in me or is just being a nice guy and feeling sorry for a lonely expat. I'm painfully aware a single woman with two kids in tow isn't so sexy and I convince myself I should stick with my budding friendship with Nora and let the cute boy ride away into the night.

A few days later, the party is enjoyable, but with Craig playing host and Nora as the guest of honor, I struggle to make conversation. The guests all seem to be acquainted with each other and take little notice of me. Most are from the university, and I'm fairly certain I'm the only mom in the room. Craig is kind and attentive, often putting his arm around me, which doesn't get past his female roommate, who he later confides is not pleased he's told her he isn't interested in anything more than friendship. It's been a long time since I've been at a party without knowing anyone, and my social skills are rusty. Suddenly, sitting at home alone on the terrace, staring at the lights of the city, is very appealing. I say goodnight to Nora and get my sweater.

"I'll walk with you," Craig offers, whispering, "I need a break." We slip out the door and start down the dark footpath.

Craig drapes his arm around me, gently rubbing my shoulder, and I'm thankful for the escort. We walk through twists and turns I never would've been able to navigate on my own. It's dreamy being with him, so easy and comfortable. I feel like we've known each other for years rather than days. Between the demands of running my store, and being a single mother, dating had been rare, so this is a refreshing change. The quiet misty streets in yellowing lamp light feel romantic in spite of the garbage and sleeping cows. When a taxi finally appears, Craig gives the driver directions in polite Nepali. He turns to me, sea-green eyes glimmering, and touches the side of my face, then softly kisses me, the sweetest, most delicious of first kisses. Then a smile, a slight bow, and a good night.

November

As the days of November floated by, I found blessings everywhere, every day. After the stresses of getting settled, normalcy bordering on boredom, was a welcome feeling. Once I realized that at almost any time of day, almost anywhere, I could catch a taxi to Summit Hotel, I became more adventurous and discovered new neighborhoods as I soaked in more of the city. Daily walks provided the quiet time of bustling markets and honking taxis in narrow streets choked with pollution and garbage. But I loved it all, and I walked consciously, one foot after another. The rhythmic crunching of gravel under my sandals brought order to my days. *Om mani peme hum.* The gentle curves of our lane, the hopscotch of colored gates, the street dogs staking out their territories, all had become embroidered across the landscape of my mind. I loved the scenes of daily life, ladies outside doing laundry in big metal basins, children chasing chickens down alleyways, men sitting in tea stalls playing cards, cows blocking traffic. Every day I gave thanks for this window of time in my daughter's country. I no longer saw it as an arduous wait. No matter how strung out from lack of sleep I was, by the time I returned from my walk, I felt refreshed, and I often configured my afternoon escape to circle back to the Summit garden to relish one last taste of sanctuary for the day.

Sitting in the Summit Lodge, Nora and I engage in shameless mountain-man-watching and chit-chat with the handsome adventurers. A party of Australians who've just returned from Everest Base Camp tell us they are on their way to Pokhara, a little tourist town in the east, to scope out the famed Annapurna Circuit. With my ability to roam wild and free on hold, I relish living vicariously through them.

"Pokhara sounds amazing, don't you think?" I ask Nora as we walk down the lane, arm in arm.

"Yeah, I'd love to check it out, but I blew a wad on that elephant trek in Chitwan. I'm terrified I'll have to eat *dal bhat* every day if I don't stick to a budget," she groans. "Speaking of which, I saw a new café, Erza; we *must* check it out. It's near Annie's place in that big building that looks like it was dropped from the sky, the one smack in the middle of the road?"

I know the spot, the haphazard construction in the Valley is frightening. With very little local timber left to harvest, the majority of buildings are brick or cinder block; the city a true concrete jungle. With no building code enforcement, whether or not the ornate pillars are reinforced with rebar is debatable. The concrete itself is a questionable mix, hauled in by bucket brigades of young men using tightly woven baskets. In some areas, the mortar literally crumbles out from between the bricks. On a daily basis I repress the fear of being buried in rubble when the overdue mega earthquake hits.

"Lunch at a new place? Sounds good to me!" I cheer. In the real world, I don't know how much Nora and I would have in common. She, a refined classic beauty, full of confidence; next to her, I am a "plain Jane" in long organic cotton dresses—I'd rather be comfortable and culturally sensitive than stylish. I long since traded a big city career for the quality of life a mountain town offered, and I never looked back.

Nora came to Nepal to do a little soul searching after her life in New York went sideways. Her work in public relations had been on the fast track, and her fiancé, Richard, was a successful Wall Street broker. She had fabulously fashionable girlfriends, the perfect apartment, and a successful career; she was looking forward to a life full of glamourous potential. Then things took a turn. Richard started working late frequently, causing Nora to question their relationship. As things unraveled, Nora discovered that Richard had lost a great deal of money, but not on bad trades; his late nights had been fueled by an insatiable desire for cocaine. When she confronted him, he became volatile, and she knew she had to leave. After retreating to her parent's Philadelphia home, she decided to visit Craig and heal her broken heart through volunteer work. That was where our spirits connected, both of us feeling the pain of the world and a shared desire to be of service.

As we walk up to my gate, Jack peeks out the arched window by the front door and hearing the clank clunk of the heavy metal latch, he flies out the door and down the steps, leaping down the last three.

"Nora, Nora, Noooorrraaaa!" he calls out, bowling into her.

"Hey there, Jackie boy," she catches him in a hug. "Where's that little sister of yours?"

"Oh, she's somewhere with *Didi*, doing some girl thing," he mumbles, momentarily deflated by the mention of his nemesis. "Are you going to stay for dinner?" He jumps up and down, holding her hand.

She looks to me with question mark eyebrows. "Do you have time for us this evening, Ms. Murphy?" I tease. Since Nora's flat has little more to offer than packages of third world ramen, sparse crackers, and questionable fruit, I make a point of inviting her for dinner often. For pennies a plate, it's worth feeding her for the cheerful company she brings to our table.

"Let me check my schedule," she sighs, reaching into her bag for a mock cell phone, dialing into her palm and speed talking to rearrange her faux schedule for her most important client, Master Jackson Saunders.

Jack squeals and giggles as Nora keeps up the game, slowly walking and talking up the steps.

An ever-smiling Dinesh serves us salad with homemade dressing, rice and chickpea *dhal*, sautéed vegetables, marinated chicken, and rolls made from scratch. A devout Catholic, Nora insists on offering thanks before we begin the meal, a ritual I appreciate her reintroducing to my family. We guzzle glass after glass of purified water, diluting the happy hour cocktails from Summit, and pass around the serving dishes. I try to ensure the majority of the rice Devi spoons out actually makes it to her plate.

"Okay, who's ready for High-Low?" Nora asks brightly. "High-Low" is a Murphy family tradition that gives everyone a turn to tell the best and worst parts of their day.

"Oh! Me, me! I have a good one!" Jack bounces in his seat, enthusiastically raising his hand.

"Okay, Jackie," I chuckle. "Go ahead."

"Well, first, my low," he says with an exaggerated frown and pouty puppy eyes, lashes beating, "Mom made me write definitions for *five* new words before I could go fly kites with Sarresh."

"Boy, sounds rough," consoles Nora. "What about your high?"

"My high was . . ." he thinks, tapping a finger on his temple, "riding my bike with Sarresh."

"That sounds fun!" I approve.

"And getting ice cream at Laxmi." He glances at me sideways.

"Jack, I've told you I don't want you going over there by yourself!" I exclaim. I'm trying to get over worrying about him being run down like a street dog by a buzzing motor bike, and I wish he would follow at least this one rule.

"I wasn't by myself; I was with Sarresh!" He says with a naughty smile. I glare at him, but he just looks to Nora and giggles.

"And how about you, dear Mommy? What was your high today?" Nora redirects the conversation.

"Well, a pigeon pooped on my head in the market this morning."

"Ew! Gross!" Jack shrieks.

"Yeah, I guess that was more like the low, huh?" I scratch my head in mock wonder.

Devi is unsure what this conversation is about, but picks up on the nonverbal cues and tries to blend in. She chuckles and laughs, clutching a roll in one hand and her spoon of sloppy *dhal bhat* in the other.

"Why do you think I came home so soon and got right in the shower?" I joke.

"I thought you had a hot date!" Jack teases.

"Oh, I did! With Nora!" I retort, and we all laugh some more.

"And your high?" Nora asks, wiping the tears from her eyes.

"A wonderful dinner made by my favorite Dinesh *Dai!*" I call over my shoulder toward the kitchen.

"Yes, Madam, I hear you," Dinesh replies kindly.

I've tried repeatedly to persuade Dinesh to sit down to dinner with us, but he never does, always faithfully waiting to share the meal with his family. He prefers to putter around the kitchen while we eat. It's hard for me to acclimate to being waited on, but the longer we are here, the more I see the preponderance of domestic help isn't merely the result of colonial influence, it is a societal necessity. The Valley is tremendously overpopulated by hordes moving in from impoverished regions fleeing civil war and looking for work, so unemployment is epidemic, hovering near 50%. Other than the brick kilns and handicraft exports, there is little industry, so hiring household staff provides much needed jobs. Realizing a portion of the proceeds from selling my business will help support this generous man and his family, I am content. This system also keeps us all from starving.

"Okay, Nora, your turn," I prompt, handing her the pot of tea.

"Let's see. My low today was my landlord's yacking wife tying up the phone all morning." She rolls her eyes. "And my high . . . the look on Antoine's face when I gave him the video game he's been wanting. That made my day!"

A couple of times a week, Nora goes to the prison to visit expats serving time for various offenses. Antoine, originally from Senegal, ended up on the wrong end of a drug trafficking venture while trekking. He is serving 20 years, and Nora has become his private entertainment committee, helping him pass the time.

"Oh, and dinner with my favorite family in Nepal, of course!" Nora raises her glass in a toast. Devi crawls into the middle of the table to clink glasses, and I haul her back before anything spills.

"And how about you Miss Devi?" Nora asks, her sparkling blue eyes locking with Devi's onyx saucers as I settle her back into her seat. She shrugs and giggles, hands to her mouth.

"What was the best part of your day, Devi?" I repeat slowly, hoping to help her connect this newest language. She squirms in her seat, tearing at her roll.

"Did you like walking in the garden with me at Summit?" I suggest.

She nods her head eagerly in agreement; spoken words are still rare.

"And what was the worst part?" I prod, brows knitted, with grumpy face for clarity. Her eyes grow wide and she studies my expression. "Was there a part of your day you didn't like?" I ask a little lighter this time. She intently holds my gaze, maintaining the connection. "Were you sad when I only let you eat one donut at the farmer's market?" I hint.

We'd had a fierce battle, resulting with me tossing Devi over one shoulder, her legs kicking, and tiny fists pounding my backside as I sped down the Summit drive. I surprised the landlord's mother, our adopted Hindu grandma, as I stumbled through the gate at the top of our compoud. My embarrassment subsided when I glimpsed her chuckling as I tried not to drop the pastries.

"That wasn't fun, but we had a nice afternoon reading, didn't we?" I trail off, wondering how much she comprehends. I speak slowly and softly, a constant practice of hoping to keep her present, but she looks right through me, down to my soul. I can't read her, she is the most stoic being I have ever encountered—a tiny secret service agent refusing to reveal crucial information.

Devi starts to pick at her food, and I give Dinesh the nod to take her plate before the remaining contents find their way to the floor. He'd vetoed my solution to this latest meal time trouble—letting our street dog, Kali, inside to clean up.

When Devi first came to live with us, her behavior at mealtimes was impeccable. Head down, she carefully and quietly ate every bite whether it was her usual diet of dhal bhat or something new. Though her stout little body told me otherwise, I'd been concerned she wasn't getting enough to eat, so I always offered her more and then waited for signs that she was full or disinterested, but those signs never appeared. Instead, she morphed into a cave girl. It became painfully obvious plentiful food was not something she'd experienced before, and she ate until she vomited. She would then continue to stuff food in her mouth, chew it up, spit it into her hand, and throw it on the floor. When this first began and Dinesh or I tried to take her plate, she would become frantic and would grab at the food, guarding her meal like a starved prisoner of war. Sometimes she would even grumble a low growl, hitting and kicking at Dinesh. These survival skills were too much, so we came up with a plan to keep us both safe and sane. When I gave the nod, I would distract Devi while Dinesh swept in from behind to remove her plate. As I scooped her up to take her toward the loft for a bath and pajamas, he had already disappeared into the kitchen. She was, after all, still a toddler, and easily redirected with the right props. Nora was a great one, who I used without guilt.

"Let's get ready for bed so we can play a game with Nora before she leaves!" I sing song as I haul Devi from her seat and swing her around to my hip, just as Dinesh waltzes in and takes her plate. She glances over my shoulder to the table, but the plate has magically vanished. Nora and Jack play supporting roles, turning up their palms in a gesture of "all gone," and up to the loft we flow.

Devi willingly puts on pajamas and even lets me brush her teeth. The best-loved reward, Nora, waits downstairs for pat-a-cake and stories. As challenging as Devi is, like an oversized puppy who doesn't know her own strength, she loves to be read to and sits patiently as the pages are turned. (I'd tried letting her turn them herself, but inevitably, the playful puppy takes charge, tearing and crumpling them in fits of excitement.) Nora graciously accepts the role of story teller, offering me a few more minutes to stare out at the Himals and gather energy for the night ahead. With colorful pictures and the sonata of a new language, Devi sits enraptured and brings book after book to Nora as Jack patiently looks on.

"Okay you two, it's getting late. We need to get to bed." I begin the literary last call.

"Awwwww, Mom!" Jack gives the expected response.

"We'll read together once Devi is asleep," I whisper in his ear as she fetches one last story.

We say our goodnights and Nora hops down the steps, blowing kisses, and I carry Devi up to bed. We've settled into a predictable routine, and she is going down more easily at night with less thrashing. I've started to give her time to settle herself, hoping she'll allow sleep to come gently. I turn on *Midnight with Mozart*, then roll her on her belly and curl up beside her, patting her back rhythmically like I've seen the *didis* do with the babies at Annie's. They carry the little ones in baskets on their backs, which are connected by a strap around their foreheads, and walk slowly, gently thumping the bottom of the basket with a hefty stick in the rhythm of a heartbeat. I feel Devi's body soften and her breathing slow as she drifts off. I hold my breath and roll from the bed ninja style, then tiptoe out of the room. Jack is asleep on the little wicker loveseat, clutching *Mrs. Frisby and the Rats of Nihm*, patiently waiting for his Mommy time. I wiggle beneath him, gathering his balled-up body onto my lap, and cuddle him close, smelling his hair. From the hint of smoke, I know he's been up on the roof again lighting matches, his new favorite pastime. With Dinesh so busy wrangling Devi, it's easy for Jack to escape to the gently sloping roof where he engages in all manner of bad boy behaviors: eating all the cookies, reading comic books, hiding Devi's favorite tea cup or dolly, and most recently, lighting wax paper matches. He loves striking them, watching the fire ignite and burn slowly, holding them as long as he can before dropping them to the concrete roof. I never thought I would be thankful to be living in a concrete jungle, but back at home, he'd have started a forest fire.

After hearing about Pokhara, I wake with thoughts of travel. While I can no longer go "extreme," I can at least go "family" and I'm aching to shake things up a bit. While conscious of how important a stable routine is for both kids, I feel ridiculous coming halfway around the world to play Ring-Around-the-Rosy on the terrace every day. Winter will be here soon, and although we can go south to Chitwan National Park or farther into India, a mountain getaway will become impossible. Pokhara, known as the City of Seven Lakes, is just northwest of Kathmandu, a short and inexpensive flight away.

I try to convince Nora to come with us, but she stands her ground, mindful of her budget. I'm anxious about traveling alone with both kids, but since Jack was such a superstar on our flight from the States, I know he'll be fine on a short jaunt in a prop plane. He's taken to being a helpful big brother, and fills his backpack with all the necessities: binoculars, journal, water bottle, prayer beads, his favorite Batman book (we are going to the Bat Cave, after all), a couple of *Tin Tin* comics, a flashlight, and as always, several small Ganesh statues. Seeing children begging on the streets spiritually wounds Jack, so he always carries at least one Ganesh with him to give to a child. He struggled to understand why we shouldn't give them money and was disturbed when I explained that it wouldn't help them, because it would only go to the adult who was forcing them to beg, and this would only further encourage the abuse.

"I can give them Ganesh," Jack suggested. "He can help them with their obstacles, like getting enough to eat." After buying the tiny trinkets from Pilgrim's Book House on several occasions, Jack made friends with the manager, Balbir, who finally asked what was becoming of all those statues. Taken aback by Jack's explanation, Balbir was visibly touched by his compassion for the street children and offered him a substantial discount from then on.

On the morning we leave for Pokhara, with Devi in the baby backpack, I haul our bags down the lane and catch a taxi to the airport. I locate the correct ticket line and we shuffle off to the departure area. The airport feels much less intimidating than when we arrived two months ago. A little white Buddha Air plane appears, and Jack is sure it's a good sign. We climb aboard and go to the back, taking seats on the right side for the best view of the

Himalayas. A smiling flight attendant gives us cotton for our ears and once the engines start up, I understand why: it sounds like we're in a giant blender. As we lift off and turn south, I smush my nose against the window to see as far up and down the mountain range as possible. The Himals stretch 1,500 miles, but we can only see a small segment of the middle. The view is beyond astounding; an ocean of rippling ridges stretches as far as I can see. Jack, meanwhile, is looking for China.

Less than an hour later, the tiny plane descends into picturesque Pokhara. The airport isn't much more than a concrete warehouse, with no luggage claim area or conveyor belt, just a line of suitcases unceremoniously deposited inside. I find our one bag, the space monopolized by Devi's cloth diapers. I can't bring myself to use disposables knowing that in a matter of days I'll see them in the trash pile down the lane from our house. Even in the face of abundant squalor, my conscience won't allow me to contribute to that particular environmental evil.

We find a taxi driver familiar with the guest house where we have reservations and hop in. As we pass a camouflaged, army-occupied gun turret at the front of the airport, I look the other way hoping Jack doesn't notice and start asking me questions I don't have answers for. While signs of civil war are all around us, the ho-hum attitude of the locals makes it difficult to gauge the true level of danger. It's hard not to feel trepidation.

Newspaper reports in Kathmandu have made me aware of the Maoist threat heating up outside the Valley, particularly in the backcountry where insurgents have been advancing in search of increased funding and fresh recruits. The U.S. Embassy has issued travelers' warnings for the area, and the warnings have also included Kathmandu; however, other than a few days of protests and closed shops, nothing of significance has occurred during our stay so far. When I asked Annie if Pokhara was a safe area to visit, her response was, "Of course! No problem! Have fun!" But now, seeing the military presence throughout the town, roadblocks and checkpoints at the ready, razor wire gleaming in the sun, I feel faint of heart.

As we wind toward the downtown lakefront strip, the familiar sights of monkeys hanging off buildings and cows meandering in the street help me to relax. We pull up to a quaint guest house, and I'm all the more at ease. At only twelve dollars per night, I'd been concerned about quality, but the travel agent assured me it would be fine. The threat of terrorist activity had caused lodging rates to drop significantly due to the lack of tourism.

The staff takes to Jack and Devi right away, offering them juice and snacks, then they show us to our room. It reminds me of a college dorm room with a tiny bathroom, two twin beds, and a perfect view of the neighbor's livestock: a lone water buffalo and a scattering of chickens and ducks happily splashing in muddy puddles.

I've studied my tattered *Lonely Planet* guidebook to find all the age-appropriate activities in the area and the best places to eat. I'm determined to avoid the infamous traveler's diarrhea as well as the rampant hepatitis. A four-day stay seems long enough to check out everything on our list, but not so long as to rattle Devi's blossoming sense of security. I'd carefully packed her little turtle backpack with her favorite things, hoping they would provide comfort and familiarity: the wooden sheep I gave her the first day we met, her blue stuffed bear, Babu (the only thing she brought from Annie's), favorite board books, and Jack's plastic Catwoman action figure which he'd let her borrow.

After the kids finish their snack, we set out for the Bat Cave, the number one stop on Jack's list. After stumbling through the language crevasse with a smiling bobblehead taxi driver, I point to the picture of the fabled cave in the guidebook, and we're off through the countryside. In Kathmandu, our view of the Himals is fantastic, but now the mountain range is up close and personal. A hint of the Annapurnas peek between the clouds, alluding to their tremendous presence. I get a glimpse of the sacred mountain, Machchhapuchhre Himal, better known as the Fish Tail, shaped in a perfect triangle and standing 22,942 feet tall. Its proximity makes it appear to be the biggest peak; however, others surrounding it top out at over 26,000 feet. Eight of the world's fourteen mountain peaks over 26,000 feet are in Nepal. The sacred mountain of our stateside hometown is only a little over 13,000 feet, a David in comparison to these Goliaths.

As we wind along the valley floor carved out over eons of erosion by the Seti River, the strata provides a brilliant display of color. We slow as we drive through small villages, then veer off the main road, winding around and about, and I begin to doubt the driver's understanding of our requested destination. The road degrades to a potholed dirt trail, and we bounce around to the jingling of bells and bangles that adorn the taxi. Then when the road becomes too rough to drive any further, we unceremoniously stop. Tumbling out, we gather our gear, and I load Devi into her baby backpack. When I swing her up behind me, she immediately grabs and twists my ponytail for tactile comfort.

"I wait. You go," our driver says, pointing to a tiny sign on a scrap of wood that may have once been part of the fence. Under an uncertain arrow, BAT CAVE is scrawled. I look to him questioningly, but he waves us on, and I hope I'm not foolish for believing he will be here when we return. We start up the gentle grade and settle into a rhythm as Jack reports everything he sees.

"Mom look at this rock! Mom, do you see the river down there? Mom look at those huge trees! Mom, how much further is it?" I respond in mostly monosyllables, consumed by the beauty enveloping us. On one side, the valley drops away into a tapestry of terraced fields, while on the other the mountain face juts up to the sky. Around the bend, a farmer plows his field with the steady assistance of two water buffalo. I want to dive in and be immersed in his simple village life. The forest is lush with ferns and is heavily treed, all brilliant Emerald City green. Insects hum all around us, but a gentle breeze keeps them at bay.

A couple of women walk toward us on the trail, carrying baskets on their backs secured by woven straps across their foreheads. One of the women also carries a baby a bit younger than Devi in a sling. I bow my head slightly, hands folded, *Namasté*, and the ladies look to each other giggling, then return my greeting. They eye Devi in the backpack, so I pause and try to resurrect my most recent Nepali lesson.

"*Es chorri, dedi rambro cha* (your daughter is very good/pretty)," I say, attempting to offer a compliment. I hope my pronunciation isn't too terrible, and the women start chattering. I shake my head, waving my hands slightly. "*Mero Nepali, mero mero,*" I interrupt, advising them I only know a little Nepali. Smiling, they speak slowly and in simple sentences I can figure out. They talk about Jack, pinching his cheeks, laughing, "*Ramro, ramro chorra, ramro, cha.*" Good, good boy.

I bid them *namasté*, ready to continue down the path, but they start talking again, and gesture to their little girl. The woman she's strapped to quickly unwinds the sling and comes to me, trying to hand me the babe. Still confused, I attempt to sort out what they want." *Bastadi, bastadi* (slowly, slowly)," I ask. Then the words and gesture make the request clear: Please . . . daughter . . . you take . . . you good mother . . . take good daughter . . . please take . . . please take . . .

Shocked, I stumble backward, away from the ragamuffin child. I see desperation in the woman's eyes, slightly gaunt and sunken. Her clothes are threadbare, and her hollow collarbones poke from under her gunny sack *kurta*. None of them have shoes. "I'm sorry," I mumble. "Boy and girl enough." I avoid their heavy gaze, unable to think of anything else to say or do. They plead with me as they watch me leave. I'm ashamed to just walk away, and unable to look back.

As we reach the crest of the hill, we spot a vacant ticket booth at the head of a small footpath that leads into the trees. Upon seeing us, a young man drops his cigarette and trots up the steps to pop into the booth. I try to decipher the hieroglyphic sign, but soon give up and ask for three tickets. I hand him some rupees, and he escorts us down the narrow trail into the forest canopy.

Up ahead is a small shack with bottled water, packaged chips, peanuts, and distant cousins of Little Debbie snack cakes. Jack is sure they'll have ice cream; I'm sure they won't. An eager tour guide approaches, and we follow him down to join two young couples. Both women are dressed in flowing silk saris and the most unsensible shoes I've seen since arriving in Nepal. The men joke with each other, ignoring the women, clearly content with each other's company. The guide asks if I would like a torch, which I'm relieved to see is just a flashlight. Jack eagerly takes one, but I have my hands full with Devi, who is now out of the backpack and on the move. The guide shrugs and walks to the entrance of the cave, which is little more than a crack between a clump of basalt boulders, and one by one our little group disappears. I hear squeals and giggles from the women as they descend, and I wait with Jack bouncing impatiently and Devi flopping. When it's Jack's turn, he quickly slips through the crack as I gather Devi. The second guide pauses behind me. With Devi balanced on my hip, I duck my head under the ominous boulder that marks the entrance, expecting to find a flight of steps, but there's nothing of the kind: no hand rail, no steps, no light. I was anticipating smooth concrete pathways lighted by unnatural yellows, pinks and blues, like the tourist trap caves that had filled my childhood family vacations, but this is nothing but blackness dotted by the distant torches of those ahead of us.

I start to call out to Jack, hoping he can shine his beam back to light the way for me, but quickly change my mind. He's already so far ahead, and since I'm standing at such an odd angle, I worry that distracting him could cause him to fall. I look back to the second guide for assistance, and he asks where my torch is.

Devi feels my tension and starts to get anxious, twining her fingers in my hair and pinching my neck.

"See where Jackie is?" I try to shift her focus. "We'll be there soon, and then back out again. Keep watching his light." Scooting along the rocks, using my backside for balance, I maneuver from one sharp boulder to the next, groping for flat ground. Soon, I realize there is no cave floor, the "tour" is just a scramble across a jumble of boulders in the dark while listening to bats chirp. I'm off balance without the backpack to strap Devi into, having left it at the mouth of the cave, since I thought she would enjoy exploring. Now, I have to stay calm, knowing Devi, like a wild animal, will smell my fear and launch into a frenzy. Her freakouts are hard enough to handle on even footing; losing her to a full-on tantrum would be impossible to manage in this pitch black, dangerously rugged terrain. I stop to formulate a plan and take a few deep breaths. The guide is clearly annoyed, but I don't care. I'm frustrated because I've fallen into yet another Nepal-trap. We've descended so far down from the entrance that it will be impossible to climb back out the way we came; our only option is to keep going. One butt cheek at a time, I crab-crawl over boulder after boulder, careful not to scrape Devi's chunky little legs.

Finally, outside light begins to filter in from above, outlining the silhouettes of the rest of our party crowded at the exit. Jack turns to me, accidentally shining his light in my eyes. "What took you so long?" he quips, and I know from his voice, he's loving every minute of this.

I just want out. Our escape requires a bit of climbing, and the women in the group are having a difficult time; their high-heeled, strappy sandals are even more cumbersome than my modest calico skirt. After much crying, wailing, pleading, pulling, pushing, boosting, and begging, the ladies finally make it out, clacking at their men like angry chickens.

Jack hippity-hops up the boulders like a billy goat, easily slipping through the mouth of the cave, then peeks his head back in and coaches, "See, Mom? It's easy! Come on, you can do it!"

Devi balks when I try to hand her off to one of the guides, so I coax her into releasing her vice grip legs enough to shift her onto my back. I take a moment to catch my breath and give thanks for the Vibram soles of my Chaco sandals, then begin my ascent as Devi's fists dig into my throat, cutting off my airway. Balanced precariously on the upward angled edge of a boulder, I'm about 15 feet up, only halfway there. I wedge my leg in a crack between the boulders to steady myself while I peel a violently protesting Devi off of me and hand her up to the guide near the mouth of the cave. She shrieks at the separation, but the guide moves quickly to prop her up on the next boulder, and she climbs the last few feet into Jack's arms. No longer caring about modesty, I wrap my skirt around my thighs, tuck the hem into the side of my underwear, and use every inch of my long legs to stride up the last several boulders and squeeze out of the cave.

"Hooray, Hooray!" Jack jumps up and down clapping, but Devi is frozen, staring blankly ahead, while her fingers pick and pinch each other, searching for something to cling to. I rush to pick her up, but she stares right through me, my zombie girl is back. We walk up to the snack bar, and I find the least grimy spot on the concrete pad to sit with Devi in my lap. Her body is rigid, but she allows me to hold her, and I suppress my instinct to stroke her back, knowing it will only cause irritation. I offer her a juice box, but she is unavailable, no juice box required.

Jack is already back at the mouth of the cave with the guides, remarking wide-eyed at how cool their job is and asking endless questions. How many bats live in the cave? How big is the cave? How old is the cave? If you work here, can you live in the cave? He sees me watching and comes running back. "Can I go again?"

I laugh out loud at this request, but now the guides, barely past childhood themselves, see Jack as a prince and are more than willing to take him back to the center of the Earth, happy for an excuse to play. I sing softly to Devi, periodically checking her expression for signs of life, but she remains vacant. When Jack reappears, we gather our things to leave, and Devi readily climbs into the backpack, a guarantee she's going with us. I try to stay positive and even though our outing has rattled her, I take this as a sign she's attaching after all.

Sleeping with Devi in the less than double bed back in Kathmandu is challenging enough; I know we won't survive the night in a twin, so I make her a Princess and the Pea pallet on the floor next to me. She's happy to try it out, especially when Jack mentions he wishes he had one, too. After watching cartoons and reading stories, I turn out the light and curl up on the floor next to Devi, patting her back as she surrenders to sleep. With a silent prayer, I cuddle into my own empty bed, knowing I will be back on the floor again in a matter of hours. Miraculously, Devi's night-waking has minimal terror attached and peaks with only subdued wails that drift out the window and into the cool night air.

The next morning, we wake ready for breakfast and choose a little café beside the lake. Between super-sprouting Jack and bottomless Devi, I decide to go all out: hot cocoa and juice, muffins and pancakes, eggs, fresh fruit, and oatmeal. Like most cafés in Nepal, they offer an outdoor seating area in the garden, which allows the kids to romp. This one also has a small playground with low swings and a merry-go-round. When we arrived in Kathmandu, I was pleasantly surprised to find that Nepalis have no expectation of children sitting patiently at the table waiting for their meal; a revolutionary concept! The kids run off to play, and I have a few precious moments of alone time before our next adventure, a pony trek.

When we arrive at the gear shop to meet our guide, I'm surprised to see only two ponies and point to Jack, Devi, and me, and to him.

"I walk, Madam," he says, and I wonder how he will keep up. Devi resists climbing on board until she sees Jack mount up, then she allows me to place her on our pony's back. With heads hanging low and hip bones jutting out from under their saddle blankets, I feel guilty adding my weight to our pony as I slide into the saddle behind Devi and hope he doesn't collapse. We start out with Jack in front being led by the guide at a snail's pace. Now I know why the he doesn't need his own ride. The ponies' hooves click-clack on the pavement until we reach the edge of town where the road turns to gravel, and we are met with open countryside dotted with the occasional homestead or guest house. Gazing out over fields of golden flowers, I think of Dorothy and her friends in the field of poppies on their way to Oz, and I want to run and lie down in them. I imagine the deep sleep would be comforting and trust the coming winter snows would wake me. The road winds along the valley floor, dropping off on the left where the river rushes to feed the terraced fields as well as Lake Phewa Tal, the layers of mountains reflecting on its glassy surface. On our right, we practically kiss the face of the mountain. The ponies hardly notice when an occasional *Mad Max* era go-cart/tractor rattles and bangs past us stirring up clouds of dust. I'm surprised these machines are even operable; they look ready for the big junkyard in the sky.

I take deep, long breaths of the crisp, clean, mountain air and settle into the pony's rhythm. Jack asks the guide one question after another, and Devi relaxes into me, her head bonking and bobbing against my chest. In spite of the gorgeous scenery, I can't stop looking at her tiny mocha hands on top of mine as I hold the reins and happy tears roll down my cheeks. I'm overwhelmed by how much I love this little squirming, pinching, screaming person. She didn't come from my body, but that doesn't matter, now I am her *Ama*. I think of the women from the trail the day before and wonder once again where Devi's mother is, and if she is wondering about Devi, too.

With fall coming on, men and women alike are busy in the fields harvesting crops. The men wear shorts, t-shirts, and cloth hats as they walk behind plows pulled by water buffalo. Women dressed in brightly colored skirts, scarves, and aprons, follow behind using hoes to break up chunks of soil, while others carry enormous bundles of hay or wheat three times their size on their backs, held in place by a strap across their foreheads. Each dwelling we pass is unique in size and shape. Some are large, two-story tin-roofed farmhouses made of limestone blocks, while others are straw huts, like something one of the three little pigs built. In a field near a homestead, a man hunts with a falcon, and Jack is entranced. Watching the bird soar and drop is exhilarating, and when it returns with a small rodent in its talons, I want to applaud. The falconer looks less pleased by the meager return. I daydream about this simple life, wishing to dissolve into this world, romanticizing the hard labor and primitive living conditions.

Eventually we come to a cluster of white rock and mortar buildings among enormous shade trees that surround a central water tap.

"We stop here," our guide says. I dismount, then turn to catch Devi as she bails off our bag-of-bones. At the water tap, several women and children wrangle ducklings and baby chicks among puddles as they peck at the ground for bugs, and now feast on Devi's *bapa* crumbs. Our ponies stretch their necks as far as their reins will allow to graze on the tall grass, their waggling lips reaching out for tender green shoots. Devi and Jack splash in the water with the other kids, laughing and getting muddy. I'm content to stay here all day relaxing in the shade while the children play with ducklings, but soon enough, our guide readies the ponies and announces it's time to go.

Jack tries to convince me we should take at least one duck with us, having already named and bonded with several puffs of yellow fluff. I convince him that our new friends need the ducks for eggs and choose to end the story there, rather than fuel his fire with news that duck was also likely on the dinner menu. Jack is quick to understand that we would be taking away from their livelihood and willingly gives up the duck. Devi, watching closely, follows suit. We saddle up and plod back to town.

After a room service lunch of grilled cheese and chips, (aka French fries), we meet Bikesh, our driver from the previous day, for our afternoon outing. He's agreed to show us around during our stay, happy to have a guaranteed fare, and I'm relieved he knows the locations of all our chosen destinations.

Sarangkot, a small village in the mountains known for fabulous sunrises, is next on our list. The thought of getting up before dawn and hiking for several hours in the dark is inconceivable, so sunset will have to do. Bikesh advises that the entire trek is lengthy, so he takes a motorized shortcut up a gravel road, depositing us half way up the mountain at a secondary trailhead, and promises to wait.

"There is curfew, Madam. Maoists," he warns. "We return before dark."

I hoist Devi up in the backpack so we can make good time. The trail is well established, a cobblestone of flat rocks that gradually become huge stepping stones as we ascend. Up the narrow ridge, the mountain drops away on both sides, providing sweeping views like a magnified version of the Rocky Mountains. In the distance, little brown Lincoln Log houses perch on vibrant green steps, and tiny puffs of clouds converge to form cotton-ball blankets to cover the sleepy town. The trail takes us through several homesteads, and, at one point, surrounded by a gaggle of goats, I realize, we're in a barnyard. Smiling, dirty, shoeless children dressed in rags, several missing the wrong teeth, beg for candy as we pass, but in the absence of adequate nutrition, I can't bring myself to hand out sugary treats. Instead, I offer biscuits that they take begrudgingly and scamper away. As we approach the home, a woman is selling *pashminas*, her loom visible through a glassless window. The wool is poor quality, but I buy one anyway without haggling, hopeful it will help her family.

Close to the summit, the trail opens to a narrow dirt road lined with several modest hotels in various blue and green hues. Beyond, an ocean of snowcapped mountains ripples through the thin gauzy clouds as the sun begins its descent, the giant fishtail peak flushing cotton candy pink.

"Yeah, that's real pretty," Jack humors me as he scales a trailside boulder.

The high-end hotel atop the ridge looks promising, but with no time to explore, we make a U-turn and head back down as Devi nods off, drooling on my shoulder. We find Bikesh waiting faithfully to zip us back to town and plan an outing for the next morning. He's eager to hear about all things America, so I indulge him. I also tell him of our life in Kathmandu, my pending adoption, and the choice to vacation in Pokhara rather than India since I have no documents for Devi.

"Oh, Madam, please be very careful. Maoist say Nepali child stay in Nepal," he warns me, eyes serious in the rearview mirror. "Some Royal Nepalese Army say no foreigner take Nepali child." He helps me understand that many people believe Nepali children belong in Nepal, while others simply see expats as a lucrative source of funding, whatever their mission. In Nepal, there simply is no defining line between yes or no about anything; everything bobbles.

The next morning, we meet Bikesh and his cousin, Sarish, a porter who will carry Devi and provide security on our next outing, a trek to the World Peace Pagoda. The guest house staff have warned me that while the trek is very beautiful, tourists are occasionally mugged along the trail, and it is wise to have a local with us. I'm happy to have a break from my heavy Devi load. We plan to hike up the ridge to the pagoda, then down the other side through the temperate forest to the lake where a boat will bring us back to town.

Bikesh drives us up the steep, rocky, mountainside as far as his little taxi is able to chug, then we gear up. Sarish is unfamiliar with the baby backpack, and good naturedly lets me adjust it for him. From my vantage point it's a good fit, but he shifts awkwardly, like he's breaking in a new pair of shoes, and attempts to readjust the straps.

The sun's only been up a few hours, but the morning mist is quickly burning off and the south side of the mountain heats up fast. I'm relieved my pack is full of water and snacks instead of Devi, and we set a good pace. Jack maintains an energetic lead with prayer beads in hand, excited to see the famed golden Buddhas while Devi anxiously turns to look for me walking behind Sarish. Since the trail is too narrow for us to walk side-by-side, I move ahead so she can see me and hope Sarish will overlook the social awkwardness of walking behind a woman.

We make our final ascent up a flight of wide concrete steps to the narrow ridge where the World Peace Pagoda sits. Magnificent views of the enormous Annapurnas surround us, and I shrink in their presence, like an ant on a hill. Through the mist, the sleeping giants loom like noble knights waiting to be called into battle. Across the valley, I spot Sarangkot sitting atop another ridge, while quaint Pokhara lies below.

The pagoda was built by Nichidatsu Fujii, a Buddhist monk from Japan, who devoted his life to peaceful resistance after discovering a kindred spirit in Mahatma Gandhi. Fujii lived to be 100 years old and founded eighty pagodas to encourage resolving conflict through nonviolence. The entrance to the pagoda is guarded by two huge, concrete snow lions. We respectfully remove our shoes and leave them with those of other pilgrims. Other than a group of Japanese tourists and a multigenerational family from

India, we have the place to ourselves. Deep peace vibrates from the angelic white glow of the *stupa* crowned with a sparkling golden spire. We walk through the impeccable, verdant grounds to a reflecting pool crowded with water lilies and lotus blossoms. Devi is anxious to get out of the backpack and run, so Sarish unloads her, then rests in the shade while we explore.

As we approach the first of the four golden Buddhas, I bow, pressing my palms together, feeling the hum of enlightenment. The larger than life Buddha sits serenely, high on a pillar before a turquoise arch framed by intricate golden flowers; a tender white fence keeps devotees at a respectable distance. Moving clockwise around the *stupa*; we meet the three other Buddhas chanting their thoughtful prayers. I imagine peace moving in all directions to touch every part of the world as it ripples from each one. Mindful of the poverty surrounding us, my struggles with Devi suddenly feel small and simple, a teardrop in an ocean of suffering, and I visualize that ocean becoming calm and peaceful.

Jack loves the standing Buddha who holds one finger in the air, as if checking the wind, though it's more likely a sign of attaining enlightenment. My favorite is the reclining Buddha, lounging his way to mindfulness. An intricately carved band circles the top of the *stupa* depicting various scenes from Buddha's life among his students and in nature; a deer lies at his feet. I'm awed by how the air feels infused with peace, permeating everything around us; even the garbage caught along the chain link fence rustles peacefully in the breeze.

We sit in the shade and fuel up on snacks for our trek down the other side of the ridge. Devi, determined to be as big as her brother, bowls down the trail after him, and I'm amazed she's able to control her tiny frame without crashing. Her burst of energy soon ebbs, and she willingly climbs into the backpack for our descent into the rainforest. Under the canopy, bird calls echo and invisible critters scurry out of sight as we pass empty homes, their occupants away tending their crops in the terraced fields. At the lake shore, we see a sign for "Typical Restaurant," and consider grabbing lunch, but the grimy conditions prompt us to move on to the colorful wooden boats lining the dock. While Sarish looks for someone to paddle us across, Jack debates the merits of a yellow versus a red boat. When Sarish returns to select a boat, Jack is relieved it is a yellow one, for reasons known only to him. As we pile in, the edge of the leaking boat comes closer to water level with each additional passenger until the boatman finally hops in, and I'm sure we're all going under. Devi is compliant, which surprises me; she's clearly enjoying the quiet glide of the boat.

"Mom, can I swim the rest of the way?" Jack inquires, confident this adventure needs more action.

"No, Jack. See the sign? 'No Swimming.'" I point to the prominent warning.

"But why?" he whines.

"The water isn't clean; it's not safe."

"I'll keep my mouth closed," he pesters, refusing to take "no" for an answer.

"Alligators in lake," the porter interrupts. "Eat you, one gulp," he emphasizes with a jaw crunching clap of his hands.

Jack's eyes pop open wide; he's shocked speechless. I don't know if Sarish is actually annoyed, or is just taking pity on me, but I'm glad he intervened.

After lunch and a little rest, we meet Bikesh for the last stop on our tourist trip. In college, while volunteering for Amnesty International, I'd become interested in the plight of the Tibetan people and was anxious to connect with the culture through a visit to their refugee camp. Also, I imagined this would be the perfect place to find a traditional handmade carpet.

I'm not sure what to expect as we creep down the pot-holed dirt road lined with prayer flags and pull through a white gate with ornate gold filigree bordering the top. The scene is like so much in Nepal, striking beauty intertwined with equally striking poverty. I'm reminded of Native American reservations I've visited in the States; dry, desolate patches of barren land assigned to be home, but here, the backdrop is the unsurpassed beauty of the Annapurnas. A small white *stupa*, wrapped at the base with a modest burgundy border and a golden spire perched proudly on top, sits in the middle of the deserted camp while the monastery and school lie behind several other squat buildings.

"Is okay, Madam. You go, see monastery," Bikesh suggests, seeing the disappointment on my face. "We leave soon," he reminds me of the dusk curfew.

We hesitantly walk around, then see a wrinkled woman arguing with a cow intent on coming into the main temple. Clearly, she's on the losing end of this battle as the cow pushes her aside to enter the sacred space. It's dinner time, and as we come up the steps, we spot the cow standing at the serving window of the kitchen, unfazed by the yells of the women within. Jack and Devi are surrounded by a crush of curious children, and I slip inside.

The quiet temple is incredibly beautiful; incense hangs heavy in the air. While the outside is the same white cinderblock we're familiar with, inside, it's ornately decorated from floor to ceiling with Buddhas, banners, and carpets of rich burgundy, royal blue, and abundant gold. In one corner, an elderly man sits spinning a prayer wheel, chanting under his breath as a giant golden Buddha watches over all who enter. I walk past rows and rows of butter lamps, awed by one golden effigy after the next, and ponder if they were brought here over all those mountains in the exodus from Tibet. I am astounded by the endurance of the Tibetan people to continue their culture after having to leave all they knew behind.

Realizing I've lost track of time, I hurry back out to the kids. They're busy playing with children from the camp after having already shared a plate of Tibetan style *dal bhat*. Slightly less grungy, wearing oversized t-shirts but still no shoes, the children flock to me. I'm struck by the vibrant beauty of their smiling moon pie faces. While this environment initially felt desolate, it is their home, surrounded by sublime beauty, where they are free to express their faith together in a community. I see love in their eyes and feel it in their laughter. They value each other, not material possessions.

The sun begins to dip behind the mountains, and knowing we need to be on our way, I gather Jack and Devi to walk toward the taxi. Word of our presence has spread, and now, lining the long dirt drive, the vendor's stalls have magically opened, and smiling women stand behind each candle-lit table. Bikesh is next to the taxi, nodding for me to come along, but I'm unable to brush past the ladies and their wares, so I hold up a finger, signaling "one minute."

I'm overwhelmed by ornate turquoise and coral jewelry, shell-studded belts and embroidered handbags, prayer wheels, and carved wooden boxes. The hopeful looks on the women's faces compounds my desire to linger. I can't choose who to support, so buy a trinket or two from each. Jack, repeatedly denied a *Ghurka* knife, finds woven bracelets to give his friends back in the States, while Devi is thrilled to pick out necklaces, draping them around her neck. I find a small, carved wooden turtle whose shell comes off to reveal a hidden chamber as well as a string of turquoise beads a rich shade of blue I've never seen in the American Southwest.

The purchases are an easy indulgence, and I hope the few dollars I've spent will help support the community.

"Madam!" A young man runs toward me. "You buy carpet?"

"Yes!" I enthusiastically reply, much to Bikesh's dismay. I follow the man to a small, dark building piled high with carpets. I don't know where to begin, so start by telling him I want something small, pointing to a nearby stack.

"What color you like?"

I have no idea, they are all so unique. As he turns them over one by one, like pages in a giant book, I'm drawn to those with traditional colors. I would love to stay up all night looking at the gorgeous carpets, learning what the symbols mean, but seeing Bikesh standing in the doorway, arms crossed and a look in his eye telling me it's time go, I quickly make a decision.

The soft, fading light drops a filter of gold through the air, and pink bounces off the river valley lighting up the strata. We zip along at a pace I didn't know the tiny taxi could manage, as Bikesh chain smokes. Darkness falls, and both kids drop off to sleep, Devi with her head in my lap, and Jack draped over her like a rag doll. I unconsciously hum along to the Classic Rock Greatest Hits cassette that turns in the tape deck, oddly thankful for the familiarity. I lean my head back, rewinding images of the faces of the women in the stalls, touching the turquoise beads around my neck. Feeling the car slow and change gears, my eyes flutter open to see a short line of tail lights shining like demon eyes moving toward a brightly lit booth. Bikesh stamps out his cigarette and turns down the scratchy stereo.

"Madam, cover your child," he says, nervously glancing at me in the rear view mirror.

"What? What do you mean?" I ask, confused.

"Your little girl. Cover her. Now!" he demands, trying not to convey his panic while pushing his canvas jacket toward me.

"Uh, okay . . ." I mutter, still not understanding, until I realize we are approaching a heavily armed checkpoint where men in camouflage are tearing apart the car in front of us.

I have no documentation for Devi, not even a letter from the orphanage giving permission for her to live with me while we wait for the adoption to be processed. I hadn't had any reason to worry in Kathmandu, but now, watching the machine gun toting soldiers swarm the vehicle ahead, I suddenly understand just how precarious our situation could be.

I drape the jacket over Devi and wiggle my arm around Jack, trying to prop him up on my shoulder. Devi twists and moans, and I say silent prayers as we pull up to the booth. A soldier steps out and approaches, eying us suspiciously. Christina's advice pops into my mind, and I look the other way, playing aloof. I struggle to slow my shallow breathing, sure the soldier can see my chest heaving. He snaps at Bikesh, blinding him with his torch, and Bikesh responds casually. I hope he's blaming me, the silly tourist woman who wouldn't stop shopping. Remaining steadfast, I stare out the window at the lights from the checkpoint that are bouncing off the razor wire surrounding the booth. Then I feel the beam of the flashlight sweep the backseat, hovering briefly on the cloaked lump between Jack and me. Devi shifts under Jack's weight, and I jerk forward to hide the movement. Momma Bear bursts out as I glare at the soldier and shield Jack's face from the light, appearing incensed that this man dare wake my sleeping son. Daggers shoot from my eyes, and the soldier steps back, giving Bikesh a sharp reprimand, then waves us through. As we pull away, Bikesh lights another cigarette and exhales slowly, "Very good, Madam."

Wind whips through the windows, and I collapse back into the seat. As we increase speed, again flying through the river valley, Bikesh turns up the stereo and the Eagles belt out "Hotel California"; the lyrics resonate with me on a new level, as I feel like a prisoner here of my own device, in this beautiful but terrifying country.

For our last morning in Pokhara, we return to our playground breakfast spot, and take our time in the garden. We walk along the lakeshore, and Jack looks for signs of alligators, warning Devi not to get too close. It is so cute I don't dare spoil their adventure.

Sad that this is our last ride with Bikesh, I tip him well when he drops us at the airport, and he's sure I'm mistaken when I hand him the extra 2000NRS (about $25). I reassure him that it is no mistake, for he has served us well. I know this is several days' wages, but he's been so kind, especially keeping his head together at the checkpoint the night before, that it's the least I can do.

With plenty of time to spare, we make ourselves comfortable by the wall of windows, and the kids watch for our plane. And there we wait, and wait, and wait for hours. Each time I ask the smiling woman behind the counter about our flight, I receive the same response, "It will arrive in 30 minutes time." In the past, this would have made me crazy, but now, it simply is what it is. So we wait, eating every snack, reading every book, reviewing every trinket from the Tibetan camp. Jack even talks me into buying overpriced mini-bags of potato-like chips from the airport vendor, as well as a bottle of water I hope is being opened for the first time. I'm surprised at my newfound level of patience; Nepal is rubbing off on me in all the best ways.

During our time in Pokhara, Devi seemed to enjoy having her own special place to sleep, so I decide to continue the practice once we get home. There's enough space at the end of my bed for a similar pallet, and she is thrilled, almost as much as I am. Though still commuting between the wood floor and my bed in the night, it's wonderful to stretch out and relax without fear of disturbing my volatile bed partner.

Knowing the local furniture makers are capable of building anything to order, I measure the space and take the dimensions to the man who sold me the Holy Grail rocking chair. Within days, Devi's own bed is delivered, with her own foam mattress and miniature cotton blanket. It's too short for me to stretch out, but it's wide enough to curl up next to her. I hadn't realized how much musculoskeletal pain I'd been in until I could sleep Devi-free for a few days. The absence of nightly beatings by tiny fists and kicking feet feels heavenly.

```
Dear Mom,
    Our latest outing to Swayambhu, the
"Monkey Temple" was great! You'll never guess,
Jack wants a monkey! I have to admit, they
are very cute, but a glimpse of their teeth
discouraged him a bit. He settled on taking a
picture instead.
    Unfortunately, Devi was especially
difficult, screaming to be picked up,
screaming to be put down, running to vendors'
tables and grabbing their trinkets, throwing
them on the ground . . . all the charms of a
2-year-old!
    I'm working with her on the attachment
activities suggested in the book Annie
gave me—little games like peek-a-boo, pat-
a-cake and ring-around-the-rosy. I never
really thought about it, but all those games
teach children to attach. Peek-a-boo, I did
come back! I didn't abandon you! The agency
suggested we play with her sitting in my
lap, her back to me, so it isn't such an
intimate (I'm learning intimate=threatening)
```

experience, and Jack sits across from her. I think it's good for her to attach to him; maybe it won't be so hard with another child? After all, chances are she wasn't abandoned by her brother, if she had one? The first night we played, she had so much fun she got carried away. After we all fell down, she got up giggling, playing in my skirt and bit me! I know it wasn't meant to hurt, but I sure did squeal! It shocked her, and she shut down, the spell was broken, she was off to her own little world, past trauma obviously triggered. I paid for it all night, lots of screaming!

    She's doing well with pooping on her little potty :) I'd forgotten how exciting an appropriately dropped bodily function can be!! Her favorite part is when she's done; she hops up, charges to the toilet and points at the handle saying "Frush, frush, frush!" waving bye-bye. Yep, in spite of it all, she's pretty darn cute.

    Okay, gonna run and take a walk before dinner. I need to recharge for the evening ahead. It's bath night!

Love,
Kate

    Once I knew I was on my way to Nepal, I'd searched my email contacts for any connection to Kathmandu for insider information. Through a mutual friend, I was introduced to Tessa, a journalist from the Netherlands who was living part-time in Kathmandu ,and she advised me about everything from weather to wardrobe. She spent the majority of her time in Kathmandu volunteering in an orphanage for severely handicapped children and serving on the board of directors for an animal rights group, Animal Nepal. She'd helped establish an animal birth control (ABC) program to curb the use of strychnine by government officials to control the street dog population. Unfortunately, dogs were not the only victims;

sometimes cattle became ill, and even worse, street children who scavenged the poisoned meat. Government workers were slow to remove the dogs' bodies, which tended to spread disease, and in the rainy season, the poison flowed into the sacred Bagmati River.

At last, Tessa and I find a time to meet at the Banana Cat Café. More than once, I'd seen the postcard-sized sign pointing to the café, packed in among storefronts and tall office buildings, but hadn't yet explored the tiny footpath that led to it. I'm amazed to find a lush tropical garden with a fountain bubbling into a koi pond brimming with blooming pink lotus. The air smells of recent rain, jasmine, and baked goods. Inside the dark wooden shack-cum-café are high-end artisan quality handicrafts: leather shoulder bags, silky soft *pashmina* scarves, gorgeous silver jewelry, and framed art. I'm stunned this oasis exists among the pollution and squalor.

Tessa is waiting at a table by a window that looks into the greenhouse where the café cultivates its own herbs, salad greens, and tomatoes. She's a tiny bird of a woman with a blond pixie cut reminiscent of Tinkerbell.

"Hi, Tessa?" I ask, hesitant.

"Kate?" She takes my hand. "You found the place ok?"

"Oh yeah! I'm glad to finally check it out."

"I love this place. When I go back to Holland in the winter I daydream of this garden and warm days ahead." Tessa's blue eyes twinkle as she tells me of her native land filled with snowy winter days.

We talk about her work as a freelance journalist, the retail pet shop Animal Nepal is planning to open, and of course, my pending adoption. The orphanage Tessa supports houses children deemed "unadoptable" due to their medical needs. She tells story after story about how the children have learned to compensate for their disabilities and work together as a family. Full-time, live-in staff care for the children, and as they grow older, they receive job training skills based on their abilities, so they have a chance at a life beyond begging. Tessa focuses on interdependence, not welfare, and I admire her strength of spirit.

"I'd love to help in any way I can, maybe with Animal Nepal?" I offer.

Desperate to ease the suffering of the street dogs, I'd already made an agreement with Dr. Devkota to sponsor spay surgery for two dogs a month, starting in our neighborhood and working outward. With so many dogs in need, it is a slippery slope, and I know I can't take them all in. The best solution is to return the dog to its home base the morning after surgery. Although it's hard to find anyone to claim ownership of a street dog, it's clear the people who live near the mongrels care about them. They are always delighted and thankful when I return a dog and explain "no more puppies," pointing to the shaved area from the surgery. Tessa tells me that often dogs are taken in for the night by locals when word gets around that government officials are laying out tainted meat. Clearly, the ABC program provides a solution in which all beings benefit.

Though Dinesh was quite happily employed with us, I knew his wife, Leena, was still looking for work. He was a "modern" Nepali man, and recognized the value of educating his daughters, so the family stretched their rupees any way they could. They lived in a small apartment building down the lane from us, renting two 10' x 10' concrete block rooms on the ground floor. In one bedroom, Dinesh, Leena, their three kids and a nephew slept. In the other, on one side, Leena's brother, Ram, slept on the sofa. The other side was a makeshift kitchen with a propane camp-style stove, a table and chairs, and a bookcase with a few cookbooks, old National Geographic magazines and a variety of outdated textbooks. Dinesh had taught himself to speak English at an early age, hanging around the southern tourist town of Chitwan. Later, when he and Leena married, they moved to Kathmandu to escape the growing Maoist threat, and Dinesh had endeavored to learn to read English as well. The textbooks represented his window to the West.

Ram was studying finance at Tribuvan University in downtown Kathmandu, a lofty goal for someone of his caste, his last name giving away his social status. I was inspired by the family's strong spirit and belief that they were capable of improving their quality of life, since things were changing in the caste system, similar to the Civil Rights Era in the United States. Some people were still labeled untouchable and were not allowed to use the same water source as others. Historically, this was a means of preventing the spread of disease, however, continuing the practice now seemed ignorant, predjudiced, and condescending. Dinesh's rooms had no indoor plumbing, but at least they could use the water tap in the courtyard.

Like a growing number of Nepalis, Dinesh had renounced Hinduism to become a Christian, and his belief in Jesus Christ clearly brought him great joy. He always invited us to join his family at church, and several times Jack went along, enjoying the Devi-free outing and time with Dinesh's daughter, Salena, one of his many crushes. I was intrigued by Dinesh's choice to change religion, having had a similar experience, only in reverse. I was raised a Christian, but my parents never had me baptized, thereby allowing me to choose the path I was drawn to, though they never expected it to fall outside the bounds of Christianity. Another twist to the great mystery of religion lay in an unspoken understanding that in the Christian world, Dinesh's family was exempt from the caste system. The love of Jesus was truly setting his family free.

When I get word that Annie is looking for someone to fill in while two of her *didis* are away on holiday, I take Dinesh and Leena over to meet her staff. It's bizarre to be the one guiding our little party after growing dependent on Dinesh for so many things. Leena is happy to help me chase Devi down the quiet lanes behind Summit, and once we reach the busy main road, Dinesh sweeps her up onto his shoulders, as Jack looks on, disgruntled. He loves every minute with Dinesh, gladly accepting him as a ring-around-his-little-finger-father-figure. Everything here is in Jack's favor; he's an American boy prince, never to be told "no," much to my dismay. I've given up on anything resembling discipline from Dinesh. Everything else about him is so perfect that spoiling Jack is the least of my worries.

As we approach Annie's compound, I hold my breath. Peering over the gate, I see her jeep is gone, then I spot Suraj, the only other driver in the house, and I know she isn't home. I hadn't been to Annie's since Jack's game of hide-and-seek had gone wrong. When I tried to discuss the incident with her, she flippantly brushed off my concerns, so I just dropped it. Then, when she found out I contacted the agency about my issues with Devi, she was furious. I supposed she hadn't grasped the gravity of my concerns, so I just apologized in hopes of smoothing things over, but her outrage convinced me I needed to limit my involvement with her whenever possible.

Once the introductions among *didis* are made, Devi and I step inside to see the cook, Chandika, one of Devi's favorite *didis*. Leaving Devi with a cool drink of water and biscuits in hand, I go to check on Jack.

Outside, I find him helping to look after the four babies warming in the sun after their bath and customary mustard oil massage. Like slippery little seals, they roll around on the big woven mat. Some are waggling on their bellies, struggling to push themselves up, while others are content to be stuck on their backs like turtles, fists in mouths, chubby legs kicking invisible bicycle pedals. Jack entertains them until the *didis* take them one by one into the nursery to get dressed for lunch.

"How's it goin', buddy?" I ask, squatting down next to him while he makes faces at one of the babies.

"Can't we just trade her for one of these?" he requests, clearly daydreaming of a different little sister.

"Uh, no," I reply, surprised by his blunt suggestion.

"Well, why not?"

Feeling irritated, I have no idea how to respond. Jack has become increasingly bratty, putting on an air of suffering at the challenges of life, Devi, in particular. I thought I was being careful to keep his first-born-son status in check by making time for just the two of us, but nothing seems to satisfy him anymore. Even during our trip to Pokhara, Jack found ways to complain, and this latest demand is about to send me over the edge.

"Because I love Devi, and I would miss her very much, that's why," I state matter-of-factly as I stand up to leave.

"Well, I was just asking," Jack laments, whining at my back as I walk away.

When I notice Leena wrapping up her visit with the *didis*, I go back to the kitchen to find Devi parked on a foot stool in a patch of sunlight. I tell her it's time to go, and she shakes her head no, cheeks packed with peanuts and raisins like a squirrel stocking up for winter. Sweeping down to haul her to my hip, I brush off the crumbs from her previous course and thank Chandrika for keeping an eye on her, then go to gather Jack.

He is with baby Arun, whose parents-to-be Dave and Elise, had contacted me via email before I left for Nepal. I'd brought hard-to-come-by supplies for their tiny babe, particularly formula, so I pause to snap a few photos to send them. They've been waiting for months for their file to be signed, but the circumstances of Arun's orphan status are unusual, and it seemed to be causing a substantial delay. One of the *didis*, Bindi, is the niece of a female doctor in the Valley who runs a small clinic that provides refuge for women without means to receive healthcare and often plays angel to young ladies in need. Arun's mother had been no different. Late one night, a teenage girl came looking for help—her friend was in labor and hiding outside the clinic gate. The doctor took the young woman in, and within hours, she gave birth to a wee baby, clearly premature. While the doctor took the baby into the next room to clean him up, the young mother and her friend slipped out the backdoor, fearful of the repercussions. The father was of a lesser caste, preventing the young couple from ever being together.

The baby was tiny and needed high-level care. Taking him to an understaffed government-run orphanage would be a death sentence, so the doctor went to Bindi, clearly gifted in the care of young children and begged Annie to take the child in. With no information about the child's parents and fearful of taking the babe to a police station to be properly processed, the secret group of women focused on the matter at hand, keeping the baby alive, and decided to figure out the paperwork later, if he even lived. Now it was later, Arun had miraculously survived, and questions and presumably bribes were flying within the Ministry. The lack of adequate paperwork to prove Arun's orphan status was preventing the adoption from going through. It was unclear what the solution would be, so I hoped the photos would lift his would-be parents' spirits.

We all say our goodbyes and head for home.

"How did it go?" I ask Dinesh, hopeful Leena has been offered work.

"Fine Madam, thank you." He replies, then, as if he had been wrestling with how to convey his next bit of news, he cautiously offers, "Madam, I must tell you. The *didis* there, they are not speaking Nepali, they are speaking *Jiri*, the language from their village. That must be why Devi does not talk so much."

Finally! Another piece of the mystery is solved! All this time, I've been working to learn Nepali, but it's a language almost as new to Devi as English. With English, Nepali, *Jiri* and, most likely, her own village dialect, four languages are swimming through her brain. No wonder she looks at me with such confusion; I can't blame her for getting so frustrated.

"Jack, come on . . . I want to do something else with my day too, you know," I beg, aching for him to come out from under the table and finish his school work. He'd struggled to fit in at school, and I took some of his difficult behavior as a sign that things were too much for him, so I'd agreed to let him quit school if he would promise to keep up at home. We'd brought workbooks from his stateside teacher, and I came up with enrichment activities like an art journal, book reports, vocabulary lessons, and weekly field trips. We created a schedule and a very official-looking contract, sealing the deal. That was the easy part; following through is a different story.

Secretly, I've had other reasons for taking Jack out of school. The political demonstrations throughout the Valley have heated up as the Maoist influence creeps in, establishing roots to stage larger protests as the King's re-election draws near. When the United Nations parked a tank in the main intersection between our house and Jack's school, my mind was made up. Although the principal assured me that in the event the road became blocked due to a demonstration and it was too dangerous for the school van to deliver him home, he would be kept safe within the compound until the commotion subsided and I was able to fetch him on foot. While I trusted he would be alright, the scenario of me on one side of a violent demonstration and Jack holed up on the other was more than my already frazzled nerves could handle. With a heavy heart, I notified the school of our decision, and as they smiled kindly, bobblehead nodding, I realized the civil war was affecting every aspect of commerce in the country.

Homeschooling seemed like a groovy cool idea I'd always wished I had time for. I assumed it would be a snap, but now, with Jack under the table, it's nothing like what I pictured.

I hear the familiar clank, clunk of the heavy latch on our gate. Not expecting anyone, we're still in our layered pajama cocoons trying to stay warm in the frigid house even though it's close to noon. I wrap my *pashmina* around my waist and look out the window to see golden locks bobbing just below the railing. Craig! Turning quickly, my stocking feet slip on the marble floor, and I lunge to swing around the banister and dash up the curving stairway while calling to Jack, "I'll be right back!" Just as I click the latch of the bedroom door, the bird call doorbell makes my heart flitter. Jack, glad for the excuse to get out of schoolwork, answers and I listen to them chat. Tearing a brush through my hair, I tie a scarf around my head to hide just how much I need to bathe; I'm at the end of my shower cycle. Since the days become shorter and the nights colder, it's late afternoon before our solar water tank heats up, so I haven't bathed yet. I pretzel-reach between layers to slather on deodorant, then wipe my face with a wet cloth. Hearing Jack and Craig coming up the stairs, I grab my book, dash out to the terrace, and hop in a wicker chair, trying to look relaxed.

As the door opens, I glance over my shoulder. "Oh, hi Craig. I didn't hear you come in," I say.

"Then why did you go running upstairs?" Jack grins, and I glare at him.

"Don't you have some homework to finish?" I suggest while he makes goofy faces behind Craig's back. "GO!"

Craig chuckles and pulls up a chair. "What are you reading?" he looks over my shoulder. "Oh, *Midnight's Children!* That's a great one; I finished it a couple of months ago. Have you read *The Satanic Verses* or *Fury?* They were both fantastic, but I think my favorite was *The Ground Beneath Her Feet.* I just love the way Rushdie develops his characters. When I finish one of his books, I feel like I've lost a friend!" He smiles and my stomach jiggles.

"I think I've read more since I've been in Nepal than in all the years since Jack was born," I say with a sigh.

"I've read forty-two novels since I got here," Craig boasts.

"Wow . . . sounds like you're either an incredibly fast reader or you've had too many lonely nights," I tease.

Conversation with Craig is easy. He tells me of his struggles with his students and the culture, often feeling that he wants their success more than they do. I liken his experience to my Stateside store with the endless parade of trustafarian-hippy-wanna-be employees and the frustration of trying to motivate them. We laugh about "kids today" and I'm relieved someone else is starting to feel old, too.

Dinesh serves us tea, looking at me sideways, curious about my relationship with this visitor. Then the gate clank clunks and I see Nora coming up the steps.

"Hey, Nora," I call, peering over the railing, "Come on up."

She arrives on the terrace and looks as surprised as I was to see Craig.

"Well, hello! Fancy meeting you here." She looks as suspiciously at him as Dinesh had at me.

"Is it already time to meet Jonathan?" I ask. We were set to have tea with a new friend at Summit, a maths professor at the British School.

"Oh, no, I was in the neighborhood so thought I would drop by early; little did I know you would have company." She looks long at Craig who flushes and turns away. "I couldn't see Antoine today, the prison was closed, something about a fight or something . . . I don't know," she mumbles. "So," Nora prods, "what brings you by here, Craig?"

"Just in the neighborhood. Thought I'd stop by and see how our favorite nontraditional family is holding up." He justifies, patting my knee for emphasis.

"Mmm hmmm." Nora concedes.

"Well, as much as I would love to spend the rest of the day on the terrace with you both, I *really* have to get in the shower," I chirp, starting to feel my own cheeks flush like a schoolgirl. "You two stay and finish the pot of tea."

"You don't have to shower for Craig and me; we don't care. We're all living the hot water rationing reality," Nora offers. "And don't you dare spruce up for *him!*" she teases, punching Craig playfully on the arm. "Just because he's Mr. Beautiful Model Man."

"Shut up, Nora . . . she doesn't need to hear about that . . ." Craig grumbles, red as the poinsettias on the railing behind him.

"What?" I sit back down, intrigued.

"Oh, didn't Mr. Gorgeous tell you?" Nora chides, letting the suspense build as I shake my head. Craig wrestles to cover her mouth, but she only gets more animated, her voice muffled through his hands. "Oh yeah, Benetton, Abercrombie and Fitch, a little Calvin Klein, right Craig?"

Once again, I'm struck by the turn my life has taken. I can't help but wonder how we all ended up here, on my terrace, in Kathmandu. It's not surprising I have such a crazy crush on this guy. It wasn't just the seminary he had left behind, but a bit of superficial success as well.

"Well, well! You are an interesting man, Craig Murphy." I stand up and smile over my shoulder as I turn to shed my layers and hop in the shower.

With my bathing routine complete, I feel like a new person. As I open the door into the bedroom, the concrete walls soak up the warmth spilling from the bathroom. I look out to the empty terrace and my heart drops.

Nora is waiting downstairs. "Kate, for God's sake, you're not falling for him, are you?"

"Ha, ha," I say, my veil of disinterest thin as the gauzy curtains. "I have my hands full." As if to help make my point, Devi runs up to swing from my arms, but Nora isn't convinced.

"Kate, you know I adore, even *worship* my brother. I would do anything for him, but really, he's not a good boyfriend. Maybe the years in the seminary stunted his emotional growth or something, but trust me, he's not someone you want to get tangled up with. So promise me, okay?"

I'm stunned. Craig has always been a perfect gentleman. "We're just friends, Nora. It isn't a big deal," I say, feeling like I've done something inappropriate.

"Kate, don't take it the wrong way; I just love you both and wouldn't want anyone to get hurt. Can we just keep this between us, booga booga?"

Booga booga was another Murphy family tradition that had infiltrated my life. It meant this is a secret, no telling anyone, ever. "Okay, booga booga . . . really, just friends," I laugh. "Besides, we have a dashing young math professor to fight over! Now, come on, before some child has a crisis that I absolutely have to be here for."

Several weeks earlier, I met Jonathan while having dinner at Summit with the kids. I'd seen him there before, always eating alone, so I finally introduced myself after Devi repeatedly sauntered up to his table and demurely took his silverware, one utensil at a time, save the pieces he told her he needed to complete his meal. She would grin sheepishly at him, select the desired utensil, turn her back, and slide it down her dress. If we'd been in the U.S., I never would've tolerated this behavior, but here it didn't matter; the staff loved kids. At the time, the only other guests in the restaurant were an older couple who thought Devi was adorable and secretly hoped she would abscond with their silverware next. Eventually, the pieces worked their way through her layers, down her leggings, and out alongside a sock, clanging to the ground. Jack retrieved them, like my good pup, rolling his eyes and shaking his head in disgust at her childish behavior. "Lighten up, she's two!" I sighed.

Over dinner, Jonathan shared that he was a maths professor at the British School, and properly British he was. He'd made a career of traveling to less-than-glamorous locations around the world where teachers were in demand. A modest, conservative man, he lived humbly, stashing away the majority of his earnings to pay off his home in Great Britain, setting himself up for a comfortable retirement.

When Nora and I join him for tea, he shows us pictures from his latest trek to Mustang, one of the most remote places on Earth. His pictures are gorgeous, accompanied by colorful commentary, and I drift with the stories, living vicariously through his adventure. Jonathan is attractive, he likes kids, he's financially secure, he has a cat. In short, he's a catch, and as much as I adore him, an intimate relationship would never work between us. I know I'd never be able to exist in his incredibly tidy world. Where he is disgusted by Kathmandu, the stench of the sewage, and the chicken carcasses in the alleys, I love it for its incense-laden temples and orange crush-clad *saddhus*. We are night and day, yet lucky enough to find each other at the intersection for tea.

When I wake up, it's light out. I've slept all night. Something is terribly wrong! I bolt upright, clambering to the end of my bed to look down at where I am sure I'll find Devi dead, the only reasonable explanation for why I haven't been awakened in the night by screams. I watch for the rise and fall of her chest, fumbling with my glasses to get a clear view. She breathes softly in and out. It's a miracle! She's finally slept through the night.

After breakfast with the kids, I take off for Boudha to meet Lori, a woman from my hometown. We'd met at Buddhist events, and she'd also been a customer at my store. She's in Kathmandu to celebrate the unveiling of a new shrine at a monastery she helped sponsor, so we agree to meet at the White Monastery to attend a teaching by the abbot, His Holiness Chökyi Nyima Rinpoche. We leave our shoes at the door and enter the prayer room packed with international students. Craig mentioned a group of Westerners who were practicing Buddhism in the Valley, so I'm hopeful this is an opportunity to make some new connections. I've been considering becoming a student as a viable option to extend my visa if it expires before the adoption is complete. Guests are permitted to stay in Nepal for six months per calendar year on a tourist visa, and although my timeclock will reset in January, I'm worried that any delay in the process could force me to find another legitimate reason to be in the country. Studying Tibetan language and culture through a program offered by the monastery for the growing Western population feels like a good fit.

Sitting cross-legged, I drink in the sentiments offered by His Holiness, and feel stronger in my path, able to see my time here with Devi as a blessing. Cultivating patience is only part of it; the growing compassion for those around me magnifies each day, and I try to remember to give thanks for my beautiful children, warm clothing, plentiful food, good health, and safe home. All these things I have taken for granted, and now realize how fortunate I am. The chanting of the monks and practitioners vibrates through me, and I settle in blissfully.

When the teaching is over, I mill around outside with Lori while she chats with other members of her travel group. She goes on and on about a recent illness that has prevented her from attending most of the teachings. I have trouble breaking into the conversation and feel out of touch with the Western crowd, disinterested in participating in their complaints. I turn to listen as another gregarious young woman, adorned in torn-in-all-the-right-places beatnik clothes and designer prayer beads, rattles on about how long she's been in Kathmandu. Eager to hear more about her experience, I listen intently to her exploits of touring temples and bar hopping in Thamel.

"How long have you been here?" I eventually inquire.

"Almost two weeks!" she says exasperated, rolling her eyes.

I quietly walk away, feeling completely disconnected from the culture I left behind.

Waiting for Lori under a large shade tree, I enjoy the cool breeze and the chattering of birds in the canopy above. I notice His Holiness making his way out of the building through a tangle of followers. When he moves to the side yard on his way to the monastery, I approach him. I bow deeply, offering a sincere *namasté*, and thank him for the teaching, then tell him of my son and daughter. He enthusiastically replies that he loves children and that I should bring them next week. I agree, feeling joyful in the warmth of his kind and loving presence. Sparks shoot down my spine at the touch of his hand on my head as I bow *namasté*. This place is magic.

I spot Lori, and we walk back to the *stupa* center for lunch at the New Orleans Café. We order fresh lemon sodas and browse the menu even though I already know I want, *thukpa*, a steaming bowl of traditional Tibetan noodles and veggies.

Lori laments, "I came all the way here to attend Rinpoche's teachings, then end up in bed the whole time. I'm missing out on so much! This place is so filthy, it's no wonder I got sick. And the bed in my room is terrible! I can hardly get any rest," Lori monopolizes the conversation with incessant complaints. She doesn't even ask about my life, Jack, or my new daughter. I try to remain engaged but am losing patience with her whining about how life had not gone according to her plan.

I smile softly and attempt to point out the bright sides of things, "Really, it's wonderful you've been fortunate enough to come to Nepal. It's such a powerful place, especially here at Boudha."

Without missing a beat, she insists, "But I didn't come all this way just to lie around in a dingy room! I'm just devastated!"

I can't take it anymore and snap, "Lori, if you really want a teaching, leave the gates of Boudha and walk down the street. You'll get a real-life experience of what true devastation looks like." She is stunned, never having heard me speak so bluntly before.

I sit quietly and finish my cup of tea, then smile, bid her a heartfelt *namasté*, and walk out to join in the evening flow around the *stupa*, a current I love to be swept up in.

This week, for Jack's field trip, we are off to see Dr. Jane Goodall! She is stopping through on a worldwide tour to promote her new organization, Roots and Shoots, whose mission is to empower kids through volunteering to address local environmental issues. Dr. Goodall is speaking within the courtyard of an old temple turned museum, lined with raised flower beds, water features, and an outdoor café. Jack and I get there early to meet Tessa and find her holding a tiny puppy, yet another victim of dog versus motorbike. The pup's hind end was hit, and she is in a cast up to her hip.

"Can I hold her?" Jack volunteers, and Tessa gently places the puppy in his lap. We leave him to save our spot and stroll to the café for fresh juice.

"So, what have you been up to?" I ask, always interested in Tessa's latest crusade.

"I'm totally consumed with the rescue center. We are renovating a barn to house street dogs while they recover from spay surgeries or if they have been hit by motor bikes. I think of it as a canine bed and breakfast." She smiles, finding light in the suffering.

When we return to our seats, Jack is surrounded by several attractive young women cooing over the puppy. Basking in all the attention, Jack is disappointed to see us, but grudgingly hands the puppy back to Tessa. He slurps down his juice, just as Dr. Goodall emerges to the cheers of an enthusiastic crowd.

"What a lovely welcome," she responds, then offers her own greeting call, chimpanzee fashion, asking the audience to return her primate greeting. Jack goes wild as a band of temple monkeys assemble on the roof above her, curious to hear what else she has to say.

I am amazed. My lifelong hero is here just a few feet away, in an intimate picturesque setting. As she floats about the makeshift stage, like Glenda the Good Witch, I am awed by her presence, her grace, her natural way of communicating, and her classic beauty. Speaking directly to the children who have come from nearby schools, she states candidly, "Grown-ups have made a mess of our planet, and now I need your help to put things right. I was so saddened to see your Holy Bagmati River clogged with garbage. We have to fix that!"

The children are enraptured, sitting quietly, heads nodding, eyes wide. She is lighting the spark in a hundred children to make their world a better place.

Once she finishes speaking, she opens the floor to questions, and Jack's hand shoots up.

"What about tigers? I want to be a vet so I can save them," he offers, puffing up proudly.

"Tigers are very important endangered predators, rapidly losing their habitat. I'm glad you're out there to help fight for them!" she replies with a twinkle in her eye.

Although we don't have Dr. Goodall's book to sign, we wait until the crowd thins so Jack can give her his pledge to start a Roots and Shoots club at his school when we return to America, even if there aren't any tigers there to save. From under her canvas umbrella, she motions us forward.

"Thank you for coming here, Dr. Goodall," Jack says politely, holding out his hand to shake hers.

"My goodness. Aren't you a proper little fellow? Tell me, what is your name?" she asks.

"I'm Jack. This is my mom. She made me come here because she is trying to make me smart since I don't go to school anymore," he states very matter-of-factly.

"So, do you think you got smarter today?" She leans in.

"Oh, yeah, I learned tons of stuff. I wanna start a club when I get back to my regular school in America, but while I'm here I'll pick up all the trash I see. And my mom, she takes care of the street dogs around our house, even if they don't belong to us," Jack glows.

"That sounds like quite a job! I'm glad you and your mum are out there trying to help. Now do you have something you would like for me to sign?"

"How about this?" Jack suggests, handing her his tattered copy of *How Ganesh Got His Elephant Head*, one of his favorite Hindu tales.

"That looks perfect," she chuckles. "Let's see, how about this: To Jack, Good luck with the tigers. Be a good monkey! Love, Jane." She smiles, handing the book back.

"Wow! That is *so* cool! OOOOO, AAAAA!!!" He jumps up and down, cheering like a monkey.

"Good job, Mum, he's a sharp one!" She compliments, turning to me with a wink. "Let's walk and you can tell me a bit about yourself."

"Oh, me? Well, uh . . ." I stammer, starstruck. "I came to Kathmandu to adopt a little girl, so we're living here while I wait for the paperwork to go through. I'm homeschooling Jack, so this was a wonderful learning opportunity for him. I'm so thankful that you came here, and he had a chance to meet you and hear you speak." I gush, eager to get in every possible word.

"You're adopting? What a wonderful gift. Please promise me you won't let your little girl forget her country. She could come back here one day and make such a difference. You are giving her a life she never would have here, but don't let her forget where she came from." Her advice is heartfelt and straight to the point. She's not preaching, only speaking kindly, like a long-lost friend. Her beauty and grace are beyond measure. She is the most extraordinary person I have ever met. As she turns to go, I look to the carved gods and goddesses all around me and give thanks.

Then we pick up garbage as we walk home.

The end of the month snuck up on me like the haze (read: Pollution with a capital P) in the Kathmandu Valley. Time was marked by the incessant repetition of stories recycled daily at nap and bedtime. Sameness created routine, which equaled security and predictability for my groundless toddler, but my mind was growing numb. I could feel depression coming in for the kill when

I found myself in tears after carelessly leaving my favorite grey hoodie in a taxi. I was heartbroken at the loss, as if it were a family pet gone missing, knowing I would never see it again. It wasn't the sweatshirt itself, or even the nostalgia of when I bought it on a trip to Catalina Island with Jack; it was the feeling of losing yet another piece of myself, slowly drowning in the sea of Devi.

I had come to accept that I had made my bed and now it was time to lie in it, even if my legs dangled off the end as I was repeatedly kicked by fist-sized feet. I was encouraged the first time Devi slept through the night, but it had been a fluke, and her night terrors returned as quickly as they left. Still, the epic suffering I witnessed daily in the faces of street children who lived in the sickening pollution of this concrete jungle kept my self-pity in check. I thanked Ganesh, our elephant-headed neighbor, for removing any obstacles in my path as I continually questioned how I had been dealt the cards to be born into a life of privilege rather than one of adversity.

I spent my days sitting on a lovely rooftop terrace, blowing through paperback novels like Chiclets, submerging myself in an international sea of literature, my escape from the growing tedium. Pilgrims Book House was my indoor sanctuary. Bypassing the brass trinkets, locally made soaps and incense, I prowled the stacks on the second floor like a child in the library for the first time, rediscovering the world of literature beyond domestic borders. An international menu of famous authors, Salmon Rushdie, Isabel Allende, Paulo Coelho, and Jostein Gardner, opened doors to works I was unfamiliar with. There was a limitless supply of writers I had never heard of and V. S. Naipaul, Jhumpa Lahiri, Kazuo Ishiguro, and Arundhati Roy became some of my favorites. I loved browsing the area of the store that housed local publications, cookbooks, traveler's guides, and sofa-sized coffee table books with breathtaking photos of the region, many by Christina's husband, Stephan, a local legend. In addition, there was a sizeable collection of multicultural children's books filled with Mongolian folklore and Persian kings, Hindu gods, and *Tin Tin* comics, picture books of animals and their accompanying Nepali sounds,

Third World modes of transportation and "colours." I found science workbooks from outside the influence of the U.S. that measure in metric units, address the weather in terms of typhoon and tsunami, and offer descriptions not often found on the five o'clock weather roundup in our little mountain town. I collected coloring books starring Ganesh and volume after volume of Hardy Boys mysteries. The manager, Balbir, and I always made polite conversation. He would ask about Jack and quiz me on the latest Nepali phrases I had learned, always patiently correcting my pronunciation. I was spending a small fortune on my reading habit, but I just couldn't help myself. At least it was books I was addicted to, rather than more destructive vices.

Thankfully, when Nora pops by, she notices my less-than-fabulous mental state and decides to shake things up. "You need a ladies' night out. I'll ring Tessa."

I haven't been out of our neighborhood in quite some time, and I'm ready for an adventure. Submitting to peer pressure, I get dolled-up, even letting Nora put makeup on me, and we step out to Thamel. It doesn't take many dark, stinky bars before I'm aching to abandon the girls and return to my peaceful terrace. The Mountain Man watching is inferior to that of Summit; clearly the chumps in these bars are amateurs. They remind me of frat boys—obnoxious and quick to show off.

"Come on Kate, don't be such an old lady!" Nora teases, knowing my Achilles heel.

"I'm having a great time with you two, and I love you for bringing me out; it's just the atmosphere that could use an upgrade," I glance at the meathead, now vomiting on the floor, who bought our last round of drinks.

"Well, I know of a lovely place, not far from here," Tessa suggests, her eyes twinkling like the disco ball overhead.

"How far? I'm in heels," ever-practical Nora asks. I questioned her sanity for taking up precious space in her luggage with heels, but then again, I don't own a single pair. And I know if she wants to, she can get all *Sex in the City* on me and run in those heels; she's just weighing her options.

"We can grab a rickshaw," Tessa hops up. "I should warn you, though. There probably won't be any cute boys."

"I don't care about boys. I just want good times with my Nepal BFFs!" Nora declares, draping her gin-infused arm around my shoulders. "Kate, if it means keeping you out later, I'll gladly change locales to please you my darling!"

I'm loving my girl time, and already feel lighter than I have in weeks. We walk to the taxi stand, dodging snake charmers and street vendors hustling rosewood Buddhas and Technicolor peacock feather fans. We vote for the rickshaw most likely to be clean, and Tessa strikes a deal with our chosen chauffer. We all squish in, with Tessa perched between Nora and me, her tiny sparrow frame nearly bouncing out when we hit a pothole. The driver strains to gather momentum, but in spite of the cramped quarters, the ride is divine. The wind, cool and crisp, blows our hair like teenage girls in a convertible. As we ride past the King's palace, I fantasize that we are going to a ball, convinced my prince must be waiting inside. We circle back to the tree-lined thoroughfare, and the sparkling city looks unexpectedly beautiful as we drift by. I imagine this world before automobiles, when a rickshaw was the top of the line transport, and I feel like I missed something. Life moving by slowly is lovely.

Tessa directs the driver to stop as we pull up to what appears to be *absolutely nothing* on a dark, vacant street. The neighborhood isn't bad, the international clinic is just around the corner, but it's not well lit, and I nervously bite my lip. Tessa hops down to the sidewalk and hands the driver some rupees as Nora and I crawl out. Down the shadowy drive with an arching canopy of foliage, there is a promising flicker of light. A building, not much more than a hut, comes into view, and we hear music softly playing and the distinct sound of running water.

"Surprise!" Tessa turns to us announcing, "How 'bout a hot bath?"

Nora and I squeal and jump up and down like schoolgirls, as we attract the attention of a hostess inside. Tessa explains the "menu" of the traditional Japanese tea house, and we order a hot bath, shower, tea and dinner.

"Umm . . . Why did you wait until now to suggest coming here?" I ask, regretting the time wasted in the bar.

"Well, I thought you were having fun!" Tessa retorts slyly.

We follow our demure hostess past the sushi bar and dining room to the women's lounge, which is more like a high school locker room shrunk to fit in a shoebox. After stripping down, we drape ourselves in *lungis* provided by our hostess and venture into the garden. We have the place to ourselves and scamper through the chilly outdoor patio to the hot spring-fed pools. At the end of a babbling stream is the largest pool, about four feet deep, with huge river rocks to sit on.

We laugh and joke, then I notice a small bell perched next to the pool, "What's this for?" I ask Tessa.

"Ring it!" she says, gleefully.

Soon, our hostess appears carrying a tray with a pot of hot green tea and three cups. We simmer and soak until our fingers and toes look like we're little old ladies, then we brave the frigid night air and scurry back to the lounge for hot showers. Refreshed, we sit down to an incredible meal and a final pot of tea. I toast my cheerleaders and their authetic friendship.

Laughter is just the cure I was needing.

With little luck finding work for Leena, (the position at Annie's was only temporary), Dinesh's family was struggling to make ends meet. It was relatively easy for Dinesh to find other employment since his English skills were far superior to Leena's, so we struck a deal. Dinesh would come in the morning while Leena got their kids off to school, then she would come to do the housekeeping, shopping, and nanny duties. This would free up Dinesh to take another day job, then return to us in time for dinner. The arrangement worked well, and Leena and I developed our own hybrid English/Nepali language, often using hilarious mime to bridge the gap.

I've lost an earring, a dangling silver leaf. Under normal circumstances, this wouldn't upset me, but I'm holding some of my personal items especially close, despite my attempts to practice nonattachment. This pair of earrings feels like yet another piece of myself lost forever.

I try to tell Leena about the missing earring by showing her the remaining one.

"Yes, Madam," she answers with a bobblehead nod, and I'm hopeful she'll find it.

Jack is having a challenging morning with Devi, so when it's time for Leena to go to the market, she takes Devi with her.

"Why does *she* get to go?" Jack complains.

"Because it would be hard for me to talk to you if you went along," I smile at him, trying to soften the edge. "Don't pout. You know Leena will bring you something sweet. Come on up to the terrace."

Jack is struggling to enjoy his new sister, to say the least. He'd imagined her to be his protégé, his best friend, his partner in crime, Robin to his Batman. But she is none of these things. She breaks his few toys, tears pages from his books, writes on his school papers, gleefully squeezes his juice box out on the floor. She is a perfect brat, and she's driving him crazy.

Spreading a blanket on the terrace, we stretch out to watch the cotton ball clouds float by while I reassure him that everything is okay; this is just how it goes between brothers and sisters sometimes.

"How would you know? *You* don't have any brothers or sisters," he challenges.

"Because *I'm* the mom and *I* know everything!" I reply in an equally bratty tone. "You know, as the older brother, you have more responsibility. It's up to you to do the right thing, even if that means walking away. That doesn't mean she wins, it's about learning to live together, and sometimes there are things you just have to let go of and surrender."

"Surrender? Like in a battle? No way. I don't wanna do that!"

"The thing is, when you surrender to some of those little things, the big things don't seem quite so big, and before you know it, there aren't as many of them to bug you."

"But then she gets away with it! She can do whatever she wants!"

"That's how it looks on the outside buddy, but really, how you feel inside, that's what matters most," I console. "When you let that stuff go, it'll feel a lot better than constantly fighting. Surrender isn't a bad thing, it's simply saving yourself. You win by not letting her make you nuts. Remember what Spiderman says? 'With great power comes great responsibility.'"

He looks at me suspiciously.

"If you increase your level of responsibility, like picking up your books, you are surrendering to the reality that if Devi gets her hands on them, they will probably get damaged. Instead of being stubborn, expecting *her* to change because it's wrong to tear up books, surrender to the reality, increase your responsibility, and you both win. Devi won't be tempted to do the wrong thing, and you won't be angry because your stuff was ruined. Everybody wins."

Jack glares at me, arms crossed, sulk in full swing, but I can tell he's thinking about it, hating for me to be right. The gate below clank clunks, and Jack is disgusted our alone time is being interrupted. Moments later, Devi bumbles out to the terrace and body slams me.

"Nice surrender, Mom," Jack chides as I lie on my back under the weight of a victorious Devi. I laugh and wiggle as she giggles with delight. Then I notice, her ears are pierced. Leena is at the door, smiling widely, proud of her accomplishment.

"*Raamro, raamro,*" she chirps, showing off Devi's earrings as I try not to look shocked. A few weeks before, I had asked Leena about getting Devi's ears pierced, since they had obviously been pierced before, but now the holes had closed. I guess when I showed her the earring earlier in the morning, she thought I wanted her to get Devi's ears pierced. Now it's my turn to practice surrender, what's done is done, and I need to let go of the missed milestone. Besides, I didn't have to listen to a single squawk or scream. Surrender is okay with me.

"What? She got earrings?" Jack yelps. "I want my ears pierced, too!"

"What?" I ask, surprised. Jack mentioned his interest to me a few times, but I thought it was just because he was noticing that many of the local boys had their ears pierced, just like the girls.

"If she gets to wear earrings, then I should, too."

I see the determination in his eyes, like when he was four and wanted a haircut, and he wanted it right then. I was busy at the store and told him I would make an appointment, but he was tenacious. He waited until my back was turned, then scaled the front counter, grabbed a pair of scissors, and right there, with customers waiting to put down their purchases, he started chopping. As a crowd of locals grew to watch the show, I played cool Mom, after all, it was only hair and said, "You know, buddy, you're doing a great job, and I think you should go with that look. Come in the bathroom and see how you're looking so far."

Shocked by my easy-going attitude, he let me pluck him off the counter and carry him to the bathroom, leaving a confused cashier to clean up the mess and weigh the next customer's vegetables. I stood him on a milk crate in front of the mirror and said, "Here's the deal, you give yourself the best haircut you can, and when you're done, it'll be my turn, and I'll get to shave it, okay?"

"Yeah!" he exuberantly agreed and was off, chunks of hair falling to the floor.

Now I feel like I'm in a similar situation. I've done my best to raise Jack to be a kind and compassionate person, not a boy or a girl, only wearing certain color clothes, or only playing with certain toys. Still, this decision about the earrings is challenging my parenting worldview, but, how can I say no? No big deal, just little holes in his ears that can close up; it's not like he's getting a tattoo.

"Okay," I sigh, giving in to my boy prince.

"What? Okay? Did you say okay? You said okay, didn't you? You said okay! *Didi, mero ama* say okay!" Jack bounces around the terrace like he's won a grand prize, and I wait for confetti to shower us from above.

Leena leads the way to where she'd taken Devi, assuring me it was the place for the best price. I can always count on Dinesh and Leena to get the lowest rates, because expats are blatantly charged significantly more than locals. Considering the difference in the exchange rate from dollars to Nepali rupees, I don't mind the sliding scale, and am always happy to get a discount.

As we walk downtown, Jack starts to get nervous, asking Leena, "Will it hurt?" and "Did Devi cry?" To which she answers "yes," and "no," the second answer clearly more bothersome than the first. He debates getting one or both ears pierced, as is customary for the boys in our neighborhood, carefully weighing his options. The closer we get to the jeweler, the more he looks like he might turn tail and run. He takes my hand and asks, "Mom, if I get my ears pierced, will you get yours, too?"

"Mine are already pierced—this one twice. I don't need any more holes in my head." I joke. "You know, you don't have to do this; you can change your mind, or we can come back another day." I offer, secretly hoping to abort the mission.

He eyes Devi, looking down at him from her perch on Leena's hip. "No, I'm doin' it. But you should at least get that other ear pierced again, they need to be even."

"Okay, I'll get the other done. Are you satisfied Mr. Misery-loves-company?"

"All right!" he exclaims, the spring back in his step as we reach the door of the shop labeled "jeweler."

We step inside what is little more than a concrete closet on the ground floor of a large, multi-use building. A jumble of jewelry in a glass case looks like a scattered collection of vending machine prizes, minus their little plastic bubbles. Leena explains to the shopkeeper that Jack and I are here to get our ears pierced, and he smiles widely. Jack's anxiety reignites, so I volunteer to go first, so he can see how it's done, and, hopefully, how little it hurts.

Courageously stepping up to the stool, I take a seat and the jeweler wipes my ear with a grubby rag wet with alcohol, then marks the spot on my lobe with a purple felt tip marker. I sit still as a statue waiting for the pop of the gun, but all I feel is cold metal, then hear a loud click, and realize the gun is hand powered, like a giant hole punch. Jack is amazed and ready for his turn.

Sitting proudly on the stool, he watches the jeweler mark his ears and heavily considers the location of each dot, eventually offering stoic approval. Then, in one last bit of panic, he turns to me and confesses, "Mom, I think they're gonna have to give me the knockout gas!"

He closes his eyes and grips my hands as the cold metal of the gun meets his ear. At the point of impact, he flinches, but it's already over. As if mentally debating how to react, he lifts his hand to his ear and wails, low and miserable, like an angry cat.

"I just want one, Mom! One is fine. I'm done." and he jumps off the stool to head for the door, while reaching up to protect his virgin ear.

"Here, let me see," I intercept him before he can escape. Clear of the gun-toting jeweler, he drops his hands so I can admire the new earring.

"Fabulous!" I compliment, then realize, it's in his right ear. Now, I don't want to make a big deal of this, and I'm certainly not going to try to explain the social signals men convey when only their right ear is pierced; I just know I need to come up with a way to convince Jack to get the other ear pierced, and quick.

"You know, you really should get the other one done as long as we're here. Just get it over with."

"Nu uh, no way. One is enough."

I say to him, "Well, you know Jack, guys with both ears pierced really look a lot cooler. Crazy Uncle Mike has both of his ears pierced." I say, reminding him of one of his surrogate fathers, now guiding kayak trips in Alaska. "Really, I can just see you, ten years from now, telling some cute girl about getting your ears pierced in Kathmandu. It will sound so much better if you get both done. I mean, anyone can just have one ear pierced, but two? Wow. *Super cool.*" As I babble, I wonder, *What bizarro world have I slipped into that I am lobbying for my child to get his ears pierced?*

"Maybe," he considers. "But you have to get another one, too."

"But I have both of my ears pierced, two times. Look, there isn't any more room, my ears are too small," I bend down for him to examine.

"Well, something else then. Your bellybutton. Those look awesome, like Eliza's!" He daydreams of his favorite deli worker whose t-shirt was always a little too small, revealing the small silver loop in her navel.

"Not a chance. There's no way he's getting that thing anywhere near my belly button. Besides, it's probably illegal here."

"Okay, then," he says thinking, finger to temple, like Pooh. "Your nose! You have to pierce your nose!" He cries out triumphantly, happy to even the piercing score.

"I don't think so. I don't want something stuck in my nose all the time. Yuck!"

"Aww, come on. All the women in Nepal have their noses pierced. Why not you?"

He has me. Feeling the strain of battle, I surrender to a souvenir I think I can live with. Leena advises the jeweler, visibly delighted, and he goes to a special drawer and takes out what appears to be just another post earring. Then he brings it to me, as if he's offering me a great treasure, laying it delicately on the faded black velvet tacked to a piece of cardboard. It's a hideous fake gold heart with an extra thick post. I try to make the appropriate noises and facial gestures to convey approval and he smiles, happy to please, the few teeth he has left gleaming in his gummy mouth as he nods excitedly. Then, to my horror, he takes out a large file and starts to sharpen the end of the earring.

Frantically I look to Leena, whispering, "Is this going to hurt?"

She bobblehead smiles and laughs. "Oh, yes, Madam!"

"Wait, wait . . . Maybe you don't understand." I point to my nose, "This. *Aya?*" The Nepali word for ouch.

She giggles again. "Oh, yes! Yes, *dedi aya!*" Very much.

Great. Now Jack's memory of this day is going to be watching his mother cry while the jeweler sticks giant pliers up her nose. Looking to Jack for a reprieve, I see the deal is done. I swallow hard and take my seat on the stool, determined not to flinch. At the moment of impact, my face feels like it is going to explode. Tears sting my eyes, and I squeeze them shut, walking past Jack, gasping, "Your turn, buddy."

"Are you okay, Mom?"

"Just stings a little," I choke out, stifling a scream.

Jack bravely takes his seat for the final family piercing of the day, and I look around for the portal back to my pre-piercing life.

"Your turn, Leena," I joke and pay the eager jeweler. As we walk home up the big hill, Leena giggles the whole way, mercilessly mocking and teasing me. "*Aya*, Madam?" she asks, then collapses into a fit of uncontrollable guffaws. Devi thinks she is hilarious, and readily imitates her. Jack is already looking forward to showing Sarresh his new brand of Nepal. I'm distracted by the giant heart protruding from my rapidly swelling nose.

"Kate, is there any chance you can get Dinesh to watch the kids tonight? I have absolutely fabulous plans for us. Tell me you can come," Nora pleads into the scratchy phone.

"Hang on, Dinesh is in the garden picking greens for dinner." So far, Nora's attempts at wild nights out have been a bit of a flop, more often than not featuring drunken trekkers, although the night we ended up three-girls-in-a-tub had been worth the risk. I'm intrigued, and Dinesh kindly agrees to watch the kids.

"Wear something nice," she sisterly snaps, bringing me to attention.

Something nice? Clearly, she has me confused with someone else. I do my best to pacify her and pull out my least worn wardrobe items, shaking out the wrinkles. Nora arrives in a private car just after seven. She's elegant as ever in all black, with a colorful silk scarf flowing behind her dark mane of hair. I slide on my battered sandals and hop down the steps, feeling like the girl next door, invited out of pity by one of the cool kids.

"Okay, so here's the deal," Nora whispers rapid fire as she

takes my arm. "This guy is super powerful in Kathmandu. He's connected to everyone worth anything. His daughter's boyfriend is one of Craig's best friends, so I know we can *totally* trust him. We're going to dinner with him and some of his business associates. It'll be fabulous, don't worry!"

A well-dressed, strikingly handsome man waits outside the gate beside a shiny sedan wedged into the tiny alley. The street dogs swarm, intent on protecting me from this strange man and his four-legged motorbike.

"Birendra, this is my dear friend, Kate!" Nora gushes as he steps forward and takes my hand, bowing slightly.

"So nice to meet you. I have heard much about you and you wonderful children. I am delighted you join us this evening." He opens the door and waits patiently for us to get settled, then carefully shuts it and takes a seat up front with his driver.

"We are going to very special restaurant this evening to meet some old friends of mine, so you girls do me favor and not embarrass me too much." He turns to look at us with a deadpan expression, then bursts into jovial laughter. "Baa, ha ha! You should see look on you face! You look so worried!" And he turns forward again, still laughing, "No, we just going to have fun time tonight," then he addresses the driver, pointing ahead like a conductor.

Nora and I look at each other, excited for a new adventure.

The driver pulls up under a burgundy awning, and Birendra politely opens the door for us. Inside the restaurant, the air is thick with the aroma of rich Indian curry tinged with smoke and alcohol. The room is dimly lit by candles in sconces on the walls and around the bar. Birendra takes Nora's hand and leads her toward the back of the room as I obediently follow. Half a dozen older, professionally dressed men sit in a wraparound corner booth, drinks in hand. They welcome Birendra warmly as he introduces us as his very special friends, and they make room for us, shifting and sliding around.

When the waiter appears, Nora orders a gin and tonic, and I request a fresh lemon soda. This draws jeers from the men, heckling me to relax and enjoy myself. I look around the room and I question to myself if some of the women here are actually prostitutes; I can't help but wonder what Nora has gotten me into. But there's something oddly comforting about this group of men; they seem strangely familiar. When the waiter returns with two gin and tonics, placing one in front of me, I take the hint, and offer up a "cheers." The men think they have broken through my shell, and now I'm really letting my hair down. They have no idea.

I'd done my share of partying in college, but the last several years of running my groovy grocery store by day and single momming by night hadn't left a lot of time for social drinking. I nurse my cocktail and try to be polite. Then it hits me: I'm in Nepal with my best, desperate-for-excitement girlfriend, at a table with a bunch of upper crust elite gentlemen. Now is not the time to be conservative and demure; now is the time to throw down and have some fun! I crawl out of my funk and offer my opinion on the topics being discussed, especially politics, and the men always show courtesy and respect when I speak. They listen intently, as if they've never heard a woman talk, even though they all have wives and daughters at home. Why are Nora and I so different? Is it because we're Americans? I trust they have no sexual expectations of us; they are almost fatherly, never once making an off-color remark. Then comes the bottle of whiskey.

Feeling the gin warm me I get brave and ask, "May I?" offering up my glass. The men within earshot look stunned, and I wonder what social custom I've just broken. They look to one another for advice, then finally the man next to me hesitantly tips the bottle up, splashing a hint of whiskey in the bottom of my glass. Looking down with exaggerated disappointment on my face, I hold the glass up to the light, as if to measure the meager amount rationed out. Then, looking to the men, I toss it down smooth, closing my eyes for dramatic effect. Their mouths hang open. Feeling empowered, I clank my glass down on the table and say, "That the best you got?" The men come undone, laughing hard, teasing the man who poured the first drink. As he pours me another, I lean over and say in the sexiest Marilyn Monroe voice I can muster, "Can I have a big girl size this time?" and the men nearly fall out of their seats with laughter. The man pouring makes it a little more generous, and I smile, looking at him sideways. "Well, that's better." They are enthralled.

The men love everything Nora and I say or do. They love it when we go to the ladies' room, they love it when we come back. They love it when we try to order, bumbling along, then order more for us, in case we don't like the first thing we're served. They make sure our glasses are full, continuously offering ways to make our evening more enjoyable. They ask endless questions, mostly about America, and hang on our every word, finding us incredibly charming and entertaining. They are blown over that I owned my own business and are dumbfounded that no father, brother, or husband set it up for me. In my pre-Nepal life, I would have been livid at the men's seeming sexism, but they are so innocent about it all that in my heart, I know they aren't malicious, they're just of another era, another world. They probably think the same of me.

By the end of the evening, Nora and I are grateful for Birendra's driver. Being encouraged by the men, I've consumed too much whiskey and have no hope of hailing a taxi, much less finding my way home. Our guard waits dutifully at the gate to our compound, ushering me in and walking me up the steps as I thank him profusely, trying not to stumble or accidentally profess my love to him. Dinesh, clearly entertained by my state, helps me up the stairs to the bedroom.

"Madam, you must be very quiet. Miss Devi was up crying and she just goes back to sleep." Dinesh cautions, the verbal coffee I need to sober up.

"Oh, Dinesh. Thank you so much," I gush, my sloshy mind unable to hold back, "I *love* you!"

"Yes, Madam," he smiles and turns to lock up on his way out.

When the door clicks shut behind him, I peel off my smoky, whiskey-splashed clothes, dropping them in the hallway, and tiptoe into the bedroom. The soft purr of sleeping children fills the room, and I look out between the curtains to the city lights below. I wish on every one of them as if they are stars, thanking them for sharing their city with me, for bringing me to my daughter, for keeping my family safe, and for holding me tightly in prayer folded *namasté* hands.

December

As the daylight hours of December became shorter, I waited with a heavy heart for the crushing cold I'd heard was soon to come. Nights grew chilly, and I found myself pulling on another layer almost hourly feeling like the little boy from *A Christmas Story*. Central heating was unknown in this corner of the world, and the concrete walls soaked up any warmth our meager space heater provided. I started bringing Kali, our chicken-shack street dog, in to sleep with us at night, for our benefit more than hers. I knew she would prefer to be outside, guarding her pack on the front stoop, but in our bedroom she was another warm body. Mornings were so frigid, my tea would cool on contact with the icy mug, but once the sun was up long enough to melt the frost, we were out on the terrace to soak up the sunny warmth.

Bright-eyed and enthusiastic, Steve and Lisa, an adoptive couple from New York, have arrived to meet their their daughter-to-be, Indra, one of the babies living at Annie's. Clearly, they are head over heels in love. They happily loan me their video recorder to make a movie of our home and new life to carry back to the

States for my anxious mother. In return, I offer to take pictures of their little one as often as I can, so they won't miss out on her precious baby time. Over tea at Summit, they tell me about the orphanage where our children lived before moving to Annie's, and their optimism is a breath of fresh air. It's difficult watching them come and go so quickly. They're already in the queue while I still have two more months to wait before I can even begin my process. While I recognize that "fair" has nothing to do with any of this, it's hard not to pout and feel like they're cutting in line. Seeing tears in Lisa's eyes as they pull away from Summit, while Devi swings from my arm, it's clear that none of this is fair to anyone. In their eyes, I'm the lucky one, able to stay here with my little girl. Looking down, watching her favorite pink bows bobbing on top of her stubby pigtails, I'm reminded of just how lucky I am.

Clank clunk goes the gate, and I know it's Nora, stopping off on her way home from a visit to the jail. I try not to feel like the pathetic next stop on her good will mission and appreciate her being my link to sanity. As the days run together, my seemingly ideal world of long walks through the city and tea at Summit are beginning to feel hollow and lonely.

"Helloooo," Nora coos, looking up to me through Jackie-O sunglasses.

"Come on up," I call down from my terrace perch.

"Nora! Nora! Nora!" Jack announces, freeing himself from the table in the raised dining area now known as Homework Island. So far, he's been content to be marooned so close to his endless source of fried rice a la Leena who plays the role of aid worker.

Moments later, Nora emerges onto the terrace, tea in hand.

"So, what are you up to? A new read?" She pulls up a chair.

"Yeah, *House Tibet*. I hadn't heard of the author, just bought it for the cover and the title. And guess what? It has nothing to do with Tibet," I grumble, disgusted by the trick the author has played on me. "Nothing at all. It's about a couple of young girls in

Australia who run away from home and become street children. Really, not what I needed to brighten my outlook right now," I sigh.

"So, you up for getting out? Maybe a foot bath?" Nora attempts to shift my inertia.

"Sure, whatever . . ." I don't care what we do, all the days melt into each other. The only day I care about is my birthday, which is still nearly two months away.

"Are you okay?" Nora asks.

"Oh, I'm just feeling sorry for myself, I guess. It was so sweet to see how excited Steve and Lisa are and hear about the filing process, but I feel like I'm in some sort of purgatory. Don't get me wrong; I'm thankful that this is what my purgatory looks like, but I don't want to waste my time here, just watching the days tick by," I confess.

"Well, what can you do?"

"Nothing, you know that. . . just sit here like a good little girl and wait to be old enough for Annie to say I can come out and play with the other mommies and daddies." The irritation building in my brain bubbles out.

"So, when you reach the magic age, then what? I mean, once Annie gives you the okay, what's next?" Nora continues patiently.

"Steve and Lisa went with her to the orphanage, and they met with Rajkumar, the Nepali facilitator. Then he took them to the Ministry, and they signed their file. But I'm not of age, and I'm not on Annie's list of things to do, so . . ." Annie had been adamant that we go to the orphanage together for first introductions, but I hadn't been able to pin her down on a day or time.

"It sounds like the orphanage is your first stop. Do you have to go with Annie? Was she helpful for Steve and Lisa? Did they need her to translate?"

"No, not at all! That's the most annoying part of this! It seems like she just shows up to make an appearance and collect her fee." I'm fired up, venting the frustration that has been brewing. "Why? What are you thinking?" I ask, knowing she's up to something.

"Well, I need to get going with my orphanage project. With the holidays, and gift giving season coming, I'd love to send pictures of a few kiddos back home to bring in some donations.

You wouldn't happen to know of an orphanage that might like a shiny, happy volunteer, would you? Maybe Steve and Lisa told you where to find one?"

"As a matter of fact, they drew me a map with directions, just in case I wanted to go over there myself," I offer.

"So, let's go check it out," Nora suggests, eyes bright, happy to hatch her plan.

"What do you mean? Just pop in? 'We were in the neighborhood and decided to drop by' kind of thing? Shouldn't I make an appointment? I mean, I don't want to bother them." Annie's intimidating words echo through my mind.

"From what I can tell, Nepalis love the pop-in. If they're busy, we'll know it, and we can offer to come back another time. Besides, they don't seem to have any trouble keeping folks waiting. Plus, you're caring for one of their children; I'd think they would roll out the red carpet for you! How much of your father's money did you donate to them?" She pauses, then asks, "Are you worried about pissing off Annie?"

"Well, maybe," I admit.

"Oh, give me a break. That woman has done nothing but put you off. Really, you're doing her a favor taking things into your own hands. Steve and Lisa said they were nice at the orphanage, yes?"

"Yeah, they said everyone was great. And really, I'd just be helping *you* out." I start to catch on.

"Come on, it'll be fun!" Nora chimes, forever upbeat. She can see I'm barely keeping my head above the turbulent waters that the months of screaming, sleepless nights have created. By concocting this outing, she's tossing me an emotional buoy to haul me in from my sea of despair without pity or judgment, just love and encouragement.

Once Devi is down for a nap and Jack has returned to Homework Island, Nora and I set out on our adventure. With Steve and Lisa's map and directions in hand, we take a taxi to Jawahalakel Circle, the roundabout where our treasure map begins. We soon find the tiny sign for the Starlight Lounge, our beacon for the alley we're looking for. Passing a courtyard where Ganesh presides over a pool of stagnant lime green water, we come to a T intersection and look for the blanket seller, and turn right. Then, spotting chickens and a trash heap, we take another turn and see a tea stall, our landmark for the tiny drive that leads to the X that marks the spot for the orphanage. The area seems oddly familiar, but with all the twists and turns, it's hard to be sure. Then, the pieces start to line up in my memory: the tall dorm-like buildings, the nails along the wall with laundry drying, the burgundy Nepali lettering on the white block wall, the words "Children's Home."

"Nora, I've been here before," I say, shocked. Of all the hundreds of orphanages in Kathmandu, I'm back at the one that opened my eyes to the reality of what Devi's life would be if I had chosen to leave several months earlier when things were so rough.

"What? Are you having some woo-woo past-life flashback or something?" She jokes, then, seeing my ashen face, stops short. "What is it, Kate? Are you going to pass out?" She takes my arm as I start to quake.

"This is the orphanage where we dropped off that little girl. Remember, the one I told you about from the bus ride?" Nora's face is blank. "The little girl from Jack's school. The one named Devi."

"Oh my God!" Nora gasps, now feeling the jolt through my arm, traveling up hers. "Well, let's just go. We don't have to go in there today. We can come back another time," Nora speed-soothes as she moves to turn me around.

"No, we're here. Just give me a minute." I say, taking a deep breath. I hear the monks from Boudha chanting in my head, *Om Mani Peme Hum*, and step forward to face this piece of my daughter's past.

When we knock on the gate, a guard opens it, and seeing we are Westerners, steps aside and bows. "We're here to see Rajkumar," I request. He motions toward the main house and tells us to go to the second floor. About twenty young children are gathered on a patch of grass playing. Above them, on a terrace, several *didis* have babies out in the warm sunshine. In a garage next to the main building, almost thirty older children sit at picnic tables. They're busy sharing pencils and paper, presumably working on school lessons, with a blank chalkboard behind them. At the carved wooden front door, we remove our shoes and leave them in the jumbled heap of various sized footwear. They look as foreign and out of place as we do.

We tiptoe inside and peek into several rooms with enough bunk beds to sleep a dozen children in each one. Next is a large room containing a mound of stuffed animals and floor pillows in a corner next to a television. At the end of the hall is the kitchen and a concrete stairwell. We follow voices up the stairs, and as we pass more bedrooms, I try to add up how many children live here, quickly losing count. We approach an office where a woman sits behind one desk and a young man behind another, both engaged in separate phone conversations. The woman glances up and smiles, waving us in, and we take a seat on a faded floral loveseat, a possible refugee from a 1970s garage sale, and nearly fall through the few remaining springs.

"How may I help you?" the woman asks politely, as she hangs up the phone.

"My name is Kate Saunders," I say, hoping she's heard of me. "I'm adopting one of the children who was staying at Annie's, Devi?"

"Oh, I see. So, *you* are Madam Saunders," she says curtly, briefly looking down at her hands, then back to me with a cold expression that doesn't match her words, "Very nice to finally meet you. I am Amita, the assistant director. Rajkumar is on the phone, just a minute." She turns away, preferring to wait for Rajkumar to finish his conversation rather than interact with us. Nora and I exchange confused looks.

"My name is Nora Murphy. I'm here for several months and would love to spend some time volunteering," Nora attempts to break the silence, but Amita continues to stare at Rajkumar, willing his call to end.

As soon as he hangs up, Amita begins speaking to him in rapid-fire Nepali with a hint of irritation in her voice as he glances our way. I wonder what I have done to upset her already and hope she is telling him about the phone conversation she was having before we showed up. Rajkumar looks at us, then back to Amita as she continues, asking questions here and there, then, finally, he addresses me.

"So, you are here to adopt Miss Devi. It is kind of you to come meet us. We did not know what had become of her."

"Well, I've been waiting for Annie to bring me to meet you, but I was in the neighborhood and thought I would stop by. I hope that's okay? This is my friend Nora, she'd like to volunteer here and help out." I stop myself as Nora's elbow pokes my ribs and realize I'm rambling. Judging by the deadpan faces of Amita and Rajkumar, I'm not off to a very good start.

"So, how is Miss Devi?" Amita asks.

"Oh, she's just great." I lie, trying to keep it simple.

"And does she talk?" Amita inquires, quite serious.

"Oh yeah, she's babbling more and more. I don't really know what she's saying a lot of the time, but she's getting better about using words, like *bapa* and juice." I feel myself babbling again and try to hold back, afraid I am irritating them.

"Well, that is very good," Amita says and smiles, looking slyly at Rajkumar, leaning back in his chair.

"So, Ms. Saunders, if you don't mind me asking, what took you so long to come see us? We knew Devi was no longer at Annie's but had not gotten word of where she was staying," Rajkumar inquires, cutting to the heart of the matter.

Shocked, I don't know what to say. "Oh, I was waiting for Annie to make an appointment," I justify, but seeing the hard looks between them, I feel like I'm in the principal's office, accused of taking something without permission. My words sound like excuses, something I can't stand, so I gather myself, take a deep breath, and say, "I'm sorry that it took so long for me to come by and introduce myself. I'm very honored to be here, and Devi is a blessing. Thank you for trusting me to care for her."

Their expressions soften as I tell them about Devi and her new big brother playing in the garden. I describe the house we are staying in, providing the usual directions, and invite them over for tea to see how Devi is adjusting. My offer is warmly received, and the conversation takes a turn for the better.

"Madam, you must understand, this is a very special situation. You must not tell anyone that you have not completed your paperwork or there could be much trouble for all of us," Rajkumar warns. I absorb his words knowing I will have to depend on him in the future to complete our adoption.

"But I thought I had permission for Devi to be with me until we could file with the Ministry," I stammer, shocked by this new level of secrecy.

"Oh no, Madam. His Majesty's government would never allow such a thing. There is difficulty with the children at Annie's already; you would never be permitted to have Devi with you. They would demand that she be returned to the orphanage until the paperwork is complete. Please, do not share your circumstances with anyone. We would not want any trouble with your file, and you still have some time before your birthday, yes?"

"It's at the end of January." I lower my head, reminded of how far I am from the starting line, not to mention the finish.

"Madam, this is very serious. Please, there are many people who are not in favor of international adoption. You should not even take the girl out until you have her travel documents in order, not even into Thamel. Crossing the wrong person could make trouble for us all," he continues.

"Yes, I understand," I attempt to show my willingness to cooperate and cringe as I slip the pictures of our trip to Pokhara back into my bag.

"Madam, please, do not take her beyond your familiar neighborhood. You have the rest of your life to be her mum and take her all number of places. For now, be safe. Stay home," Amita chimes in.

"Yes, of course." They have scared me straight.

"Now, would you like to take a tour?" Amita asks, standing up and motioning toward the door, her glittering red fingernails flutter like a game show hostess. We follow her down the long hallway to a large room filled with rows and rows of cribs; the back door open to the terrace. We step out into the bright sunlight to find at least a dozen babies on mats being tended by *didis* changing diapers with one hand and administering bottles with the other. Amita stops to check on one obviously sick little bundle with weepy eyes and a nose clogged with thick, yellow-green mucus. Her baby bird stick arms flail about, shaking, as her tiny fingers grip invisible security blankets. She makes breathy, raspy cries, her little lungs unable to produce significant volume. I feel like my chest is tearing open and turn away as my throat clenches off the shriek inside. Amita glows with pride at the facility she oversees, and I struggle to keep the crushing sadness off my face as I blink back tears. Nora takes charge of the conversation asking questions with genuine interest.

"We have over 100 girls and young children living here," Amita explains as we walk back downstairs. My limbs feel heavy as my feet thud down the concrete steps. "Eighty boys live in another facility outside the city where we are building a second home. It's about a year away from completion."

We gather our shoes and cross the concrete courtyard to a building next to the gate, where we climb a flight of narrow metal steps. "This is the toddler room," Amita announces, and I know, this is where Devi stayed. We enter a large bedroom with about twenty-five toddlers bumbling about as three *didis* try to wrangle them. Two little girls with striking facial features much like Devi's cry and cling to each other, their heads freshly shaven to prevent the spread of lice. Nora sees that I'm unable to speak and continues to carry the conversation while my heart pounds in my ears. I imagine Devi here, scared and hiding in a corner, and wonder which pallet she slept on. I look from little face to little face, and question what mystical force brought Devi and me together. Why her and not one of these other little people? Their eyes look back at me, dark hollows to their fractured souls. Some of them are crying, snot running down and pooling on their upper lips. A *didi* with a dirty rag wipes at one as she trips through the crowd and tries to stop another little boy from scaling one of the few cribs in the room. I'm relieved when Nora turns and leads me out the door.

I'm overwhelmed seeing so many children in need. I knew the facts of adoption in Nepal; families are only permitted to adopt a child if they don't already have one of the same sex, meaning if you have a boy, you can only adopt a girl, and vice versa. I could have ten sons and still adopt a daughter, but only one. Those two little sisters, desperately holding each other, would be split up and sent to different homes, and the adoptive parents would likely never even know a sibling existed. As for me? I can only rescue one child, and she is already home, where I'm determined she will stay. Nora sees me shutting down just as I've watched Devi do so many times and casually intertwines her arm in mine. She brings closure to our visit, and I somehow manage a sincere goodbye before stumbling out the gate. By the time we reach the top of the lane, tears are rolling down my cheeks like boulders in an avalanche. The reality of my little girl's past crushes me, now having viewed the set of her midnight terror movie.

"Come on Kate, let's go," is all Nora can say, the only words that make any sense. Her New York experience comes in handy as she quickly hails a taxi. "Summit Hotel," she directs the driver, and I'm comforted to know she is taking me home.

Nora stays for dinner, deflecting much of the kid energy and then she sneaks into the kitchen to give Dinesh, who is clearly concerned, a recap of the afternoon's synchronicities and less-than-comfortig events. Once the kids are off to bed, Nora and I settle on the sofa in the loft under a scratchy yak wool blanket as the night grows chilly.

"Kate, you've given her a different life now. There was nothing you could do about her being there; you didn't know about her yet. You got here as soon as you could." Nora tries to lift the darkness clouding me.

"Yeah," I choke out as tears begin to flow again. "There are just so many of them. So much heartbreak in such a small space."

"I know, I could feel it, too. But the kids out in the yard seemed pretty happy. I mean, of course it isn't ideal, but it's better than the lives of the street children, right?" I nod, seeing her silver lining.

"You can't take the weight of the world on your shoulders, Kate, even though I know you wish you could. You are just one mum; there is only so much you can do, and right now, you have a pretty big project on your hands."

"Those little sisters just broke my heart, and we know they'll be separated . . ." I trail off collapsing, as I put my head in her lap.

"Oh Kate, your heart really is too big for your own good," Nora sighs, stroking my hair, brushing away my pain. "Thank God Nepal has such an asinine law that you can only have one child of the opposite sex, or you'd be chartering a flight for all the kids you'd take home. You'd have your own Nepali soccer team," she teases, and I laugh ever-so-slightly. "Now that's better," she smiles down at me.

"I'll have a bowl of cream of mushroom soup and a side of rice, *dhanybhad*," I ask, using the now familiar Nepali "please."

"And I'd like the chicken satay," Nora adds, completing our order as the demure waiter bows slightly and turns toward the kitchen.

"So, you know the drill at the visa office?" I confirm, sucking mango *lassi* through what I hope is a first-use straw.

"No big deal, just wait in line in the stuffy, crowded concrete block office until you get to the front of the queue. Nothing you aren't familiar with, eh?" Nora jokes.

"I wish I knew. I'm not even in the queue yet, remember?" I say, chuckling, glad to make fun of my own circumstance.

"Well, this way you're getting plenty of practice! Plus, you have fabulous *me* to keep you company!"

"And for that, I am truly thankful," I offer a toast.

We finish our late lunch at Erza Café, a cross between a deli and a retro salon. It seems they are aiming for a coffee house atmosphere, but like so many things Nepali-trying-to-be-Western, they've missed the mark. The floral tablecloths are homey, but the sticky plastic cover makes it feel like a greasy diner. The seating area is quaint, but with out-of-date tabloid Hindi magazines and bowls of potpourri in every nook and cranny, it's reminiscent of a beauty shop. The twist, and there always is one: the seemingly endless volumes of Seventh Day Adventist literature. Proselytizing is illegal in Nepal, so Christianity exists underground, and we assume the literature is on hand for clandestine meetings. Still, the price is right, the food is pretty good, it's never crowded, and it's conveniently located halfway between Nora's flat and my place.

We top off our meal with a bad piece of something trying to be cake and hop into a taxi. The driver speed-swerves us to the Ministry office, a terracotta brick building with a concrete floor and a long row of service windows looking like a decrepit bank. After bobbing and drifting through the sea of expats crowding the visa office, we finally drift up to the counter and hope we are at the appropriate window. A small cranky man snaps instructions at us in Nepali and pushes forms across the counter.

"English, *dhanybhad?*" Nora asks, batting her long dark lashes and flashing her pearly whites.

The man scowls, then pivots and walks away. We start to fill out the forms while other anxious expats jostle for a turn behind us. With rumors of another coming *bandh*, the office is packed. Overstaying a visa, no matter the reason, even if the government offices are closed, is a very bad idea. Ever since the 70s when hippies descended on the Valley in drug-induced soul-searching journeys, Nepal recognized tourist visa fees were a lucrative business and increased enforcement of their regulations. Work visas are several times more expensive, which I learned when working for Kidz, and that had dampened my thoughts of an unpaid internship with an environmental organization. My budget didn't allow for a high-priced visa so I could engage in volunteer work.

The cranky man returns to take our forms and passports, looks them over, and disappears for several minutes before reappearing with another man, now scowling as well. They aggressively stamp Nora's passport and receipt in the appropriate places, hand them to her, and shoo her away from the counter. I wait expectantly for my own series of stamps and slams, but the second man looks at my papers, looks at me, then looks at the papers again. Lifting only his eyes to meet mine, he ticks his head to the side and says, "Come with me."

I look back to Nora, assuming I am being pulled aside due to

Jack's absence, though I had previously been told he didn't need to be present. Nora lunges through the crowd, grabbing my hand and I pull her to me, making it clear that wherever this little man is taking me, I'm not going alone. While disturbingly grumpy, these men pose no real threat; their body odor is their greatest weapon.

We're shown to a back office with surprisingly high ceilings and out-of-date office furnishings.

"Madam, there is problem. You overstay visit in His Majesty's Kingdom. We cannot reissue visa. You pay fine and leave country."

"There must be some mistake. Our passports were stamped for ninety days at the airport when we arrived," I stammer.

"Madam, at airport visa only approved thirty days," he says sternly and pushes my passport toward me, pointing at the date.

There it was, the expiration date, now almost two months ago. I don't understand how this could've happened, then suddenly flash back to the discussion between the men at the various counters at the airport when we flew in and realize that must have been the point of miscommunication. Now, all I can do is mitigate the damage. Leave the country? Not an option.

"So, how do we remedy this situation," Nora jumps in, smiling sweetly, ready to fix my latest fumble.

"Nothing to do," he glares at me. "Pay fine or go to jail."

I'm about to fall off my chair as the room begins to spin, when I hear Christina's voice in my head: "Show them pictures of your kids, all Nepalis love kids." I hesitate, anxious these men may not be in favor of international adoption, then looking across the table at the smug little man, I decide to gamble.

"Sir, please," I say as I reach into my bag for the pictures saved for such an occasion and gently place them before him. "I'm staying here in your lovely country with my son while waiting to adopt my daughter."

He looks at the pictures briefly, then tosses them back at me. "I see what to do."

Shaking ever so slightly, I turn to Nora.

"It's going to be fine, don't worry about it!" she says lightly, as if I've bounced a check.

We wait for what feels like hours, while various men come in to make the same accusation: "You have overstayed visa many, many days."

And I offer the same response: "Yes, I see. I'm very sorry, I thought it was stamped at the airport for ninety days."

Finally, the first man returns with someone I can only assume is the Head Man, though the office is so chaotic it's impossible to tell. "Madam, we discuss your circumstance and will make exception for you to stay in our country, but there will be a fine, and you must pay today."

"Oh, thank you. Anything, please, this was just a mistake. I promise, it won't happen again." I notice a group of men forming at the window to my side, watching the pathetic foreigner show, starring.

"Thirty-four thousand rupees," he says, the hint of a smirk curling at the corners of his tobacco stained mouth. Five hundred dollars. The cost of a monthly visa was only thirty. I could only imagine how much would go straight into his pocket.

"I don't even have that much money in the country right now," I gulp, distracted by what sounds like a bad sit com laugh track coming from the gawking staff as my sentence is delivered.

"Perhaps you friend help?" he smirks.

Nora and I look at each other. "I'm sorry sir, but that's terribly high. Isn't there something you can do?" my personal public relations manager negotiates.

"Madam, you don't understand. You friend has committed very serious crime. I have done all I can. She must pay fine."

"Well, the wire will take a few days to arrive, so I'll plan to come back next week. What's your name? Can I ask for you?" I rattle out, digging in my handbag for pen and paper.

"You will have money today, or I cannot help you," he snaps and stands, taking Jack's and my passports. "You have one hour."

Nora and I maintain a confident facade as we stroll through the visa office, but once out the door, we sprint to catch a taxi to the nearest bank where I empty my account at the ATM, and Nora goes inside to take a cash advance on her credit card. From there, we slip into a tea stall and start making calls. Craig isn't home, so we try Tessa. Through the crackle, I make out she'll stop by the British School to hit up Jonathan, then meet us at the visa office. Nora and I high-tail it back to wait under a shade tree.

"Nora, I have no idea what I would do without you," I sigh.

"Are you kidding me? What would I do without you? Nepal would be terribly boring without these wonderful adventures," she teases, patting my hand. "Kate, you're the sister I never had. I would do anything for you!"

Just then, Tessa pops out of a taxi and skips over to the tree where we huddle like drug dealers, counting piles of 1,000-rupee notes. We have thirty-four, just enough to cover the fine and buy me one more month. Finally, thirty-four is the magic number for something.

We strut back into the office with Tessa leading the way, speaking flawless, fluent Nepali. The weight lifts from my chest, and I can breathe again. As I watch first Jack's passport, then mine, take their blows from the Head Man's stamp, I give thanks for my amazing friends.

```
December 16, 2005
Subject: Important Security Message for
American Citizens in Nepal
```
    This Warden's message is being issued to alert American citizens that some members of the seven political parties have called for a "bandh" (closure) for Kathmandu on Friday, December 16, 2005 in response to the killing of civilians by RNA personnel in Nagarkot.
    While it is unclear at this time how widely the bandh will be observed, American citizens are advised to minimize non-essential travel, maintain a low profile and, if you must travel, to wait until a pattern of traffic is well established. Taxi and bus services

may not be available. Moreover, during past closures, a number of buses, taxis and other personal vehicles have been attacked. Aviation authorities advised the Embassy that domestic and international airline companies are expected to continue to provide service during the bandh, but this could change with little or no advanced warning.

The notice lists contact information for the Embassy, and at the end states, "In the event of a communications blackout, security information will be left at all of the major hotels in Kathmandu." I'm confused . . . if we aren't supposed to leave our homes, and there is no phone or internet service, how will we get information from a hotel?

The winter holidays of Dashain and Tihar have brought out the best in all sides of the political conflict, and they have agreed to a cease fire. However, with the return of the King from holiday in India and the coming election, things are heating up again. Luckily, bandh days are announced ahead of time so we can prepare, since no taxis run and all businesses are closed. Foot traffic is permitted, so Dinesh and Leena have no trouble getting to our place. The lack of motorized travel makes for strangely quiet days and brings a whole new flavor of peace to our lovely terrace.

It's easy to forget the time of year in the Hindu kingdom in the absence of Western-style Christmas marketing, which for me is a welcome relief. My father died suddenly eight years ago, just days before he and my mother were to arrive for the holidays. As a result, this time of year is filled with painful memories.

The call had come as my boyfriend, Ned, and I were on our way out for an afternoon movie. I answered to an unfamiliar man on the other end of the line, claiming to be an old college friend of Ned's, which sounded fishy since I knew all of his school buddies. I cheerfully assumed it was a Christmas surprise being set up by my ever-mischievous, holiday-loving father and played along, handing the phone off and walking to the door. I glanced back; Ned had his back to me, with one hand braced on the kitchen counter shaking his head. Then, he turned in slow motion, hung up the phone, and held out his hands to catch the fall his news was about to deliver. "Kate, that was your mother," he said in the deep, soft voice of a late night DJ, inconsistent with a Christmas surprise, "Your father died."

A gutteral groan like a sinking ship grew, gathering intensity as primal screams of soul death roared from my chest only to clog in my throat and clamp off the pain; refusing to hear the news that would force my brain to accept the truth. Ned gathered me up as I shrieked and shook, melting into the kitchen floor, refusing to leave, waiting for a call that never came to say it had all been a mistake.

I arrive home earlier than usual from my afternoon walk to find Jack happily reading *Tin Tin* comics on the roof. Once again, he's escaped from Homework Island. I am furious and out of ideas. My father was like a Jedi who led me to righteous behavior through stoic silence. Taking a page from his book, I tell Jack he has to decide his own punishment. His first suggestion is that he can't play with Devi, which seems more like a reward. Then he offers to give up his comics until his schoolwork is done, but that is an empty promise I've already fallen for too many times.

"You'll have to be more creative."

"How about an Iroquois punishment I read about. You pour a bucket of cold water over me." Jack suggests, eyes gleaming.

"Okay, let's go . . ." This punishment seems innocuous enough and certainly less damaging than my Grandmother's tales of having to cut her own switch. So, with Devi and Leena as witnesses, he stands in the shower while I dump a bucket of icy water over him and hold my breath, expecting wails of displeasure. I can't bring myself to dump the second bucket over him, but he laughs, eyes dancing above a jack-o-lantern grin.

"What next?" he giggles and douses himself again.

I feel nothing like a Jedi.

I sit, propped in a nest of pillows on Devi's bed and watch as the fading rays of sunlight turn the Himals cotton-candy pink. I feel empty, hungry for more than dinner. From the café behind us, John Denver sings: "Country roads, take me home . . ." It's near the anniversary of my father's death, and I beg his ghost for some magic parenting tip. "You just do the best you can," he tells me with a twinkle in his eye as he shakes his head over my latest crusade. Whether it had been taking me to the beach to look for a lost surfer boyfriend or waiting in the car when I offered homeless men my leftover dinner, he always supported me, no matter how far left of center I strayed. The other side of the world was the farthest I could go, and the inheritance he left behind allowed me to push to my limit. But without him, life had never been the same.

I open an email from the property manager where my store used to be. She updates me on all the drama within the building: who is dating whom, barroom brawls upstairs, the hothead landlord's latest threats, and then, my heart drops as I read, "I have some bad news. Last week Jeremy Steven's wife, Jennifer, was killed in a car wreck on her way to work; the funeral service was today. Life isn't fair, their little girl is only two."

I've known Jeremy for years, his office was next door to my store. We'd shared a secret kinship, both coming in to work pre-dawn to plow through paperwork before our employees showed up and the phone started ringing. Now, as I'm already aching for Devi's mother, who will never get to see her daughter grow up, I find myself mourning another little girl on the other side of the world who will grow up without her mother. My mind spins at the ties that invisibly bind us.

Within days, there's more unsettling news that my grandmother has taken a turn for the worse. I'm sickened by the thought of never seeing her again and ache to be by her side, but she insists my mother call and relay this message: "Don't you dare leave your little girl just to fly around the world and watch me die." I take her words to heart, but I want to share my life in Nepal with her before she leaves this world. Since my father died so suddenly, at barely 53, I never got the chance to tell him goodbye. I never even considered the things that needed to be said, and I won't make that mistake now, so I sit down and write my grandmother a story.

```
Dear Mimi,
    I have so many things I want to share
with you! I'm amazed by where I am not only
geographically, but with what has become of
my life. You've always been so supportive,
reminding me that I'm a strong woman. I've
stepped so far out of the norm, but I always
knew I could come back and find you waiting
for me, cheering me on. When I got pregnant
with Jack, and I wasn't married to his father,
you didn't see it as a mistake, you told me
it was a miracle, and you were right, Jack
has kept me afloat so often. Then, when I
chose to expand my family, I was comforted
by your approval, it has meant so much to me.
Knowing you love a little girl you haven't
even met, on the other side of the world,
brings me great peace. I wish I had found a
husband to share my life and family with, but
you and Pops gave me an incredible example
of what love truly is, and I won't settle for
anything less. I will tell my children and
grandchildren your love story, but for now, I
have a story for you.
    It is a beautiful day in Nepal. I'm looking
out the large arched windows at the layers of
snowcapped Himalayas in the distance against
the backdrop of a turquoise blue sky. I imagine
you here with me, having tea on the terrace
and admiring the poinsettias the size of
small trees in full bloom. There are women
in a rainbow of saris walking down our lane,
```

ringing their puja bells and carrying marigold garlands to place on the altar for Ganesh, the elephant-headed deity found throughout our neighborhood. We hear a street vendor announcing his wares; this one is balancing a basket of reed brooms on his head. You remark on the ornate architecture of the houses surrounding us, with their carved teak doors that pay homage to mysterious deities, the flowered spindles of our terrace railing, the intricate vines that wind around our ceiling molding. All the houses have dozens of flowers, every color imaginable—huge roses bloom blood red, delicate purple monkey flowers, pale pink geraniums, Shasta daisies, and marigolds everywhere, like little bursts of sunshine. Our persimmon tree is heavy with fruit, weighed down with branches that droop like a willow. The didi is in the garden picking guava, fresh greens and cherry tomatoes for lunch.

   The kids are on a blanket in a patch of sunshine in the playroom. Devi has brought Jack yet another book to read to her; this one is about Little Bunny learning the colors of the rainbow. Devi repeats after him—wed, ouange, lellow, geen, boo, popou. You are impressed when Jack starts naming each of the colors in Nepali and energized by how smart he is, as well as kind and gentle. I wish he were that enthused about doing his math! You smile knowingly and reassure me he'll be just fine. Devi comes bumbling in, chubby bare feet pitter-pattering on the marble floor. She greets you with a smile and climbs into your lap to give you the sweetest of sticky toast and jam kisses. You look into her onyx eyes and see the miracle of a childhood rerouted from a life of poverty and suffering to one of joy and opportunity. You know what a gift she has been given, and she is giving that gift right back. "NOSE!" She accurately locates yours with a tiny cappuccino finger, giggling and smiling so that her own nose scrunches up, her eyes crinkle and disappear. She wiggles back down to chase the street puppy we found in a ditch. "Puppy! Puppy!" she squeals with excitement, and she is off, playing hide and seek through the bright white linens hanging on the line to dry in the sunshine.

Jack saunters in. Being a big brother has given him a new sense of self and he has grown out of the little boy he was not so long ago. His developing swagger hints at what is to come. "Mimi, why can't you stay just a little bit longer?" he asks, with a pinch of boyish whine still lingering in his voice. "Oh Jackie, I would really like to, but I have to go. Don't worry, I'll see you again," you say, smiling the kind of smile only a great-grandma can, the pride of your family dancing in your eyes. Jack tiptoes up and knots his hands around the nape of your neck in the tight embrace of overanxious boys. "See you later alligator!" he sings out, grinning and pecking you on the cheek before he hops down and skips off to see what his sister is up to.

I know it's time for you to go, but I want to savor every last drop of our time together; it's the sweetness of the lemonade you would make for Jack and Pops to share on a hot afternoon; it's the gentle grace of the lace curtains softening the view of your garden; it's the compassion sewn into every angel you made for a Christmas bazaar. It is the limitless love that you have instilled in each one of us. It is eternal, so that is what I hold onto.

For all of these things, I give thanks.
I love you,
Kate

Sitting on the terrace, I'm overwhelmed as grief closes in from all sides.

Dinesh brings up afternoon tea and senses something wrong.

"My grandmother is not well," is all I can say. "Would it be possible for you stay late tonight? I'd like to go to Boudha." Craig told me about the full moon ceremonies at Boudha, and it feels like the time to go.

"Of course, Madam. You go, I will mind the children." He sympathizes.

I sit silently in the taxi watching familiar scenery drift by. The driver has chosen a route through a part of the city where the streets narrow, and the vendors are practically stacked on top of one another. It feels cozy and personal, like I'm going home. I duck into a side path as I hear the sound of monks chant *Om Mani Peme Hum* over the loud speakers, their words enveloping me in the warmth of spiritual comfort. As tears break loose, I merge into the flow of practitioners and feel the river of prayer fill my heart and carry me round the *stupa*. Prayers stick in my throat, croaking out in sobs, so I settle for a whisper, knowing Buddha won't mind. The all-knowing eyes see my pain, a teardrop of sadness in a sea of worship.

I stop at a table of butterlamps, their flames dancing in the gentle evening breeze, hand the woman enough rupees for thirty lamps and start lighting them. Ten for Jeremy and his family: *May they find peace in this tragedy.* The vendor looks at me with softness as tears fall from my eyes, and I hope they don't extinguish the flame of prayer I've just sent out. Ten for Mimi: One, two, three—*may she be free of suffering.* Four, five, six, seven—*I hope she can feel how much I love her.* Eight, nine, ten—more tears flow as I think of her never meeting my daughter, just as my father never met my son. I take a deep breath and rest my focus on my dad, seeing his smile of approval in my mind, and the stab of loss digs deeper into my heart. I thought I'd come to accept his absence, but here, now, I feel so alone, the grief is unbearable. I light ten more lamps for him and silently plead with the All Knowing Eyes above, *take this pain away.*

With the lamps lit, all that's left to do is walk. Around and around and around the *stupa* I flow until the flood of tears recede, leaving me wrung out like the laundry before Leena hangs it up to dry. I pause to look up to the starless sky, searching for guidance, and there it is: a light in a tiny window high above. Like the North Star, it guides me to a narrow hallway that runs like a spoke off the *stupa* center of the wheel, leading to a staircase. The passage is dreary and uninviting, but I've lost my fear of muggers, especially since in this part of the world, I'm a good four inches taller than any would-be assailant. At the top of the creaky metal stairs, I see a door slightly ajar, and the guiding light calls me in. I peek through the crack to see a tiny, ancient man behind a stack of hand-woven blankets. I tap on the door, and his head draws up slowly, like a wise turtle.

"Please, come," the turtle waves me in with kind eyes and a soft smile.

The air is thick with a dank earthy aroma laced with incense and wool. The room is packed with blankets and shawls, brass trinkets and Buddhas, archaic weapons of every size, all ornate and impossibly old. I start to tell the shopkeeper who I am, what I'm doing here, how I like Kathmandu, but my usual monologue feels hollow and cliché. This man deserves authenticity, so I move to the counter and look into his dark eyes. they remind me of my daughter's, but his are cloudy and almost blue with cataracts, surrounded by a storybook of wrinkles.

"Please, sit," he offers and begins to tell me the origin of his wares. He is from Tibet, and I am surrounded by its history. My anthropological mind ignites as I float away across the Himalayas to his home, and I drink in every detail of his simple peasant childhood through his family's exodus from Tibet. I'm amazed by his life experiences, far more challenging than anything I have encountered, and my grief feels smaller.

"I have something for you," he says and disappears behind the sofa-sized counter to resurface holding a wooden box and hands it to me.

I take his offering humbly and examine the hand painted

auspicious Buddhist symbols: a white conch shell, a pair of golden fish, an endless knot and beautiful lotus flower. I feel the electric buzz of history and culture through my fingertips as he explains what each of the symbols means.

"The shell, to hear teaching of Buddha. The golden fish, good fortune, help you swim with no fear. This, endless knot, for wisdom, compassion. And lotus flower, for pure mind, enlightenment. Is good, yes?"

"Oh yes, it's very beautiful." I screw up the courage to ask, "How much?" I'm sure this museum piece is beyond my budget.

"Is for you," he smiles.

"Yes, I understand, but how much does it cost?"

"For you, Madam. This box for you. It belong to you," he repeats, gesturing for me to take it. Seeing the confusion on my face, he continues, "When something belong to you, it find you."

I have no idea how to respond. He smiles, folding his hands in prayer and bows his head slightly.

I don't want to leave the tiny shop, finding comfort in the rich history within, but know it's getting late, and Dinesh must be wondering about me. I thank the Wise Turtle, hands together, *namasté*, and bow to the God within him. I give thanks for the light in his window, for reigniting the light in my soul. *Om Mani Peme Hum.*

Cuddling my awkward box like a baby, I make one more trip around the *stupa*, and my eyes gush again, now looking up to the All Knowing Eyes with tears of thanks and gratitude. In the face of pain and loss, I found kindness and compassion, and have been brought back to my center. I recognize how incredibly fortunate I am for all I have: health, family, home, friends. I vow to take all my sorrow, pain, fear, frustration and put them in my box, to let them transform, like the lotus growing out of the mud, into something beautiful. Just like the transformation going on in my little girl.

I feel trapped in a constant battle with Devi over one thing or another. I focus on helping her use words, modeling *"bapa* please"

rather than her grunting, screaming and whining. This forces her to give up some control, which she fights relentlessly.

Most recently, she refuses to use her pink plastic potty, winding herself up to the point of screaming, hitting, and kicking when directed to use it. Resorting to bribery, I've tried giving her a date, one of her favorites, when she potties successfully. Unfortunately, she often prefers control over sweet treats. The moment I give up, figuring she doesn't have to go, in spite of the glass of juice she drank an hour ago, she stands up and pees on the floor, splashing her bare feet in the puddle. Then she gives me the creepy grin, and I feel crazy trying to guess what's going on in her head. *What makes her do this?*

As with her sleeping problems, I'm at my wits' end trying to figure out what has shifted to cause her to rebel like this. I've started catching her up on vaccines, but she was on potty strike before that. Maybe something happened on the potty . . . Was she pinched by the plastic pieces? Does she have a bladder infection? If I took her to the doctor, could I get a urine sample? Maybe she's just pissed off? I slide into the world of inside-out, upside-down parenting and accept this for what it likely is: an attempt to control something in her world, and peeing just happens to be one thing on a very short list. I'm learning that due to her attachment issues, as she feels closer to me, safer, and more secure, the harder she pushes me away. This way, in her mind, if I abandon her, she won't be hurt; after all, she never needed me anyway.

Ready for a break, I head to Summit to sip tea in the lounge and skim the local paper where I find an article to lift my shaky spirits:

```
No Monkey Business
By D. Radhakrishnan
   Udhagamandalam: A dog may be man's best
friend but it took a monkey to turn saviour
to a puppy at Lovedale near here. For the
past few days, people in the town are witness
to a rare display of love and affection.
   The puppy, all wet and shivering in the
winter cold, was first seen near the railway
```

station on Sunday, according to the Station Master, N. Pramond. Even as the locals were wondering what to do, a monkey descended on the scene from a nearby tree. It did not waver, didn't have a second thought. It patted the puppy affectionately, cuddled it, and then lifted it up and ran into the nearby forest.

The locals looked on amazed. On Monday the savior and its charge could not be spotted. Come Tuesday, the monkey, holding the puppy close, appeared atop Mr. Pramond's house. When people tried to get close, the monkey fled up a tree with the puppy clutched to its chest.

It then proceeded to eat some nuts, feeding the puppy too.

After a while, the monkey came down and sat on a roof and accepted some food from onlookers. It shared the tidbits with the puppy, cuddling and kissing it all the while. As more and more people converged on the scene, monkey and friend walked off into the forest.

And, thereby hangs a tale of love.

Remembering the monkey that taught me to cross the street, I endeavor to go home and try again, my compassion reignited by the monkey tale.

Dear Kate,
I arrived in Holland in one piece, despite the wet snow greeted me! Such a strange experience to land in a pitch-black world in the heart of winter, everyone behind thick glass windows. Even at 9 am it was still dark, endless headlights on their way to work, like neatly arranged stars headed for Bethlehem.

My village is lovely as ever, with the sea so close I can almost hear it at night.

```
I am blessed to live close to both the
Himalayas and the ocean, equally powerful and
comforting.
    Life is busy preparing for guests and
thinking of what to cook for Christmas.
    Wishing you all happy holidays, keep in
touch over the coming months.

Much love,
Tessa
```

The holiday season is upon us, though largely without the influence of Christmas—the one stuffed Santa I've seen in a shop window looks horribly uncomfortable, aware the red suit is merely a costume here in the Hindu Kingdom. While I'm enjoying the break from overly abundant holiday marketing, for Jack, the lack of festivities is cause for concern.

"How is Santa going to find us if nobody here celebrates Christmas?"

"I sent him our forwarding address," I offer, hoping to end the anxious nagging.

"We don't have an address." He catches me on a technicality. "And we don't have a fireplace."

Feeling the spirit of my mischievous father, I play the oldest trick in the book, and tell him he'll just have to wait and see, which drives him nuts.

"Santa doesn't bring stuff for grown-ups cuz they don't play anymore," Jack whispers to Devi, thinking I'm still asleep and eager to scamper downstairs to check for signs of Saint Nick. To his relief, Santa has indeed made a stop at our house. For Jack, there is a cursive writing book he had been eyeing at Pilgrims, a paper airplane kit, an origami kit, and a new book, *The Little Prince*. For Devi, there is a necklace, a flute, some bells and a wooden elephant on wheels.

I'm pleased our low-key holiday has fulfilled him, and I love the way he shares it with Devi. I realize how little the material items themselves mean and watching them having fun together makes the day special. By Nepali standards, they are spoiled with so many gifts.

I have all sorts of grand plans for the holiday. Since Dinesh and Leena are off, we are on our own for meals, something Jack is sure is a very bad idea. I attempt to reassure him that I do, in fact, know how to cook, reminding him of the organic deli I presided over since shortly after his birth. I get busy in the kitchen while he dresses up as an elf in red and white with a big stuffed belly and runs around excitedly singing carols while waiting for our guests to arrive.

I've spent a small fortune on ingredients for our meal: miniature vegetarian lasagna—to fit in our miniature oven—with mushrooms, spinach, artichoke hearts, and goat cheese. Dinesh baked fresh rolls the day before and prepped the salad greens and homemade dressing. Unfortunately, like all else in Nepal, dinner is delayed for reasons beyond my control. After lunch, the power goes out because workmen have taken down all the lines, lying them in the street to remove branches from a nearby tree. Not only does this prevent my masterpiece lasagna from cooking, it also stops the water in the tank from heating up. Hot showers were to be my humble gift to my guests. With Tessa and Jonathan gone for the holiday, it is just Craig, Nora, and me, plus a couple of new faces.

Nora arrives early, not to cook, she's quick to qualify, but to bring the kids their gifts. For Jack, she has a traditional Nepali game akin to chess, played with tigers and goats. Devi is thrilled with a stuffed rabbit in a pink dress and bloomers. Nora has a gift for me as well, a lovely set of batik napkins.

"You can never have enough of these!" she looks to Devi, munching peanut butter crackers at the table. "Plus, once I leave to go back to the States, it'll be like I'm still here having dinner with you!"

"Ugh, I don't want to think about that right now," I say. Then, hearing a strange rumbling, I ask, "What's that?"

Nora and I look to each other quizzically. It sounds like heavy rain, but there hasn't been a drop of precipitation in the Valley for weeks. That's when Jack bursts in the back door, shivering and dripping wet.

"What happened?" I gasp, all holiday spirit extinguished.

"I was looking for Santa." Jack wails through chattering teeth. "I thought maybe he came through the water tank, so I went up to the roof to see." After climbing the water tower, he'd swung down one of the pipes that attach the tank to the house and snapped the connection, causing hundreds of gallons of water to gush out onto the roof.

I dash up the back steps to fetch the landlord while Nora helps Jack out of his soggy clothes. By the time we return, the tank has nearly run dry. All that's left for the landlord to do is to turn a ball valve on the side of the tank to stop the trickle.

"I'm *so* sorry." I apologize profusely.

"Is okay, is okay," he says as he bobbles and smiles, though I see from the strain on his face, all is not okay. The repair, and subsequent compensation will be addressed in the morning.

Luckily, Craig arrives with a bottle of wine in one hand and a bottle of whiskey in the other followed by a professor friend, Jason, who is visibly entertained by the chaos.

"It's like a missing scene from *Christmas Vacation*," Craig laughs.

"Oh, don't worry," Nora reassures me, "eating late is very European; you're incredibly chic."

As I serve cheese and crackers to hold us over while we sip cocktails, Dave, our last guest, arrives. An adoptive dad-to-be, Dave has come to wait out the final steps of his adoption of Arun, one of the babies at Annie's. He's just flown in from the States and is happy to have new friends to share the holiday with. Right away, I like him and appreciate his laid-back attitude in spite of the atmosphere. I stop fretting over making the holiday perfect and sit down to sip whiskey with the boys while Nora wrangles the kids into pajamas before the long-awaited lasagna is finally ready.

We huddle around the table saying what we're thankful for, and when Jack's turn comes, he somberly says, "I'm thankful for still being in my body," and seeing the confused looks of the adults around him, he adds, "because my mom didn't kill me!" This elicits guffaws from everyone but me. I feel my face turning Santa-suit red. "It's not me you have to worry about," I tease. "We'll see how many days the landlord will have you scrubbing pots at the outside tap to pay for all that lost water."

```
Dear Kate,
   What a wonderful Christmas present! I
just got the video from Steve and Lisa and
have watched it over and over. I can't think
of anything that would make me happier than
seeing you, Jack and Devi! I loved hearing
your voice, and am delighted with my new
granddaughter, she's so smiley! Her eyes just
twinkle! Jack is growing so fast and looking
tall now! What a big jack-o-lantern grin with
all those teeth missing! Your house is so
much prettier and more spacious than I had
imagined. I can't wait to share the video
with the rest of the family!

Love to you and your beautiful children!
Mom
```

Photo Gallery

Above: Kate & Jack on their way to the airport.
Below: Kate & Jack meet Devi.

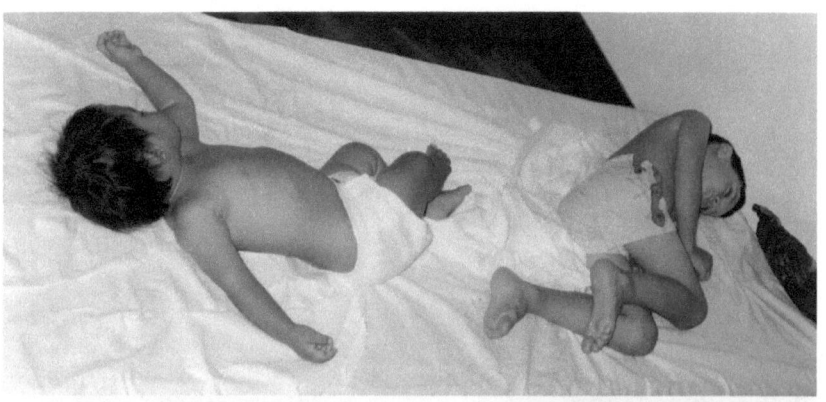

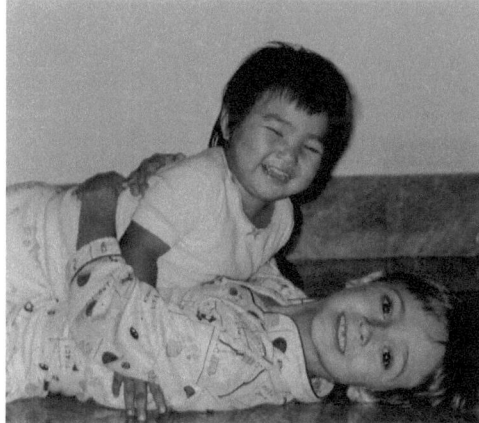 

Above: hot nights in Kathmandu.
Middle: Devi loves to wrestle! Out on the terrace.
Below: after the laundry is done, Devi gets a bath.

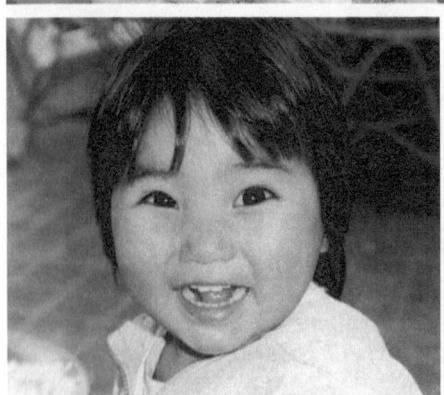

Above: Devi loves reading with Jack.
Middle: Devi excited for a walk in the Summit garden. Our little house on the hill.
Below: Devi and Leena.

Above: Jack's favorite rule to break—relaxing up on the roof.
Below: A view from the terrace of our bedroom and the water tank above.

Above: "Good Dog" on Kukur Tihar.
Below: Tenzing.

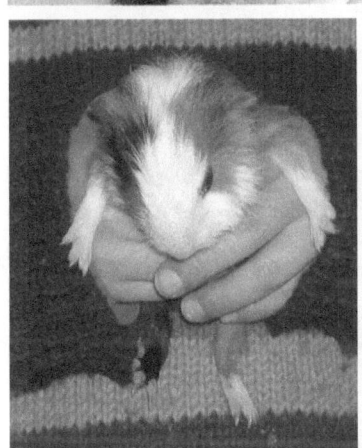

Above: Jack and Bilbo Baggins, one of our many street pups.
Middle: Squeaky (left), Norbu (right).
Below: our collection of street dogs: Bilbo, Zelda, Perro and Kali.

Above: Jack circumambulating at Boudha.
Below: Boudhanath Stupa, Kathmandu.

Above: World Peace Pagoda, Pokhara.
Below: crossing Phewa Tal.

Above: Happy Birthday, Jack!
Below: family photo on the terrace; Devi loves swimming!

Above: the mud fight.
Below: Jack has an audience with Chökyi Nyima Rinpoche.

Above: Jack is ferocious!
Below: Best birthday with my favorite people: Dinesh, Jack, Devi and Leena.
(photo credit, Nora)

January

Dear Friends and Family,

    Happy New Year from Nepal! We had a wonderful day with Dinesh and his family. After surviving an insane bus ride on a bumpy road with livestock and a squirmy two-year-old on my lap (the sheep didn't respond to her insistent "moo" greetings, so for her, the party was over) we arrived at a beautiful park in the foothills. Jack ran around climbing trees with the other kids, and when Leena bought them cotton candy (I'm surprised it even exists here) he was ecstatic! Devi did her best to keep up, but her favorite part of the day was the picnic—eating, eating, eating—with so many adults offering her this and that, she was in heaven! I had fun passing an underinflated volleyball around a circle (no net) but it took a bit to get used to hearing, "Madam!" when the ball came my way. I haven't decided if this is how they refer to me out of respect, or because they have a hard time remembering my name, haha. It was wonderful to be included in this kind and loving family. We were all sad when the day came to an end.

We have a new pet guinea pig! Leena took the kids to the bike shop to get a new pedal for Devi's hunk-of-junk-trike and returned with a bizarro third-world pet vendor. He carried a big bamboo pole over one shoulder with baskets hanging off either end packed with a variety of rodents and illegal feathered friends. He quickly handed Jack a pathetic, skinny guinea pig (much to his delight) and Devi two baby ones. He continued to pull rabbits out of cages by their ears, while lime green parrots with blood orange beaks squawked, white and turquoise parakeets beat their wings in flightless frenzy, and tiny, iridescent jade finches fluttered and chirped as he told me they would change color every month. Seeing so many captive little souls, it was hard to resist the urge to buy them all, especially the birds, and set them free. I finally made peace with rescuing the guinea pigs and a parrot. One of the babies died the first night, and the momma the next day, so now we just have Squeaky, who is being spoiled to epic proportions and monopolizing our single space heater. I give thanks for his continued survival every day since he has become a necessary tool in the homework battle with Jack. The new rule is: No Squeaky time until the homework is done. It is amazing how fast lessons can be accomplished with a rodent reward! I'm sure Jack imagines himself riding off on Squeaky's back, like his favorite god, Ganesh, with his mice. I'm wondering if there will be a quarantine on a guinea pig, it would be a tragedy to leave poor Squeaky behind!

Devi is doing well, sleeping more, hitting and biting less. She continues to learn more English, as well as Nepali. I'm feeling less inept when I have to ask Leena to translate for me; most of the time she doesn't understand her either. Devi is incredibly hard-headed and determined to not need anything from me, so when she has softer moments, peeking out from behind her wall, I drink them up. She and Jack couldn't be more different; none of my previous parenting tactics work with her, and she has more stamina than me any day of the week. I'm terrified what the teen years will bring! She's quite bright, and unexpectedly catches on to things. And, oh my, such a girly girl! Ramro (pretty) is one of her favorite words, especially when combing her hair (or mine, ouch!). She loves pulling out all of her clothes and trying them on. "Ramro!" she says grinning as she smooths the folds of her dresses, feeling the fuzzy velour fabric I found in the market.

Our sunny terrace, looking out to the Himalayas, is a welcome sanctuary from the chaotic polluted city. And what do I miss the most from home? FRESH MOUNTAIN AIR! And of course, all of you. Happy New Year!

Namasté,
Kate

January drifts by like the lazy daydreams that float through me, light and puffy as cotton ball clouds while I sit huddled under layers of wool sweaters and blankets that still smell like sheep. I plant myself in a pocket of sunshine on the terrace and watch the Himals go bubblegum pink as night creeps in. There is a chill in the air, but it feels warm compared to the concrete cold inside our house. Third World standards equate to no central heat, but I'm not ready to make our experience thoroughly authentic by burning garbage for the kids to huddle around in the evening just yet. As the winter drags on, however, it seems more and more like a viable option.

Changing clothes in the morning is torture, and I rarely peel off my silk base layer. The mere thought of exposing my skin to the icy air gives me goosebumps. Full-fledged showers are sporadic as the sun hovers low over the black haze of pollution that blankets the Valley, preventing the solar panels from heating up the water tank beyond lukewarm. This is fine with Devi; clearly, hot water was an unknown luxury in her village, the orphanage, or even at Annie's, but I crave steamy showers and justify heating the tank with the electric backup as an excuse to entertain friends. Sharing the warm comfort means shorter shower time so there is enough to go around, but I don't mind.

Nora is at a Zen retreat center for a couple of weeks, and I feel lost without her, but Dave is filling in the gaps between attempted meetings to move his adoption process forward. For some reason, neither Annie, nor the Children's Home staff, are impressed by Dave's bold move to come to Kathmandu to wait on the doorstep of the Ministry to complete his adoption. He and his wife had hoped his presence would light a fire under the Ministry, but so far, Dave seems to be the only one fired up in his strong, silent way. I appreciate his patient nature and realize that when he has something to say, it's often of great value. I'm eager for any tips he can share to help me navigate this process. I'm trying not to count the days to my birthday, but catch myself doing the mental math relentlessly. Knowing it's almost time to get in the queue is exhilarating.

The power goes out often and without warning in the evenings due to low water levels in the hydroelectric dams, so I've stashed matches and candles around the house, out of reach of busy little hands. Last night I was watching *The Bourne Supremacy*—it was even in English—when, POOF, no power. I felt irrationally angry, then took a deep breath and waited for the lights in the house behind us to click on, powered by their noisy generator that illuminates the room enough to light a candle so I can stumble to bed. The phone lines and TV stations are also cut at random, and rumors say this is all intended to weaken the Maoist insurgency. It's becoming a bit surreal.

I don't know what it is about the frequency Devi emits from her tiny lungs in the night, but it's driving me insane. She isn't crying, it's just a relentless, unbearable whine: "Aaannnnaaah! Aaannnnaaah!" I try to ignore it, but she goes on and on and on. I tell her to roll over and go back to sleep, but she just doesn't stop.

I get up to comfort her, and she pushes me away. From the vacant look in her eyes and the creepy grin, I can tell that nobody's home, and I dig deep to cultivate more patience.

I keep hoping it's just a phase, but then I worry, maybe this is just who she is, a manipulative, defiant, creepy-smiling kid who seems to relish doing anything and everything to drive me over the edge. I can't understand why she looks happiest when she's antagonizing Jack or me. I feel like everything I do is wrong. I don't want to be a perpetual police mom, but there are too many things I just can't let slide: standing on the kitchen table, carrying the kitty by the neck, throwing food she's decided she doesn't like. Even more disconcerting, she seems unable to learn from her mistakes. When she repeatedly stands in a chair and falls over backward, is she trying to prove the chair wrong? Is she determined to defy gravity? Or is she just trying to get my attention? Does this all relate back to the theory that she never had a stable home life, so she needs to shake things up, shocking her system into knowing she's still alive? All I can do is try to stay as calm as possible and wait for the days to pass.

```
Dear Kate,
    Mimi is home! After leaving the hospital,
she was transferred to a dismal nursing
facility, but we knew it was temporary,
so didn't worry too much. But then, they
said she wouldn't be released until she met
certain physical therapy goals. She took
my hand and pulled me close, whispering in
my ear, "You've got to get me out of here.
They're going to kill me!" So, while I
distracted the nurses, your Uncle Jim scooped
her out of bed, got her in a wheelchair and
headed out a back door where Aunt Jenny was
waiting with the car and they took off! I
packed up her bag and left a note at the
nurse's station saying, "My mom really wanted
to go home. Thanks!" and that was it!
```

>   Once she got home and into her own bed, she asked me to bring her the lotion you sent just before you left the country—she's been rationing it out, she loves it so much. She was so cute as she rubbed it into her hands, smelling them and saying, "Now it's like Kate's here with me, too."
>   We had fun laughing about our big getaway, then decided we need to come get you and Devi next!
>
> We love and miss you,
> Mom

On my morning walk, I keep to a gravely pace with silent chants of *Om Mani Peme Hum* and try to occupy my monkey mind as it hops from one branch of anxiety to the next. How many more days until my birthday? How much money do I have left? Do I need more funds wired before another *bandh*? What if the King isn't re-elected? What if the Maoists come into the Valley and the country falls apart before the election happens? How many more days until my birthday? Without Nora to listen to me ramble, the voices in my head have taken on a life of their own. I try to settle my mind, crunch crunch crunch crunch, *Om Mani Peme Hum*.

Then, a sing-song voice penetrates my fog like a beam from a lighthouse, pulling me back to the present.

"Kate, my darling! Come in, come in!" It's Birendra, the Nepali businessman Nora introduced me to, standing at his gate with a pre-afternoon cocktail in hand and a charming grin. "Please, please, grace us with your beauty and fantastic wit! We are a bunch of old men tired and bored of each other's company. Please, breathe some life into this old bunch."

How can I decline such an offer? I gladly step through the gate, offering *Namastés* to the other vaguely familiar men, and in the blink of an eye, a gin and tonic appears before me. I try to refuse, since it is barely past eleven, but Birendra is a gracious host, as well as a bit of a jester.

"Darling, you must stop worrying and live your life! Drink up and enjoy the beauty surrounding you. Join us in our guilty indulgence, or kindly, show yourself *out!*" he snaps with a deadpan expression, and I worry I've offended him. Then he, along with his wingmen, burst out laughing. I feel like a guest on *Candid Camera*.

As the spirits take hold, polite conversation gives way to raucous laughter. The men appreciate my humorous commentary on all things Nepal, punctuated by my questions they find hilarious. Though I intended for this to be a quick stop, soon a delicious traditional lunch is served in Birendra's ornate dining room. Although it feels odd to be hanging out with three older men, it's wonderful to laugh among other adults, especially with Nora away. The men find me endlessly entertaining, a great boost to my shrinking self-esteem.

Once we finish our meal, the men take their leave, in spite of Birendra's heckling. They know it's for show, and once they leave, he turns to me, "Now that we're rid of those guys, we can have some real fun!"

I protest, explaining I'm out searching for a new cage for our parrot, Pete. His current perchless prison is sickeningly small, causing his tail feathers to get caught in the crudely fashioned wire bars as he desperately tries to turn around. "So, once I help you find a new home for this feathered friend of yours, then you will come with me to Godavari? I have something very special to show you there."

"Okay, okay," I sigh in mock defeat.

"All right! You wait here!" Moments later, Birendra pulls up to the gate with a honk and smiles broadly from behind the wheel of his car. "Get in!" he calls. I'm hesitant, after all he's had to drink, but I figure with the crazy clogged traffic, we can't get up enough speed to do much damage.

In the congested market Birendra leaps out, haggles quickly, and triumphantly returns with the coveted cage. It's as flimsy as the squatter's shacks along the Bagmati, but it's better than poor Pete's current housing. I thank him profusely, and he soaks it up, glowing.

"Now, we go to Godavari," he says sternly to quash any other stipulation I might come up with. As we cruise out of the city, the crisp, clean air and gorgeous landscape divert my attention from Birendra's questionable driving, and I relax into the moment. Fields of crops and rice paddies, vibrantly green, stretch as far as I can see. We wind around, climbing into the lush, rolling foothills, and the road narrows as we creep into the quaint village of Godavari. We pass the communal water tap where women are doing laundry and children chase chickens. Located at the southernmost end of the city, nothing is beyond the village but forest and mountains for hundreds of miles. The chaos of the city feels far away.

"My wife and I built this house for retirement, but when she fell ill, we moved back to the city. Travel was hard on her," he shares. "When I come to Godavari, I feel her all around me." His wife had been diagnosed, far too late, with cervical cancer, and through his smile I see the pain in his heart is still tender. Returning to live in the house alone would be too hard, especially since their two children, a son and a daughter in their twenties, both left the Valley for school and work. With the exception of his man friends and staff, Birendra is alone.

When we pull up, a guard opens the large black gate with ornate curls and twists of gold, and we roll down the long brick drive lined with avocado, guava, persimmon, and pomegranate trees. Huge gardens pop with a riot of color springing from every available spot, interlaced with meandering footpaths and an overflowing greenhouse. The house, of tasteful red brick with white trim, and terraces on every side, is gorgeous. At the door, a smiling woman bows *Namasté* as we step inside, and Birendra takes me on a tour. There is a giant kitchen and larger living spaces, layer upon layer of bedroom suites with private bathrooms and attached terraces, and, finally, on the fourth floor, an extravagant *puja* room for deities. We step out to the roof top terrace and admire the view.

"Kate, it would please me very much for your family to live here. It is so lonely now, your children would bring new life. Your own staff are welcome, of course, but my driver, guard and cook will all be at your service. What do you say?"

"Oh, my! Well..." I'm stunned, "I guess I'll have to think about it," is the only response I can come up with.

"What is to think about? You love it here and your children will be safe to run about in the gardens." He continues, trying to sell me on the idea.

"Thank you for such a generous offer, I'm just not sure what to say..." I trail off, imagining a quiet life, close to the mountains.

As we make our way down to the ground floor, I fantasize which room would be mine, and the many guests I could invite. Looking out at the patchwork of the idyllic valley below, breathing in the clean air, I am incredibly tempted, but apprehensive. The village is along the main route the Maoists are using to enter the Valley. Although I'm a Westerner, which affords me some protection, I'm also aware of how they view international adoption and question if I would ever feel safe here. I'm not sure about giving up my Summit security blanket.

Birendra drops the sales pitch once we head back down the hill into the Valley, and we finish our outing in comfortable silence. I long to help fill his void and ease the pain, but as kind, funny and handsome as Birendra is, he's also old enough to be my father. Although I don't believe he has any romantic intentions, I have no idea what strings might be attached if I take him up on his offer and am concerned about what trouble my naïveté could get me into.

"Please, come in for dinner," I offer when we arrive back at my house. But he politely declines, teasing, "You've been distracting me all day! I've got work to do." He smiles and I bid him *Namasté*, bowing to the God within him, shining brightly from his heart.

Jack has been feeling crummy for a few days, with fever coming and going, but it has shot up to 103.5 degrees, and he's delirious. I'm starting to panic, so I call Dinesh; I don't know what else to do. He brings medicine from the hole-in-the-wall pharmacy where Leena buys the antidote for Devi's persistent intestinal parasites, but the cryptic writing on the side of the box makes me nervous.

I sit up most of the night holding a cool rag to Jack's forehead and pumping him with herbal immune support tinctures I stashed away from my store back in the States. When morning comes, I pull his blanket-wrapped body onto my back and hail a taxi to the international clinic. The driver is kind and is obviously worried about Jack. The steady fares from one decrepit warehouse-like lab to the next for numerous tests ensure his loyalty, giving me one less thing to worry about. At one point, trying to engage Jack, he asks his father's name, to which Jack mumbles, "Bud," and closes his eyes again. He hates when strangers pry about his father, but it's a relief to get a glimpse of his wit. Several hours later, appendicitis, pneumonia, typhoid, and meningitis are ruled out, and we are sent home with two different medications to control the fever. The doctor calls morning and night to check on his progress, which brings me some relief. Since I'd purchased high-end travel insurance, I know we will be whisked off to Bangkok if he continues to decline.

By the fifth day of the mystery illness, I'm near my breaking point. The doctor tries to reassure me that if Jack contracted one of the horrible diseases I've read about, he would be much, much sicker, stopping short of bluntly saying "he'd be dead by now." This offers me a few degrees of comfort, in a strange, otherworldly way. I'm struck with a whole new level of compassion for the street women and their sick babies, helplessly watching and waiting for their children to die. The fact that one out of four children in Nepal perishes before the age of five hits way too close to home.

On day six, just as the Himals are starting to pink up with sunrise, I find Jack soaking wet, his fever finally broken. Slowly turning his head, he speaks more coherently than he has for days, and asks for an egg, then eats two. He still complains of stomach pain, but I attribute it to not eating for several days. Finally feeling that I can leave him for just a little while, I dash to the market for fresh vegetables and broth to make a hearty soup that he downs with vigor.

The next morning, for the first time in nearly a week, he wants cereal, and I love watching him slurp it up. Within days, Devi, too, is ill, but with an immune system of steel, innoculated by life on the street, she's over it and playing again before I have a chance to worry. I conclude that the three out of four children who live past childhood are true survivors, immunized by nature and consequence. I'm beyond thankful Devi is one of them.

Once Jack recovers, he takes a new interest in his schoolwork, continuing to read like a madman, and has developed a renewed interest in playing his violin. I'd trusted Annie that it would be easy to find an instrument in the Valley, (another bit of flawed advice) so left his behind. Luckily, when his Nepali instructor traveled to Bombay to play a concert, he gladly bought a violin for Jack. It is far too big for his little body, and he has to stretch his arms to reach the strings, but in this world, it's perfect. Jack is learning to read sheet music and having fun decoding this new language.

Math is a challenge for Jack, so I decide the best way for him to get past his aversion is to practice it daily. This new approach brings us to the multiplication lessons in his workbook, and, to my surprise, he becomes excited, discovering ways to use this skill all the time, especially in the market. If a mango costs five rupees, how much will five mangos cost? He joins me on walks, and we recites times tables as we go along, imagining various items along our path multiplying before our eyes: chickens, papayas, rickshaws. It's a wonderful way to spend time together outside the compound.

Then, one day, we notice we're being followed by a huge, white tom cat. This is a rare sight in Kathmandu, since most locals believe that only witches keep cats to do their bidding in the night. The cat is being pursued by a gang of kids throwing rocks to ward off his evil intentions, so he follows us all the way up the steps and into our front door. When Jack offers him some chicken, the deal is sealed, and Bruce Wayne becomes the newest member of our family.

After lunch, while sitting in the loft catching up on email, I hear the shrill sounds of Leena scolding Devi. I roll my eyes and don't think much of it, but as the commotion continues, curiosity gets the better of me and I go down to check it out. After much laughter, mime and broken Eng-pali, I get the story. Devi decided to give Bruce a bath in the dish water, which, of course, he didn't like; however, he has learned when in the hands of Devi, it's best to just go with the flow. When she tried to put him in the refrigerator, he was happy to comply, smelling the meat for the dogs, but Leena drew a line, and the battle began. Devi has been doing so much better using her words, making two-word sentences like "good night," "no puppy," and "up please;" this event, though hilarious, makes me realize that I have no idea what's going on in her head.

I swoop her up mid-tantrum and head upstairs for nap time. Finding comfort in routine, she willingly lies down on her bed for me to roll her up burrito style in her favorite woven blanket. She fights the constriction for a few moments as we rock away the drama, then listens intently as I sing:

> "Once upon a time in a land far away,
> there was a little girl named Devi.
> Once upon a time in a land far away,
> was a Mommy and a boy named Jackie.
> They went to the land of the Himalaya,
> to find the little girl named Devi.
> They stayed for a while
> at the Roof of the World,
> and there they became a family."

I feel her body soften as her breathing slows and I peek under the top of the blanket that is flopped over her eyes to shade them from the bright afternoon sun. Seeing one eye at half-mast, I drop the flap before the lookout eye has a chance to focus. Like an amusement park ride slowing to a stop, I wait for the momentum of the rocker to wane before fluidly departing to glide into the bedroom and kneel on her bed. I hold her out like an offering and lay her cautiously in a nest of wool blankets. Vigilantly, I click the lock on the door to the terrace to prevent her from wandering when she wakes up, then tiptoe out of the room. I slip over to Summit for a cup of tea and run into Annie. She mentions that she'd like to see Devi, so we agree to meet later in the afternoon when we are out for our afternoon stroll.

We find Annie and sit down for a visit, but Devi's reaction stuns me. Seeing her former caregiver, she refuses to smile or talk; she won't even look at Annie. She clings to me fiercely and completely shuts down. I wonder if she is afraid Annie is here to take her away. After all, Annie had been the one to take her out of the orphanage.

"We're just visiting," I whisper gently in her ear. "When we're done talking, we'll go home and see Jack." While it's reassuring to feel her attaching to me, it breaks my heart to see her react with fear, her tiny closet overflowing with skeletons.

Back at home, reunited with Jack, we happily engage in playtime, rolling around on the floor, tickling and wrestling. Then, out of nowhere, Devi lets out a bloodcurdling scream and runs at Jack, knocking him down, and wraps her tiny hands around his throat. She's totally out of her head and so incredibly strong, it's difficult to get her off of him. Jack bolts upright, his eyes filled with terror and tears, as he coughs and shakes. Even more disturbing, Devi isn't present anymore. She has become catatonic. I plant her on the sofa and walk Jack to the kitchen and the security of Dinesh.

"I don't know what happened, but I'm sure she didn't mean to hurt you," I try to console him, but it's a hard sell. "How 'bout you help Dinesh with dinner?" I suggest, rustling his already disheveled hair and he smiles weakly.

I take Devi out to the terrace and sing softly as we rock. I try to bring her back, but she just stares blankly ahead, my vacant zombie girl. As the night goes on, she wakes screaming almost hourly, and falls out of bed with endless thrashing. Just when I thought her demons were releasing their grip, I'm smacked by the incredible hold they have on her. The kind sentiments of faraway friends echo through my head: "All she needs is love!" and I desperately wish it were that simple.

I've been counting down the days to file my paperwork with the Central District Office and officially begin our adoption process, however, with the coming election, the political scene is heating up. The city is buzzing with talk of coming *bandhs*, and Maoists are targeting government offices with attempted bombings, clearly marking them as unsafe places to be. Rajkumar is in no rush to get me to the CDO, and it looks as if I may have to wait until next month, after the election, to file our paperwork. I'm haunted by the foreshadowing of the Eagles song on the radio after our near disaster at the checkpoint in Pokhara and wonder if I will ever be able to leave.

I try to be proactive and renew my visa early in case the office is closed, then stop off at Saleways to stock up on groceries in case I can't leave the compound for a few days. I keep telling myself it's more the idea of the *bandh* than real danger. Somehow the sixteen boxes of cereal and containers of aseptic milk, with their turquoise sky, green fields, and happy cows on the boxes bring me comfort.

"Oh, don't be so worried," Birendra placates me yet again. Due to lack of refrigeration, Nepalis are accustomed to eating fresh foods, so he doesn't understand stockpiling is what eases my anxiety.

```
Dear Mom,
Just a quick note:
   We are all doing well, but I may not be
in touch for a few days. With the coming
election, tensions are running high and there
are mandatory curfews. Also, the phone lines
and power are being cut from 9pm to 9am, but
that can change at any time without notice.
All cell service has been indefinitely cut
to prevent the Maoists from communicating
as effectively. It's hard to know exactly
what's going on between the democratically
```

leaning Seven Party Alliance, the King and
the Maoists, but all the opposing forces are
pounding their chests, creating an inevitable
standoff. If you get worried, you can contact
the Consulate. I got an email from the Warden
and our emergency rallying point isn't far
from here. The landlord kindly checks in,
holding my gaze with apologetic eyes, making
sure we know when not to leave the compound
and when it is safe to go out. I know he
feels protective of me, alone with two small
children. Just remember, we are living in a
safe area, and military action is minimal on
our little lane. Boy, these curfews sure are
cutting into my social life :)

Gotta run before the power is cut!
Love,
Kate

I didn't want to share everything about our situation with my mother, afraid it would send her into a tailspin of worry. I had the sense she thought I was exaggerating, and there is only a slight chance of her hearing about our little "yam between the boulders," as Nepal is referred to, as it sits, wedged, between China and India. I've looked into a visa for Jack and me to go to India. We could send Devi across the open border with Leena, no questions asked, and meet up with them on the other side to wait things out if it gets really rough. But then, we would be stranded in India for who knows how long. Besides, we may not even be able to get out because the Maoists are controlling more and more of the Ring Road that surrounds the city.

For the most part, Jack isn't able to leave the compound to play with other kids in the neighborhood; he and Dinesh were going on a walk yesterday but turned back after seeing all the soldiers in the street. Two big pro-democracy demonstrations were planned, but the King issued all day curfews to force everyone to stay home. If there are no people, then there are no demonstrations, and nothing negative can be said about the King. In addition, he's jailed all the political leaders of the Seven Party Alliance indefinitely, further weakening the leadership for the democracy movement. The reality that the People's Movement looks like a revolution is starting to sink in, and I am here, living it, day by day.

```
Dear Kate,
    Happy Birthday! I hope you do something to
make it memorable since you won't be able to
file. Be sure to do something for you!
    Thank you for the continued updates on the
political hubbub. I'm glad you're being very
cautious, keep your head down! Where are all
the women leaders? Surely they must have a
different take on all this!
    I admire you more and more for making this
trip alone with no one there to tell you what
to expect. Your father would be so proud of
you, his ever-so-strong willed, independent,
confident, kind and wise little girl. I can
see him smiling down on you now.

Love,
Mom
```

I wake to Jack crawling across me, placing a card on the window sill by my bed. "Don't get up, Mom, I'll get Devi's breakfast. Happy Birthday!"

I roll over lazily to peek at a hand-drawn card with a cow on front; their perpetual presence in the road is one of Jack's favorite things about Nepal. "I'm so lucky you're my Mom," he'd written inside, but I know, *I'm* the lucky one. After Dinesh prepares a jovial breakfast, I take off for a little quiet time in Pilgrims Book House. But first, I have an important stop to make.

At the orphanage, Rajkumar is planted behind his desk,

surrounded by piles of paperwork. He looks both pleased and exhausted to see me.

"*Namasté*, Rajkumar." I fold my hands and bow slightly.

"Oh, good morning, Madam. So nice to see you. What brings you by today?"

"Today's the day! My magic thirty-five is here!" I say triumphantly, thrilled to reach this milestone.

"Of course! Congratulations!" He smiles with relief, knowing the importance of this day.

"So, when?"

"When are you going to take me out to dinner?" he jokes.

"Right after we go to the CDO. Are you ready?" I ask with a grin, knowing today is still not the day. As charming as the Nepali way of never wanting to say no to anything is, what I need now is a straight answer.

"Ha ha ha," he chuckles. "Oh sure, let me get my coat."

"Really Raj, please tell me. When?" I plead. I've fantasized what this day will look like, seeing my name and Devi's on the same piece of paper, linking us in a way that will assure me all of this is real, not just a five-month-long dream.

"Oh, Madam, I know you do not want to wait, but I will call you when it is a good day. With the *bandh* and elections coming, I don't know, maybe in one month?" He bobbles and smiles, making it impossible to hate him for keeping me guessing.

"I understand this is a very difficult time, but I'm worried about not being in the queue yet, and my visa expiring." I remind him of my very real time frame. My hourglass had turned over on January first, so I now have only five months to complete a process estimated to take four to six. The sand is spilling fast.

"I am sorry Madam, but if we go now, it will look suspicious. We must wait at least a few more weeks." I trust Rajkumar to know how to best navigate this system. Arguing with him is pointless at best and potentially detrimental.

"Please, have some tea and let us be friends," he smiles as a young woman appears at the door with a tray of steaming cups. I accept the kind offering, warming my hands, and look past him out the window at prayer flags fluttering in the distance. My impatience melts away.

I hop in a taxi and mull over my visa issue. A student visa is no longer an option since the University next to the King's Palace is a hotbed of political instability and is not an area safe to frequent. I've heard about a visa for "exploring a business opportunity," but I still feel a bit singed around the edges after my last business venture. The landlord's slimy brother continues to ask for my hand in marriage, by far, my least favorite option, but I have to figure something out.

At Pilgrim's, I take a deep breath and leave my worries behind as I disappear into the stacks. No more CDO, no more screaming, no more homework battles, no more visa anxiety; just me and all these books. After weighing endless options, I select a couple, then smile when I see Tom Robbins' *Skinny Legs and All*, remembering when I read it while visiting a boyfriend on Oahu; it feels like a different lifetime.

Before entering our gate, I take a deep breath and prepare to return to my world of screaming, hitting, and general dysfunction, then look up to see a bright and sunny Devi peeking out from between the rungs of the terrace railing and my battery is instantly recharged. *"Ama!"* she squeals and turns to run through the house and meet me with sticky hugs and sloppy kisses. Leena has my favorite lunch ready, egg salad on Dinesh's homemade bread. She offers to rock Devi into nap time while I shower; she's even heated up the tank for me. The frustration of not being able to file at the CDO slips from my mind as I emerge from the showery bliss appreciating the little things. I take my time slathering on lotion, peaceful in the knowledge that no little hands will knock at the door. Refreshed, I sneak out to Summit.

Jonathan is waiting for me, tea on the table and gift in hand.

"Happy birthday!" he says, giving me a proper hug. "I hope you like it." I can tell from the shape and feel that it's a chocolate bar.

"Oh, Jonathan, you shouldn't have!" I gush dramatically. We'd discussed the tragedy of poor-quality chocolate in the Valley, so he knew what would mean the most: rich, dark, and imported.

"I picked that up for you on holiday. Really, you should be impressed," he teases in his sweet British accent. "There are only a few bites missing."

Nora, back from retreat, Dave, and Janelle, another adoptive mom-to-be, soon arrive, and we shift from tea to cocktails. When Craig appears in the doorway, I feel my face flush and look away to avoid divulging my secret crush. He strides over to give me a lingering hug and kisses on both cheeks, holding my face in his cold-from-biking hands. As I make birthday wishes, the room spins with love and libations. It's a great time with wonderful friends, filled with stories of travels and traumas, kids and crabby roommates, and, of course, best birthdays.

When the party winds down, Nora and I walk back to my house, arm in arm, pausing to thank Ganesh for such a lovely day. Stepping inside, the aroma is intoxicating, and I know my birthday celebration isn't over yet. Dinesh has made a beautiful dinner of all my favorite Nepali foods: *dal bhat* for Devi, accompanied by curried potatoes and okra, beans and rice, fresh rolls, garlic *tsog*, salad, and fresh squeezed lemonade. While Leena wrangles Devi into her seat, Dinesh beams at his spread, giddy at the surprise on my face. I practically beg them to eat with us, but once again, they humbly refuse. Tears of gratitude start to flow as I look around the table at my family; not just my children, but Nora, Dinesh, and Leena.

"And now, for the grand finale!" Jack announces as he turns off the lights and scrambles into the kitchen. Then, the familiar cat squalling of a squeaky violin begins my song of the day, and everyone joins in singing "Happy Birthday" as Dinesh carries in a cake glowing with candles. Maybe it's the cocktails, maybe it's the chronic lack of sleep, maybe it's just being present, but I can't stop the happy tears. I'm so touched by the loving kindness surrounding me, I'm unable to hold them back. The cake is just like the one I'd ordered for Jack on his birthday from the German bakery, rich with heavy cream and fluffy frosting, things uncommon in this part of the world. Dinesh has gone above and beyond. This cake is not in his family budget, nearly $20, and I'm ashamed he's gone to such lengths to make this day special for me. His kindness and generosity are beyond compare. I have no doubt if he had a way to get me to the CDO himself, he would, without hesitation. This time I won't take no for an answer, insisting he and Leena share the cake with us and even convince them to take some home for their children. After all, it will never fit in our tiny refrigerator.

As Dinesh, Leena, and Nora prepare to leave, a last round of hugs and birthday wishes are repeated at the doorway, and Jack piggybacks Devi upstairs to get ready for bed. I look out the arched window to the rainbow of city lights and am washed over by the realization that this is not purgatory or prison. I fold my hands and give thanks for all the people in my life who have shown up today to prove to me that I'm not in this alone. And then, the power goes out.

The good news I need comes when Rajkumar calls to advise me he's preparing my paperwork to file with the CDO "sometime soon." I'm elated things are moving along, but then my heart drops. He tells me several important documents are missing from my file. I'm in shock, and frustration with Annie rises again.

Once my heart rate settles back to something close to normal, I phone Annie. Her flippant attitude and lack of interest is infuriating. She sighs and drearily drones, "It's already been such a hard day, why don't you call me back on Monday?"

Fighting to maintain my composure, I say, "I don't mean to be insensitive to your challenges, but I have been here for five months waiting and feel that I have been very patient. Now it's time for me to move forward with my process, and I would appreciate it if you could please give me the information I need so I'm able to do so." As if by magic, my assertive tone strikes a chord in her, and she assures me she will locate the documents "right away," and then curtly hangs up. I'm still at her mercy, but I know better than to wait for her to act. I email the stateside agency and explain my latest bump in the road.

A few days later, Annie calls to say the missing documents have arrived via Fed Ex and although she promises to take them to Children's House "soon," I hightail it to her house to pick them up, all too aware of what "soon" means to her. I personally deliver them to Rajkumar, relieved my file is complete.

Watching Dave navigate his own sticky process has led me to believe that waiting patiently is not necessarily rewarded, and I'm glad I pushed to get my affairs in order. However, I'm groping to find the balance between "gently reminding" and "annoying American," so I resolve to check in with Rajkumar in a few more days, hoping to make the trip to the CDO sooner than later. Political tensions are building like a thunderstorm, and I'm terrified the Ministry will collapse before any legal connection has been made with the little girl I already call my daughter.

Luckily, after the latest Annie issue, the agency sends me a clear checklist of the documents I need from whom and when. I'm relieved to be able to continue the process bypassing Annie entirely. Still, I second-guess myself, afraid I'm being too hasty, and over cocktails with Dave I lament, "I know I just need to be patient. In the big picture, a few days won't make that much of a difference."

Looking intense, he coaches, "Oh, yes it will. One day here can cost you a week. Don't let her do that to you; keep doing what you have to do and don't worry about her." Unfortunately, Dave has the experience to know. After a month of lobbying to finalize his adoption of Arun, Dave thought he was finally on his way home, but now, the U.S. Embassy is asking questions and are not liking the answers. They've opened their own investigation to determine whether or not Arun is a legitimate orphan. Since his mother disappeared into the night, and the doctor isn't willing to come forward for fear of losing her license, there is no proof of Dave's story. As far as Nepal is concerned, Arun is Dave's child; that part of the process is complete, but without a visa, Arun still isn't able to enter the United States. "Welcome to the Hotel California" we sing to each other, clinking our glasses in mock cheers.

Soon, Janelle joins us with her knitting, her practice to chase away the demons of adoption anxiety. She's a part-time musician, active in the arts, and a general do-gooder. Her husband is a neurosurgeon, and through the hospital where he works, she volunteers with a group that hosts international orphans when they're in the States undergoing complex medical procedures. She has grown close to a nine-year-old girl, Sujani, who has been staying with her family while undergoing multiple surgeries. As a small child, Sujani fell into a cook fire, and the resulting scar tissue has restrained her growth. After being injured, Sujani grew up in a small orphanage for disabled children since her family was unable to care for her. Janelle is going to great lengths to keep Sajani with her family in the U.S., having already traveled to Nepal multiple times. Once she located Sujani's mother in a remote mountain village, she asked her permission to adopt the girl, and chartered a helicopter to fly her to Kathmandu to sign the appropriate paperwork, allowing the adoption to move forward. Now, Janelle is waiting in the queue with the rest of us, but with a bit more urgency. She's hoping to complete the adoption process before Sujani's medical visa expires, and she has to return to the dismal orphanage. Janelle has enlisted Annie as a consultant to guide her through the adoption maze. I hope her success will be speedier than Dave's or mine.

    I wonder if other agencies who use Nepali facilitators have these issues. I'm curious if they are better suited to work within the Nepali system since they are not held to the same standards as Annie, an American who is bound by American laws. In the eyes of the State Department, omission of information is the same as perjury; therefore Americans are compelled to tell every known detail of a child's past out of fear of prosecution. As I'd seen with Stephanie and now Dave, it seemed knowing a child's history could be detrimental. Once information is provided, the State Department in turn is obligated to inquire, and this prompts a higher-level investigation as a means of preventing child trafficking. Other agencies are one degree removed. Without firsthand knowledge of a child's past, the burden shifts to the adoptive parents who are able to honestly answer "I don't know" to any Consular questions. Parents just want to get their children home, and they trust the agencies to refer legitimate orphans; the last thing they need is more heartache just as they reach the finish line. Without knowledge of a child's past, all the questionable stories, suspicious police reports, and mysterious disappearances of possibly fictional parents aren't even a whisper in the ear of the Embassy; the child's past blows away silently in the wind. But, my mind begs to know, *what is best for the children?*

New York Times January 31, 2006
Nepal, in a Climate of Contradictions, Prepares to Vote
By SOMINI SENGUPTA

```
KATHMANDU, Nepal, Jan.28—King Gyanendra, the
man who sacked the government a year ago,
calls for elections but jails political party
leaders. The main political parties demand
the restoration of democratic rights but call
on voters to boycott the polls. At least one
mayoral candidate has been assassinated by
suspected Maoist guerrillas. And in anti-
election protests nationwide, dogs have been
paraded along the streets with signs dangling
from their necks that read, "Vote for Me."
```

*Bandh*s have become more common with the election on the horizon, and an eight-day *bandh* is scheduled to begin in a few days. As long as there isn't a curfew, Dinesh continues to ride his bike through the city to get to his other job. "Be careful," I call out as he leaves in the morning, casting a spell over him to keep him safe. I know Leena worries as well, but she covers her concern with a sweet smile and bobblehead laughter. Rumors are flying that the Maoists are moving into the Valley to prevent the election, and turnout is expected to be poor. While the people want the right to elect their own representatives, it's obvious the election is rigged, and the men on the ballot are merely puppet candidates propped up by the King. Wherever I go, the election is the topic of conversation. Craig and Jonathan gather good information while at the

University and British School, and we meet up most afternoons at Summit to share news and settle our nerves. I feel ridiculous sipping tea while right down the road people are dying as they fight for what they believe in. The other expats don't seem to be panicking and leaving the country, so, for now, I feel safe waiting it out. The consensus is to stock up and stay home. Maoist roadblocks are preventing supplies from entering the city and prices in the market are soaring, making all those boxes of cereal not so alarmist anymore. So far, police stations and government offices, none of which are in our immediate neighborhood, have been the primary targets for Maoist bombings. While that brings me comfort, it fuels my indignation over the injustice happening in the country. Our insulated expat neighborhood feels more and more like an ivory tower, with neither side wanting to create an international incident by bringing harm to expats. All sides vie to remain in good standing with the lucrative NGO community. I'm ashamed to feel my mind shutting down, only able to focus on protecting what is mine as we sit safely tucked behind high compound walls.

My instinct to take Jack out of school proved to be a good one. There are more tanks in the streets near targeted government offices, the UN headquarters, and the petrol station between our house and the school. I've made a point to shield Jack from what's happening around us, which is easy enough, since within our compound, he is immune from any news from the outside. The curfew is lifted, but the taxi drivers are still striking, so our lane stays quiet. Jack gets a temporary taste of freedom, riding his bike with Sarresh and the other children in the neighborhood. It's a strange dichotomy to the danger blocks away. The temple where Leena usually takes the kids to play is now off limits since a child was killed after he found a homemade bomb there and curiously picked it up. I show Jack pictures in the newspaper of what a pipe bomb looks like, quietly explaining why we *never, ever* touch one. I then instruct him that if we are in a taxi and I tell him to get on the floorboard, he needs to just do it, no questions asked, and I imagine myself shielding his body.

"But why?" he asks, eyes wide.

"Well, sometimes when people are angry and arguing, they throw things at each other. If we were accidentally in the wrong place, at the wrong time, we might get hit." I explain as lightly as possible, trying to simplify the very real danger.

"What would they be throwing?"

"Bricks." I'm not ready to mention the danger of gunfire.

The things you see on CNN are here, now, life-sized and in full color.

February

From: Warden, Kathmandu
Subject: Important Security Information for American Citizens in Nepal
Embassy of the United States of America
Kathmandu, Nepal

This wardens' message is being issued to alert American citizens that His Majesty's Government of Nepal has ordered that only vehicles associated with voting will be permitted on the streets on Wednesday, February 8, 2006, a national holiday. There is also a possibility of demonstrations on Wednesday, February 8, 2006 to disrupt the election. The Communist Party of Nepal (Maoist) bandh remains in effect until February 11, 2006. The seven political party alliance has called for a "blackout" from 7:00 pm to 7:30 am on Tuesday, February 7, 2006. During the blackout there is a risk that houses showing lights may be attacked with rocks or bricks. The Embassy has also received reports that telephones may be disconnected for 48 hours, starting sometime Tuesday, February 7, 2006.

While it is unclear at this time how widely the Maoist bandh will be observed, American citizens are advised to minimize non-essential travel, maintain a low profile and, if you must travel, wait until a pattern of traffic is well established. Taxi and bus services may not be available. Moreover, during past closures, a number of buses, taxis, and personal vehicles have been attacked.

The Consular Section at the Yak and Yeti Hotel will be closed on Wednesday, February 8, 2006 and the Embassy will be at minimal staffing. American citizens needing emergency assistance should call the Embassy at 977-1-441-1179 and ask for the Consular Duty Officer.

Given the recent bombings and attacks within the Kathmandu Valley and threats against a US-affiliated NGO in Dolakha and Rautahat, American citizens are reminded to exercise special caution and to be particularly vigilant about their personal safety. American citizens are strongly urged to avoid demonstrations.

Rumor has it, the government is soon to impose curfews to curb the demonstrations and resulting violence. Rajkumar has told me several times I'll have to wait until after the election, but I worry if the Maoists gain influence in the government, they could bring a halt to international adoptions. I'm fairly certain he'll say this isn't a good day to go to the CDO since another *bandh* is in effect, but I have to try one more time.

"Hello Raj, any chance we can get to the CDO before the election?" I ask hesitantly, feeling like a nag.

"How soon can you be here?"

"Oh! Uh . . . I'm on my way," I stammer, shocked by his unexpected response.

Trembling with anxiety, I dress quickly, then clumsily kiss Devi as she lumbers by, and give Jack a peck on the cheek in between bounces on my bed. I can't bring myself to scold him for crumpling the blankets Leena just straightened, so just say, "I love you."

"Yeah, Mom. I love you, too," he replies with a suspicious look in his eye, then bounces off again, laughing with Devi.

Stopping by the recessed altar on the balcony, I put my favorite picture of my father in my handbag, feeling his presence. I look through the various incense in my stash, "Strength," "Awareness," "Power," and try to decide which to offer Ganesh on my way out. "Safe from Roadside Bombings" isn't an option, nor is "Immune from Stray Bullets," so I settle on "Devotion." It seems appropriate; my devotion to Devi is the only thing sending me out on such a potentially violent day. I strike a match and light the sticks, offering the first one to the Buddha presiding over our home, asking for my children to be kept safe in my absence, and begin whispering *Om Mani Peme Hum* as I step out the door.

I look into the empty lane between the walls flanking our alley. Several soldiers stand at the bottom of the hill. They glance in my direction, their nervous hands holding tight to their machine guns. I smile weakly and turn to make my offering to Ganesh, feeling like a fair-weather friend. Lately, I've failed to stop by with sticks of sweet-smelling prayer due to the curfews, only now showing up when I need help. I make my request and notice several rickshaws pass the soldiers below, so I walk down to ask about a ride. It's clear that they have no interest in pedaling up the steep hill in order to stay off the main road, where the *bandh* is sure to be enforced and violence is a probability. A rogue taxi pulls up, like a mirage, and as the driver and I debate a safe route, I see a half dozen rough looking men walking down the middle of the road toward us. My eyes settle meekly on one who holds my gaze. He gives me a hard look, cocking his head ever so slightly, and then, like a gangster, slips his hand into the fold of his half-zipped jacket and gives a little pat. It hits me like a rock slide, the rumors of Maoist rebels coming into the Valley are, like most of Nepal, a bit delayed. The insurgents are here, *now*, right in front of me. I gulp, forcing the lump of fear down my throat, and back away from the taxi. *Om Mani Peme Hum*. The driver, now seeing what I see, speeds away leaving me in a cloud of dust as the group comes within striking distance of the soldiers. With discipline and grace I didn't know I had, I turn and saunter back to the security of our winding little lane. I quicken my step as I round the bend, put the brewing conflict behind me, and I don't look back. I guess Ganesh isn't holding a grudge so far. *Om Mani Peme Hum.*

As I reach the crest of the hill, familiar shops come into view, now shuttered and desolate. The air feels strangely fresh as the lack of traffic allows the perpetual pollution and dust to settle. A few boys are out playing games in the road among the soldiers standing at attention. Their smiles give away their naiveté, unaware of the games being played by big boys only a few feet away. Some toss a grungy ball, while others look at a communal comic book. One little boy, wearing a camouflage t-shirt with a U.S. Army patch on the breast jumps rope like a prizefighter. Maybe they aren't so unaware? I ponder what the view is like from inside their minds.

I walk on, unconsciously hugging the walls and scanning for alcoves I can duck into should shots ring out, channeling my father's military training. I make my way down a long stretch of road past the British School, and notice a few others out walking. They seem unfazed by the tension that has me in a stranglehold. *Om Mani Peme Hum.* At the haphazard junction of several narrow roads, a group of soldiers stands with their backs to a central garden, watching intently, guns at the ready. They look long in my direction and I can practically hear them thinking "What is she doing out?" I hint at a smile, then look down submissively, hoping the anxiety rushing through me isn't visible, like a flashing red panic button. Quickening my step to clear the vulnerable intersection where too many lanes converge, I imagine the possibility of attack coming from all sides. I've never been this close to so many guns. *Om Mani Peme Hum.*

I continue on, passing more closed shops, one with rolling doors less than half open, like lazy cat eyes. Only the lower halves of men sitting on stools are visible, their heads bob down with a "who goes there" expression as I hurry by. Once outside our neighborhood, there are no more civilians, not even at the temple or the water tap, usually a flurry of activity. At the next major intersection, I turn the corner onto a main road where high-ranking generals reside. It's deserted, except for heavily-armed soldiers on high alert. I cross the street briskly and stick close to the compound walls, constantly making note of which gates are closer, those behind, or those ahead, where I can duck and cover. With a few hundred feet before the next footpath, I hear thunderous rumbling rushing up behind me, and glance back to see a military truck coming. *Om Mani Peme Hum*. I take cover in a private drive, huddled by their gate, and feel the draft before the rush of the lumbering truck. I squeeze my eyes shut and hold my breath as it billows by in an all-encompassing wave of dust and black exhaust. My heart races as I peek through my lashes to see soldiers in the back of the truck, rows and rows of them, stacked in graduated lines like pineapples on display at the fruit stand. Their knives rhythmically swing from their belts, vacant looks in their eyes, the expressions of young men with little option but to be sent to war by older men behind high walls.

When the blue storefront of the German bakery comes into view, I sigh with relief and slip off the road and into an alleyway. Passing Nora's flat, out of habit I think of checking in to see if she will join me. Yesterday, when we met at Summit, I had been advised by Father Glenn, a Jesuit priest with deep ties to Nepal, to stay home and far away from any government buildings. As Nora left, she gave me a stern look, "You're not really thinking of going to the CDO tomorrow, are you?" I knew better than to say yes; so instead, I reassured her I would check in at Summit first, our unofficial news source, to determine when it was safe to go out.

Up ahead, I glimpse more soldiers watching rooftops and alleyways, and I duck into a footpath before they notice me. The sweet aroma of orange trumpet flowers bursts from the vines overhead, and I breathe deep, slowing my pace and congratulating myself for having made it this far. This isn't so bad; really, the weather is quite nice. I chuckle at my own ridiculous denial of the risk I'm taking, and wonder, *whose life is this anyway, and how did I get here?*

As I come to the end of the footpath and emerge onto yet

another major road, I find more soldiers stationed in an empty lot where days earlier, the kids and I'd watched a group of teenage boys play cricket while we ate ice cream on the steps of the café. As I approach Pulchowk, a square for various vendors, I glance into the intersection, making note of a newly stationed tank, and decide to slide down another side road. I stride past more closed shops, empty vehicles, and sunbathing street dogs. They're enjoying a welcome day off with no vehicles, rocks, or kicks to dodge. It's eerily quiet as I creep up to the intersection, my floodgates of anxiety open as I look toward to Jawalakhel Circle and spy more soldiers than I can count around the central fountain like candles on a cake. *Om Mani Peme Hum.* I take a deep breath and step out of my hiding place, willing my legs to move with ease rather than break into the sprint they are begging for, and walk confidently past the pharmacy and into the four-lane road. A few more steps and I am off the road and onto another series of footpaths and alleyways, out of sight of the soldiers. A man calmly paints a gate as I pass, and I want to shake him and yell, "Don't you know how dangerous it is to be out?"

I have only one more turn before the lane to the orphanage. Sidling around the brick wall, I look down the alley, and am relieved to find it clear of soldiers, so I break into a trot for my final stretch down the hill. At the gate, I'm ushered in by the guard who is shocked to see me. He looks like he wants to yell at me the way I wanted to yell at the painter.

In his office, Rajkumar stoops over his desk pasting photos of Devi and me onto cryptic papers in a folder.

"Do you have your passport?" he asks. "And is your visa up-to-date?" He smiles, teasing me with his favorite new joke since the fiasco that nearly got me kicked out the country.

I try to steady my hand as I sign a gazillion places on treasure map forms. I gaze out the window to a terrace in the distance where a mini *stupa* is adorned with garlands of marigolds. I hold the vision and feel my heart swell. I will be forever indebted to this country for allowing me to raise one of its lost daughters. *Om Mani Peme Hum.*

"Madam? Madam?" Rajkumar pulls me from my daydream. "Are you ready? We should be going before the protests start."

"Oh, okay. I'm ready."

A large white van waits for us at the gate with signs in the back, clearly marked TOURIST ONLY, my only source of security for this mission other than Rajkumar, my tiny, ineffective body guard. He instructs me to get all the way in the back, and if we are stopped or hear gunfire, to immediately get on the floor and cover my head. The driver is ready to get this chore (me) out of the way.

With speed metal thrasher music blasting, we careen down alleyways and onto streets, faster than any vehicular experience I've had since arriving in the Kingdom. I'd like to think it's just because there's no traffic, but I know it is due to the risk these men are willing to take to get me in the queue. As we blast down the road, a Western man with a giant backpack tries to wave us down, seeing our TOURIST ONLY signs, but there's no way the driver is stopping for him. Clearly, he is clueless about the danger that surrounds him.

The van twists and turns through lanes I never knew existed, and I'm beyond lost. We screech up to a heavily fortified gate, and as the driver tells the guards our business, Rajkumar instructs me to keep quiet; he will do the talking once we're inside.

The guards look hard at me, but I won't meet their gaze, and eventually they wave us through. When we get out and walk toward the entrance, I feel exposed and vulnerable as the men in the yard eye me, in spite of my conservative dress. In what was once a front garden, now just a neglected, dusty patch of earth, they seem immune to the tension that hangs in the air, sitting lazily in groups talking and playing cards, smoking and spitting, waiting for something to happen. I walk submissively behind Rajkumar; if I had a tail, it would be tucked between my legs. *Om Mani Peme Hum.*

Finally, we're inside and I rejoice that there is no queue, just two men sitting behind Cadillac-sized wooden desks. One is clearly grumpier than the other, so Rajkumar approaches the less grumpy one and presents my file. The man gazes coolly over scratched clouded glasses and snaps at Rajkumar, the only word I understand is "*bandh*." Rajkumar smiles and speaks in a respectful tone. I assume he's sucking up with a story about the silly American woman who made him come down here today when, of course, he knows we shouldn't be out. The man shuffles through the files on his desk, apparently in a show of "see how many I have already?" I glimpse at the names and pictures to see if there is anyone I recognize, then quickly look away, afraid of being caught doing anything that could derail this fragile process. I stand politely while the men talk and keep my eyes fixed on the faded carpet and my street-grunge-covered toes gripping my Chaco sandals like a bat clinging to a cave.

Just as I'm about to pass out from the anxiety, the grumpy man barks at me, shaking me from my trance. Rajkumar gestures for me to sit, and the man begins flipping through my file. He comes to the page with a picture of Devi in one box and me in another, then rifles through his desk to pull out an ink pad. I dutifully follow orders as the grouchy, noticeably smelly man inks my thumbs and mashes them down in the appropriate places. And then, it's done! We're officially in the queue! I bow deeply to the man, who now holds my future with Devi in his hands and offer a sincere *namasté. Om Mani Peme Hum!*

Walking out of the building, the sun shines a bit brighter, the birds chirp a bit louder. I'm so overjoyed with relief, I want to bow and *namasté* to every man in the yard but tamp down my enthusiasm and climb back into the van. As we pull out, we pass a soldier shining his boots. Such a simple activity looks out of place here amid the palpable tension. At the gate, an ambulance driver is being questioned while his vehicle is surrounded by soldiers, machine guns at the ready, and I remember, I still have to get home.

Safely back at the orphanage, I tip the driver generously and present Rajkumar with a small gift of chocolate, wildflower seeds and sage. He looks puzzled, so I explain that each of the items is from my home in the States. He is most excited by the seeds, saying he will give them to his sister for her garden.

I walk home swiftly, careful to stay clear of main streets, as I'm washed over with waves of gratitude. Gratitude for my safety on this most auspicious day; gratitude for the grumpy, stinky man who stamped my file; gratitude for the little girl I have traveled halfway around the world to find; gratitude for my son, my guide, my moral compass, my teacher; gratitude for the opportunities life has presented. I send that gratitude into the sky to rest on the gathering clouds and move across the landscape to rain drops of gratitude. I wish for the children of Nepal and throughout the world to have kind and loving homes where their bellies are full, their clothes are warm, and their minds are engaged. I say these prayers and send out any merit I may have accumulated to ease the suffering of all sentient beings. *Om Mani Peme Hum.*

Then I head to Summit for a drink.

The election passes without much incident, the King is unsurprisingly reelected, and the Maoists call an end to the *bandhs*. While no one really believes the ten-year civil war has come to an end, the streets are again busy with motorbikes, taxis, and buses. In spite of the rumors that the Maoists are simply regrouping and planning their next move, the anxiety of recent days burns off with the morning fog. There is a renewed brightness to the neighborhood with the familiar return of giggling girls in uniforms hurrying to school, the shoemaker at his usual corner, and sari-clad ladies sweeping storefront steps.

Walking home from the farmers market at Summit, I spot Stephan hanging out the window of a private car, calling to me, "I was given strict instructions to check up on you! You must email Christina straight away and verify all is well!" This surprise encounter has my heart smiling. Christina's no-nonsense advice has saved me time and again without her even knowing it.

After shooting her an email, Jack and I take a walk to pick up his bike. A few days earlier, an ill-fated attempt at independence resulted in a blown tire. Luckily, a kind shopkeeper, forbidden by the Maoists to be open, clandestinely shuffled Jack's ride into his shop.

"I sure hope you can remember where you left your bike," I sigh, wishing to end this errand sooner than later.

"I think the place had a lot of steps," Jack offers, lost in the memory of his accident, now traumatically etched in his seven-year-old mind.

We find the right shop on the second try, but the bike isn't ready, and we're told to "come back in an hour," a favorite Nepalism. We decide to visit Nora and run into Craig on his way out. He'd moved in after things turned sour with his former female roommate. "Well, don't you look nice today," he smiles, pecking me on the cheek, then leaves me with butterflies and rubber band knees.

After so many days of *bandh*-induced seclusion, Nora and I catch up: who we got email from, what we're reading, her phone status (working or not), my Devi status, (sleeping or not). Jack, not usually privy to our girl sessions, is spellbound at first, but quickly deteriorates into boyish attention-getting antics like using us as human jungle gyms and farting on us. Finally, in a last ditch grab for sympathy, with sad puppy eyes and drawn out whine, he plays the "I'm hungry" card. Granted, earlier he casually asked, "so, what do you eat around here," but rejected the mushy orange offered by our very un-Betty Crocker hostess.

"Hey, let's go to lunch!" Nora suggests. "There's a new place up the street. The menu looks good, and the prices are great. Besides, I feel so bad for them, the place is always empty."

"Well, we *are* waiting for Jack's bike to be ready," I debate.

Taking this for a yes, Jack and Nora skip out the door before I can complete my thought. Jack is first to the street, relishing the lead role on our expedition, but falls behind after turning the wrong way. He willingly takes my hand and walks close to the compound walls, safe from bleeping taxis and zizzling motorbikes.

Roots Café
Demanding Café in Town!

The sign reads. Then, even more entertaining:

Your Satisfaction is Our CASH!

While it looks clean from the outside, we walk into a cloud of smoke. Four shady-looking men sit at the bar, their identical black motorcycle helmets lined up, like futuristic talking heads. We move deeper into the darkness of the Roots Café to choose a table. The decor is low-budget Vegas-style, vinyl-topped tables in the shapes of a giant red heart, a black spade, and a red diamond; the club is missing from this incomplete deck. Jack selects a spade, dramatically pretending to be slain on the sharp tip, then opts for the flat, narrow base. Laughing, Nora and I take up seats on the swooping sides where we perch on matching vinyl-cushioned stools that could be out of a 50s diner. We decide this must be where bad casino furniture comes to die.

An overeager waiter appears with grungy menus and a nervous smile. He takes Nora's drink order, but then disappears before I have a chance to place mine. He returns several minutes later with her warm, flat orange Fanta soda and a grimy cup she wipes clean with her less grubby thumb. As the waiter denies Jack's drink requests one by one, I look across the table to find Nora struggling to stay Zen. Out of the confines of the retreat center, this dining experience is challenging her to keep her New York spirit at peace. Finally, a deal is struck, but just as I open my mouth to make my request, he's gone again. Accepting that our orders will be taken one at a time, when the waiter returns, Nora tries to make it as easy as possible, succinctly ordering fried rice for us all. He obediently repeats the order back, accurate in both dialect and enthusiasm.

Noticing Jack's filthy hands, I spy an ominous curtain in the back corner opposite the kitchen, with "Restroom" scrawled on a sign above it and suggest he clean up. Always up for an opportunity to explore, he ducks behind the curtain, undoubtedly hoping to find a secret passage. Since my beverage order still hasn't been placed, Nora offers me a sip of her soda and peels her cup off the sticky table like naked thighs stuck to hot pleather car seats.

After too much time has elapsed, we begin to wonder if we will ever see Jack again, and debate going to look for him. He finally emerges from behind the curtain, cleaner in outward appearance, but with a mildly disturbed look on his face. He cocks his head to the side and ponders, "Did you ever see a door and wonder what kind of yuck is on that door?"

Seriously?! Is this how he's cataloging his experiences in Nepal, by the kind of "yuck" found on doors? Does this survey include alleyways, corners, cracks in walls? I can't wait to hear what he tells his class back in the States about his time in Nepal.

In the end, Jack has the least to eat, and, consequently, is in the best condition gastronomically.

Walking home, we stop back by the bike shop where Jack's bike hasn't moved since we were there hours ago. They say to come back in one hour.

According to Nora, our Nepali Events Coordinator, it's time for a night out on the town. She's itching for some nightlife and talks Craig, Dave, and me into going to Thamel for dinner and drinks. Another tortuous night of being teased by my flirtatious crush feels like more than I can muster, but we're on a mission to keep Dave from losing his mind. He's still waiting to hear from Delhi whether Arun will be granted a visa or not due to the inconsistencies in his file. At the same time, he's experiencing the fatigue of being a new parent. Arun had been with the *didis* at Annie's since birth and is struggling to adjust to life with a single dad, away from all he's ever known. Dave is cautious to make the change gradually, but still, there's only so much he can do.

Dinesh and Leena agree to watch Arun, Devi, and Jack at our house and bring their three kids over to play. Nora, Craig,

Dave, and I squish into a taxi and cruise to one of Dave's favorite spots in Thamel, OR2K. We climb the dark stairwell to the café and leave our shoes at the door, then slip through a portal to the 70s Freak Street era. We make our way through the crowded bar to a low table and pull up oversized cushions. The space has an acid-induced psychedelic dreamscape mural that covers the wall behind us and is draped in glittery gauze curtains and tapestries. Much of the menu is Middle Eastern, a welcome change from the usual Nepali and Indian fare. We order cocktails and appetizers, then a few main dishes to share.

Dave is a master storyteller and shares vivid descriptions of the characters he's met while traveling by train through countries near and far. I admire his free spirit and love living vicariously through his surreal experiences. Immersed in his stories, I'm relieved when he finally gets picked up hitchhiking to Alaska, anxious he'll run out of cash trying to catch his plane from Buenos Aires, and am miserable when he's sick on the floor of a train station in Calcutta. I contemplate if there's anywhere Dave hasn't been. No wonder he can take all of this adoption drama in stride. International travel-related strife seems to be a recurring theme for him.

After far too many plates of food and a few too many cocktails, we reluctantly accept it's time for the evening to wind down. We've stuffed ourselves, but there's still plenty more than we're able to consume, so Craig happily volunteers to take charge of the leftovers. Out on the street, the cool night air feels wonderfully crisp after the humid, crowded nightspot. Dave, debating what to bring home to his wife, and Nora, being the obvious consultant on jewelry, stop to window shop, as Craig and I continue on, his arm around my shoulders.

"It's so nice being with you, Kate," he whispers in my ear. "You just make everything so easy. Why can't other girls be like you?" I tingle from head to toe, intoxicated by his soft voice as he nuzzles my neck.

"Are you two telling secrets?" Nora bounces in boisterously, shocking me back to the reality of being just friends.

We pile into a cab and say goodnight to Thamel, just as the

nightlife picks up. For Dave and me, with anxious little ones at home, our night is just beginning. Leena and Dinesh are absolutely trustworthy, but Devi and Arun thrive on routine, so our night out, while worth it, comes with a price.

Craig and Nora wait in the taxi while Dave and I help each other up the steep front steps. Jack, forever on the lookout, unbolts the door and we tiptoe in. Trying to be quiet only makes me giggle, still giddy from cocktails and Craig whispering in my ear. Nora had directed him to the front seat of the taxi, which blocked the back seat make-out session I was secretly hoping for.

Devi is crashed unceremoniously on the wicker sofa, and Jack has covered her with her favorite blanket, and tucked Babu, her stuffed bear, under her arm. Leena is pacing with wide-awake Arun, singing softly, but as soon as Dave is within striking distance, Arun dives for his familiar arms. Leena gathers up Dave's bag to expedite their departure before Devi wakes up in the commotion. We convince Leena to get in the taxi with everyone else since her flat is on their route, and Dinesh has already gone home with their kids. As they start out the door, I stuff a 1000 rupee note in her hand, which she vehemently tries to give back, but I refuse. Dave and I agreed to split it, about $7 each. This begins the joke that often carries us through some of the rougher days as we pretend to be of the pretentious elite, throwing around $1000 bills.

As I watch the clown car reassemble and slowly back out the alley, I see how connected we all are. Halfway around the world I've met a crush that went to a rival high school, a woman who is like my long-lost sister, and a father desperate to take his son home. In spite of the cold, quiet house, I know I am not alone.

"Mom! I don't like Sarresh anymore!" Jack wails as a burst of liquid emotion springs from his eyes. Suspecting kite-flying foul play, I casually look up from my literary escape to meet his horrified expression.

"There's a goat tied up at the top of the steps, and I think they're going to kill it!" he gasps between sobs. "And it's just a *little* one!" He collapses on my lap in panic and despair. We'd heard the goat bleating earlier in the day, and Jack, always on the lookout for adventure, had gone in search of the mystery goat.

"Oh, Jackie, I'm so sorry. I was afraid that might be where it was." Seeing I've failed to comfort him, I offer, "Do you want me go up and see it with you?" I instantly regret any further familiarity with the doomed goat. Jack nods with glassy saucer eyes, and I put on my shoes. We stop in the kitchen for a bunch of lettuce from the neighbor's abundant garden and scale the stone steps at the back of the compound to meet the condemned goat.

And there she is, just as Jack described, tethered to the iron staircase, surrounded by urban fodder. She is smaller than those I've seen in the market, and oh so pretty. Dainty hooves hold her angelic, fluffy, white body, and a sable stripe runs down her back. Erupting from her softball-sized head, her tiny horns are barely the size of a child's thumb. I kneel down to rub her face and her dark, curious eyes close softly as she leans into my kind touch while her ears flop gently with pleasure. I can feel the landlord's family behind me watching, undoubtedly wondering what the crazy American lady is doing now.

"Mom, do you think she knows they're going to kill her?" Jack whispers, hoping the goat, as well as the family, doesn't hear.

"I don't think so, Jackie. Right now, I bet she just wants something to eat." I offer her a lettuce leaf.

"I think she doesn't want us to leave her here," he says weakly, falling to his knees.

We stay for several more minutes petting the goat while the Grandma of the house tells a story, complete with grand gestures and smiles. I struggle to feign attention and laugh at hopefully the appropriate times, but I don't understand a single thing she's saying. I hope she doesn't take my interest in the sacrificial goat as desire for an invitation to the slaughter.

"Jack, I'm going back home, but you can stay as long as you'd like," I say softly, hating to leave the little goat whose pleas have haunted my day. He nods slowly, and I leave him to make his peace.

Soon, I hear the kitchen door creak open followed by his footsteps tapping up the steps to the terrace. He tells me they moved the goat to a shed, then Grandma went in and started waving something around, yelling at her. I wished for something to say to ease Jack's distress, feeling his silent plea for Magic Mommy to make it all okay. My mind floods with *Mission Impossible* scenarios to free the doomed goat, financial incentives I could offer the family to spare the goat, prayers for the happy and auspicious rebirth of the goat, and finally, I wonder if Father Glenn would be willing to offer the goat last rites. I feel helpless knowing nothing will ease the pain of the reality Jack is facing, so all we can do is listen to the bleating of the goat and pray the knife is sharp.

"Devi hungee, Devi huuungeeee," is the morning mantra I wake up to, finding her perched on the edge of my bed, chanting while patting her belly. She's so cute, it's easy to get up. We shuffle downstairs for some cereal and juice, Devi's first breakfast before Dinesh arrives to serve the usual pancakes and jam. Hearing the slap slap slap of her feet on the freezing marble floors I'm awed by her sturdy constitution. No matter how many times I try, she refuses to wear slippers and pulls off shoes and socks in the taxi when we go out. I'd been disturbed when we first met because the pair of sandals she was wearing were several sizes too big, flopping around like clown shoes. I could only assume she'd never had proper footwear before. I'd been so excited to provide her with cute, comfy shoes, but what I thought of as a loving gesture had been yet another cause of discomfort for sweet Devi.

I'm trying to take her to a once-a-week play group with an international potpourri of other expat moms who take turns hosting. Unfortunately, more often than not, the fallout hasn't been worth the social interaction. The overstimulation of being in a new place with lots of other kids and numerous light-up toys with their blurps, bleeps, and sirens proves more than my little mountain girl can process. For the most part, I let her explore each new world we're invited to, but the propensity for her to lose her head and whack, bite, or kick another child is always close to the surface, making it nearly impossible for me to relax with the other moms. Occasionally, when a cry rings out that Devi is in no way connected to, I puff up with pride that my little bundle of disaster isn't the cause of the havoc.

As I gaze across the table at her, I'm amazed we are together. She was a dream child in my mind for so long, that even at this point, it's hard to believe. Now that we are officially in the queue, I realize it isn't just her walls that need to come down. I've unconsciously put up a few of my own, cautious about letting her into my heart, fearful of the pain of losing her if things don't work out. But now I know, as the days tick by, the ties that are binding us cannot be broken. I think back to summer camp and swimming across the lake, getting to the middle and deciding whether to keep going or turn back. As a kid, I would never stop halfway, but now I'm the Mommy, swimming with a toddler on my back. I've rarely doubted my stamina before, but I'm swimming for two now, and the stakes couldn't be higher.

Devi slurps down the last of the sticky sweet milk from the bottom of the bowl, and I move to a wicker chair to check my email.

```
Dearest Kate,

    I'm in the Valley for a quick photo shoot.
    Would love to see you and those beautiful
children. Stop in to Summit.
    But make it quick.
    I don't want to miss you!

xx
Christina
```

Suppressing the urge to run straight to Summit in my pajamas, I know the grown-up response is to wait patiently until Leena arrives to mind the children. I'm thrilled for Christina to share a new secret about Kathmandu, so I brave the cold and strip down to change into clean clothes. Once Jack is settled with his lessons for the day, I dash up the back steps, out the gate and down the lane to Summit. I find Christina on the patio drinking tea and browsing the local paper.

"Kate, my sweet, how are you?" she calls out, greeting me warmly with a hug and kiss kiss on each cheek.

"Great, now that you're here!" I cheer. "Tell me about your flat, how are the renovations coming? Have you started a new film project?"

"Well, you know me, leaping from one thing to the next all the while juggling the mommy and wife duties." She rolls her eyes as she sips her tea. "Dear Stephan mentioned seeing you a few weeks ago. He said you were looking good, but of course I had to come see for myself." She reaches across the table to take my hand. "So, really, how are you?"

"I got my file in to the CDO just before the election, so it feels great to finally be in the queue. Now I have part two of the wait, but at least I'm halfway there!"

We catch up on her kids and mine, her fabulous life in lovely Paris, and my lack of a love life in Kathmandu. She fills me in on her current film and I tell her the story of my near disaster, overstaying my visa. Then, the moment I've been waiting for, she asks, "Do you have time to go to lunch?"

"Well, I have so many other obligations," I joke. "What did you have in mind?"

"It may sound odd, but I have really been craving Caroline's," she says dreamily. Then, seeing the blank look on my face, she continues, "Don't tell me you haven't found Chez Caroline?"

"No, I don't think so." I search my memory of all the dives Nora has dragged me to.

"Oh, if you'd been there, you'd remember. It's close to Singha Durbar, where all the government offices are? It's in the Baber Mahal compound, an old palace where the Ranas, who ruled Nepal, lived for almost a century. It fell into disrepair until several years ago when an American architect helped renovate the entire compound. Now there are several cafés, garden courtyards and museum quality shops inside. Oh, it's fabulous, you'll love it!"

"Sounds fantastic!"

"Well then, that settles it. Off we go! But first, I'm hoping you might be up for a little shopping?" she asks with a twinkle in her eye.

"Gladly!" Shopping with Christina is always an adventure. She knows the intricate passages of Kathmandu better than I know my own name.

We dash through the market and I find a terracotta goat planter, missing an ear, for Jack, as a tribute to his heartbreaking encounter with the sacrificial victim.

"That seems about right," Christina laughs, alluding to the ever-evolving band of misfit animals residing at my Kathmandu home. Once Christina finds the jacquard silk she is looking for to decorate her Paris flat, we climb back into the private car she's rented for the day and cruise over to Caroline's for lunch.

As we pull up to the gates of Baber Mahal, it feels like we are entering an exclusive country club. The walls are whiter than white, and lush, emerald green gardens are peppered with a bouquet of bright blooms. Businessmen in sharp suits and dark sunglasses are whisked off in private cars, making ours look like a rusted tin can. Following the basket-weave brick walkway, we pass shops displaying delicate *pashminas* and ornate brass works, then wind through a courtyard to a brilliant white fountain and round a corner to enter Chez Caroline, an exquisite outdoor café.

We order fresh lemon soda, then lose ourselves in the menu of divine culinary possibilities. Eventually, I decide to start with a spinach and goat cheese salad, followed by quiche boasting exotic wild mushrooms and imported cheese. Christina orders a salad and fluffy crepes.

"I feel ridiculous coming to Nepal from Paris to eat French cuisine. Maybe it's the atmosphere that makes everything taste so much better," she confesses.

"This place is amazing! I've avoided this part of town since all the government offices are so close by."

"You are carrying on very bravely, little dove. Soon enough, all of this turmoil will be over, and you and Miss Devi will be back in the States bored to tears, wishing for some action!" She teases, then holds up her glass. "Here's to you and your little one."

"And to you and yours." Sunshine sparkles off the crystal as we clink goblets.

We share a chocolate torte, the most decadent treat I've had in Kathmandu, and soak up the ambiance. For a little while, we forget that we're within striking distance of His Majesties offices, and a revolution ready to ignite.

When Dave found out that the State Department was investigating his less than typical adoption, he knew his wait would quickly exceed his funds if he stayed on at Summit. In early January, he moved into a room at the home of an expat who had been residing in Nepal for over thirty years. The multi-level house was lovely, in a nice neighborhood nearby. Best of all, several *didis* were there daily, cooking and tending to the house and were thrilled to have a baby around. It was great for Arun to finally be in a home, surrounded by loving women, rather than a hotel room or the concrete servants' quarters at Annie's. My visits always raised an eyebrow among the whispering *didis*, and Dave and I laughed at what they must be saying about us. Women callers could only mean one thing in their minds, and as much as I loved Dave's company, he was a married man, and that was a line I would never cross. I couldn't imagine how hard it was for Dave's wife, Melissa, waiting at home.

Dave is anticipating that he'll be cleared to pick up Arun's travel documents in the morning, so I go over to wrangle the busy baby while he packs, unpacks, and repacks. He's waiting for a call from the Embassy, expecting to schedule his final interview later in the afternoon. The State Department elevated his file to the regional office in Delhi for further investigation due to the inconsistencies between the information he and Annie provided compared to what is in the Nepali file. While Dave is lucky to know the true story of Arun's early life, unfortunately, now there are more questions than answers. As happy as I am for him to be on his way back home, I have to admit, I'm sad to see him leave. Dave is experiencing aspects of this adoption ordeal that no one else can really understand. We connect in a different way than I do with free-spirited Nora, philosophical Craig, or perfect-gentleman Jonathan. We often find comfort as one another's "am I crazy?" parenting barometer.

"Thanks so much for your help, Kate. I couldn't have gotten this done without you to keep Arun busy," Dave smiles, excited to be wrapping things up.

"Oh, you're so welcome. I'm sorry to ruin all your fun, Arun," I squeeze his leg playfully as he makes another attempt to crawl off the bed to freedom. "Are you sure you won't join Nora and me for lunch?"

"Nah, I gotta get him down for a nap and wait for the call."

"Well, we can celebrate later then!" I suggest and head out to meet Nora.

After a delicious meal of fresh fruit and pastry at the Banana Cat Café, Nora and I decide to stop in at the orphanage so she can show me all the good deeds she's done. Through her personal crusade, hitting up friends and family during the holidays, she's raised nearly a thousand dollars for the orphanage. Jonathan advised her on teaching supplies for the children, and Tessa connected her with the international clinic for staff workshops on hygiene, food safety, and sanitation. I'm amazed by how much thought and energy Nora has put into her pet project, and I can't wait to see all she's accomplished.

The children in the garage-turned-schoolroom flock to her beaming, showing off their papers filled with letters and numbers. The kitchen is stocked with new cleaning supplies, and in the nursery, disposable wipes and hand sanitizer abound. No more communal snot rags.

"It's amazing what a little money can do at a place like this. The US dollar stretches *so far!*" Nora whispers excitedly as we walk toward the steps. "Everyone has been so appreciative. I was afraid I would come off as condescending, or they would reject the ideas the health workers gave them, but really, they just didn't know. Education *really* is the key. I bet next winter the kids will be much healthier, too!"

"I'm going to pop my head in and say hello to Raj. I'll meet you outside," I turn toward the office, happy for a purely social visit, and enter the room smiling, but am met by a heavy look from Amita. I try not to take it personally and fold my hands, bowing slightly, *namasté*.

"Please, Madam, come in. Sit," she says flatly. Feeling like I've been called to the principal's office, I glance at Rajkumar, stone-faced as well, and slink in to take a seat.

"Madam Saunders, I need to inform you there is a problem with your file." Her hands clasp before her in clear frustration.

"Whuh . . . What? What do you mean?" I stutter as I try to stay calm.

"Your file has been rejected by the CDO. Nepali law states that a single woman cannot adopt if she already has a child. You have a son, therefore you cannot adopt. I am sorry," she states flatly.

"What?" I practically shriek.

"What Amita is saying, because your file shows you have a son, we need to fix it so you do not have any children, then there will be no problem," Rajkumar says kindly, as if he is telling me the menu item I have ordered is not available, but they have a lovely substitution.

"What?!" I blurt again, incensed.

"Really Madam, we just have to fix your file, removing all information regarding your son." Rajkumar pseudo-soothes, smiling like a used car salesman.

"But how is that possible? I was told the law stated because I have a son, I could only adopt a daughter."

"The law says many things, it depends on who is reading which part of it," Rajkumar continues, as if this is logical.

"But they already know I have a son. He's mentioned in my file over and over again."

"Your file will be fine once we remove anything about your son," Amita interjects, hoping I will buy into their plan. "Otherwise, adopting Miss Devi will not be possible."

Tears sting the corners of my eyes and I'm ready to tear my hair out. I know I have to get out before I freak out, so I rise from the sofa and say as calmly as possible, "Let me call the agency. I need to think about this and figure out what to do. Can I call you tomorrow?"

"Yes, Madam, I understand. But please know, this is the best way for your file to be accepted, and we must act quickly before any more questions are asked," Rajkumar offers, and something in his tone warns me not to fight this too hard.

I stumble down the steps and the world starts to blur. I feel my knees wobble, and I grope for a nonexistent handrail. Outside, I frantically shuffle through the pile of shoes to find my own while glancing around for Nora. Tears spill over the levees of my eyelids as I wrestle with my sandals to cinch them on tight, ready to run, run, run all the way home. Some of the older girls notice I'm upset and look on cautiously. I ask if they know where Nora is, and one girl offers me a softly apologetic "no," but then quickly assures me she will find her. I croak that I'll wait outside. On the other side of the gate, I feel as if I've stepped onto a tilt-a-whirl, spinning out of control. The tall office building adjacent to the orphanage ominously blocks out the sun. I stumble to the block wall to steady myself, lean against it, and vomit. I try to breathe, gulping for air as I wipe my mouth with my sleeve.

Nora appears, clearly concerned by my quick departure, and I collapse into her arms.

"My file was rejected," is all I can say. She looks at me, stunned. She asks all my same questions, but I just shake my head, unable to get any words out. All I want is to get away from this place of perpetual despair.

As we walk, I regain my composure, and tell Nora all I know. Seeing the disbelief in her eyes, I realize what I must have looked like just moments ago. I'm not crazy—this is a disaster. At the nearest tea stall Nora calls Dave, and he agrees to meet us at Saleways. In a flash, he pulls up in a taxi. While Nora loads me in, Dave dashes into the store and returns with a Twix bar and a brown paper bag.

"Your favorite," he says kindly, handing me the candy bar, one of my few vices. Then he pulls a bottle from the bag, Teachers Scotch Whiskey. "Don't worry, Kate, the Teacher is in," he comforts. "We'll end up broke buying drinks at Summit tonight, so let's go local and bring our own."

Nora holds my hand as we bump along, while Dave, in the front seat, gives directions and makes small talk. When we pull up Dave takes my arm, and we stop by the front desk to use the phone to call Annie, desperate for this nightmare to end. She answers sleepily, and I feel guilty for waking her, especially when she sounds wholly unimpressed by my troubles. She sighs and says she'll be over in a little while. Dave leads me to the lounge where we sit by the fire while Nora trots across the lane to update Leena.

Sipping my overly full glass of whiskey, I stare out the window to the room where Jack and I stayed all those months ago and remember when life was so idyllic. I feel like I've aged a hundred years, and I wonder how much more I have left in me. The solution to my "problem," removing all trace of Jack from my file, echoes through my head and makes me shudder at the karmic implications of disappearing my own son. I'm sure I don't want to find out.

"Kate, this is going to work out. It has to. You're Devi's mom now, they can't take her away from you," Nora quietly consoles, and I want to rip her head off for being so calm. My world is going black, blocking out any ray of hope.

We brainstorm possible options: removing Jack from my paperwork life, risking further investigation from the State Department (something Dave assures me I don't want to deal with); having my mother adopt Jack, thereby leaving me childless (but question if that could open the door for child protective services to get involved); having Nora adopt Devi (we'd heard stories of women doing this to keep siblings together); having Dave adopt Devi (as if he and Melissa didn't already have enough to deal with). Then there was the recurring theme of marrying a Nepali man. Desperately crazy schemes become more illogical and extravagant as the spirits infuse my brain.

We wait and wait for Annie, but she never comes, never calls. Nora offers to check on the kids since I'm expected to be home by now. I don't want them to see me like this, with puffy, red-from-crying eyes. Dave leaves to take a phone call, and my mind quiets as I watch the Himals light up in their evening show. I breathe deep and try to pull myself together, thankful for Dave and Nora, my rocks in this sea of despair.

Nora returns, cheeks flushed from the chilly night air, and assures me Dinesh has everyone under control and is getting dinner ready. I'm comforted by another island of support. When Dave comes back in, he pours himself another drink, and tosses it back quickly, his face ghostly white. "That was the Embassy. Seems as if bad news is going around today." He fills his glass again and downs it. "Word from Delhi is, they're issuing a Notice of Intent to Deny."

My heart stops. "Oh, Dave," is all I can say as my eyes pool again.

"Don't start again, Kate, you might just get me going with you. I gotta go and call Melissa, she'll be waking up soon. I need her to get started stateside, contacting the agency, maybe some Congressmen. I don't know what to do," he trails off, shaking his head. "You'd think in a country like this they'd be happy for us to take these kids and give them a home, you know?" He looks to me, but I don't have any answers.

"Yeah, doing a good deed isn't supposed to be this hard," I mumble as tears run tracks down my street dirty cheeks.

"No, it's not. I'm pretty sure we both have a hard night ahead of us," he offers up a toast. "So, here's to life being hard."

"And getting through it anyway," I add, clumsily clinking my glass to his as Nora looks on, unable to ease our pain.

Once home, I tell Jack I ate the wrong thing and am not feeling well, then head up to the terrace to look out at the city lights. Soon enough, Nora joins me after settling Jack and Devi on the couch reading books.

"How is this happening?" I ask.

"What doesn't kill us makes us stronger, and I know you will find a way to work this out. You didn't come all this way for a horrible ending; I just know that in my heart. God only gives us what we can handle, and you can handle this. You are the strongest woman I know, if anyone can do this, it's you."

"But how? How am I going to fix this?"

"You just will. Like my mother always says: how do you eat an elephant? One bite at a time," and I'm reminded of Nora's fairy tale mother I met in the Summit garden so many months ago. I long for the comfort of a mother like her. "Now let's take that first bite and have a proper dinner with your children."

"Oh, I can't imagine eating, and I don't want them to see me like this. I don't want to scare them."

"Well then, I'll go be chipper while you pull yourself together; then you can get them off to sleep and call the agency in private; it's only a few more hours until they'll be in the office."

Before leaving for the night, Dinesh appears on the terrace with a cup of tea and some toast. "Madam, you must eat something," he says softly, setting the tray down on the table. "I apologize for all the trouble my country is causing you. In Nepal, things are often very difficult." Ever-faithful Dinesh, with his kind heart and gentle eyes, pleads with me to forgive him for something he has no control over. Too many Nepalis questioned me about adopting this little girl, looking down on her as worthless, when I already have such a blessing, a *son*. But not Dinesh, ever. Forever respectful, he does all he can to make our time here pleasant, helping us to feel at home and part of his family. It's no surprise he's here now, offering his support.

"It's okay, Dinesh. Someone will figure this out," I say, smiling slightly and taking a piece of toast to choke down. I can't say no to him.

"Yes, Madam. Well, goodnight,"

"Thank you, Dinesh. *Namasté*." I say, bowing to the God clearly within him.

"*Namasté*, Madam," he says softly and is gone.

And I am alone. I lean my heavy head back against the wicker chair, and wish I could float away, into the night sky.

Once Nora has done all she can to exhaust Devi and Jack, she says goodnight and takes off. I lay down with the kids until they drift off to sleep, then sneak out of the room. Flipping a mental coin, I decide to call the agency first. I want more information before I totally regress and call my Mommy. The office manager at the agency connects me to Lauren and she is shocked, alternately asking if I'm okay and reassuring me this will be taken care of.

"Eliminating Jack from your file is not a good idea," she advises. "It might help on the Nepali side, but it will definitely create problems with the State Department. I'll be in touch, Kate. Try not to worry."

I take a deep breath before calling my mom. Knowing she's at work, I ask her to move to a private line, not wanting her to cause a scene when she inevitably breaks down.

"I have some bad news. My file has been rejected." I tell her somberly, starting to cry again at the reality of the news I'm sharing.

"What do you mean *rejected?*"

I rehash the day's events, groping to explain the inconsistency of the law, concluding with my conversation with Lauren, trying not to fall apart. I need to share this burden with her, to hear sympathy in her voice.

"Well, I'm sure this is all just a big misunderstanding," she chirps, and I wonder if she has heard a word I've said. Whenever I had trouble growing up, whether it was with friends or a disappointing grade in school, her response had always been that I must have misunderstood. But there was little to mistake about what Rajkumar and Amita had told me.

"Mom, this is serious. I could lose Devi," I try to make her understand.

"Oh, I'm sure it'll all work out. Have you asked Annie what to do? I bet you just need to speak to a supervisor," She says dismissively. I hear her whispering to someone in the background, distracted, and I feel like it was a mistake to call her.

"Well, Lauren is going to see what she can find out, so I'll be in touch once I hear back from her." I accept that she isn't able to grasp the severity of my situation and shame myself for expecting anything more of her.

"Sounds good! Keep your chin up, it'll all be fine," she concludes. "I love you!" I hear the click of the phone.

Sleep is elusive, and when I finally drift off, I dream of botched files, scary government offices and lost children, sometimes Devi, sometimes Jack. I beg the sun to come up, and I stumble out to the loft to check my email for news from the agency, though I know there will be nothing. Dave and his disaster float through my mind. I wonder how he is faring, and briefly consider calling him for the midnight company. I'm sure he's up, also sick with worry.

Finally, with the first hint of daylight on the horizon, I give up and call the agency. I get the answer I was expecting: they need to talk to Rajkumar, and he won't be in for a few more hours. My head pounds with a hangover, but not from the whiskey; it's from all the crying and epic stress crushing me.

Morning drags into afternoon as I sit on the terrace, staring numbly into the chaotic city. Nora, her phone perpetually out of order, drops by after lunch, and conveys Craig's good thoughts. She's hesitant to leave me but gets the not-so-subtle hint that I have little interest in being distracted or cheered up. She excuses herself and moves on to visit Antoine, her incarcerated project. *Now there's a silver lining*, I think—*at least I'm not in jail*.

Then the phone rings. "Yes, hello, Madam? Is Rajkumar. I have good news. Your file has been accepted," he says with nonchalant pride in his voice.

"What?"

"Your file has been accepted. You are now in the queue," he states again, triumphantly.

"What? I mean, how did this happen? What did you do? How did you fix it?"

"Oh, Madam, this is not important. You are in the queue; that is what matters now. What more do you need to know?"

"Well, uh, I guess you're right. That's all I need to know. Thank you, thank you, thank you!"

"All right then. Enjoy your day and please, bring Miss Devi by so we can see how she is coming along," he says cheerfully, unfazed by my traumatic event.

And it's over, just as suddenly as it began. I call the States immediately, leaving voicemails at the agency for Lauren and then my mother. I call Dave next, hesitant to share my news since he's still in the throes of battle, but I can tell by the sincerity in his exhausted voice, he's happy for me. He, too, has been up all night on the phone with his wife, brother, the agency, lawyers, and the strain in his voice is palpable. I ask if there is anything I can do, but know what he really needs—a visa—something I can't provide.

"I just don't get it," I ponder out loud. "What changed for them to suddenly accept my file?"

"Sounds like the right person got the right bribe," he says. "I'd guess the only thing that changed in your file was a wad of rupees."

The hair stands up on the back of my neck, and I feel in my gut he's right, but I really wish he wasn't.

March

March blew in like soft wispy clouds on a dreamless night. It may have come in like a lamb, but as the days clicked by, we soon found ourselves trapped in a lion's den.

The moon is full tonight, so Nora, Craig, Dave, the kids and I, are off to Swayambhunath, the Monkey Temple, nicknamed due to the abundance of holy monkeys living in and around the ancient religious complex. Squishing four adults into a tiny taxi has been challenging enough, but now we are up three kids. Arun easily squeezes onto Dave's lap in the back seat, next Nora climbs in the middle with Devi on her lap, and Craig completes the backseat lineup. I cram our cumbersome baby backpacks into the envelope hatchback and hop in the front seat with Jack on my lap. In this land of no seat belts, I typically worry for our safety, but now, smashed in like sardines, I'm sure that if we're in a crash, being ejected is impossible.

We pass through shanty towns of tarp tents sheltering vendors and eventually arrive at the lower entrance of the Temple complex.

Legend has it that long ago the Kathmandu Valley was filled with water, creating a huge lake, and the hill on which Swayambhu sits was an island in the middle. The complex, over 2000 years old, is one of the oldest Buddhist temples in the world and a renowned pilgrimage site for Buddhist and Hindu practitioners. Prayers said here are believed to have special powers, and with the full moon, they are even more auspicious.

Opting to bypass the 365-step staircase lined with huge, colorful Buddhas, we continue along the winding road to the top of the hill where more of the sought-after deities reside. As the taxi inches up the steep slope struggling under our heavy load, we all join in a chorus of, "I think I can, I think I can, I think I can," cheering on the little taxi that could.

We peel out of our sardine-can-car thankful to stretch. Dave and I load our little ones into their backpacks and make our way toward the entrance that is climbing with monkeys. Pondering the legend that the monkeys are holy descendants of the Hindu God Hanuman, it's hard to keep a straight face as they swing from strands of prayer flags and munch chips out of plastic bags discarded by slovenly tourists. It's as if they are showing us the greatest of all life's secrets: don't take it all too seriously.

At the entrance of the temple grounds, we're greeted by a golden Buddha in the center of a pond. Visitors throw coins in hopes of landing them on the platform Buddha presides over to ensure the wish will be granted. We follow a winding path to the top of the hill and find one of the giant Buddhas. Jack climbs up to sit cross-legged in his open palm, like a meditating yogi. Bells ring from above, and as we reach the top of the hill, we enter the temple complex. The *stupa* is guarded by large, plaster snow lions. A stocky pillar sits between them displaying each of the twelve animals of the Tibetan calendar, crowned by a golden *vajra*, an auspicious Buddhist symbol that depicts the uniting male and female energies. Elaborate pillars are topped with various gods, goddesses, and deities that preside over the elements of Fire, Water, Earth, and Air. Like Boudha, at the center is a giant white dome crowned with a golden cube. The all-knowing eyes of Lord Buddha look out through hundreds of strands of prayer flags that flutter wishes into the night sky. I bow, hands folded, thankful to be within the temple I often gaze at from our terrace.

Captivated by chanting monks within the Hariti Temple, I lose all sense of connection to my comrades and begin circling the *stupa*, spinning prayer wheels as I fall into rhythm, *Om Mani Peme Hum*. I pass four Buddhas who each face in a different direction; each Buddha locked behind an ornate gate, presumably to prevent their theft. A man walks next to me, then stops to dip his finger in the red powder adorning the deities, and smudges his forehead in self-communion.

After circling the *stupa* three times, making sure to spin every one of the two hundred prayer wheels, I come to the table of butterlamps and set my intention. I light ten for my grandmother, still recovering from her hospital stay; then ten more, offering thanks for Dinesh and Leena. The next ten are for Devi and me, may our process be smooth and successful, and ten for Jack, may he remain healthy and intact. Finally, ten for Dave, wishing for his family to be reunited and whole. As if waking from a dream, I look around to see night has fallen, and everything is golden in the glow of butterlamps and moonlight.

Devi jiggles and squirms in the backpack, and I come back to the present needs of the little people in my life, namely dinner. Our party reunites, and we make our way down the epic staircase, passing giant Buddhas and ornate peacocks. Suddenly, I understand Birendra's secret to good health: he scales these steps every morning at dawn, feeding his spirit as well as his cardiovascular system. I'm awed by the pilgrims who not only climb all these steps, but prostrate along the way.

We squish once more into a taxi and head to Thamel for dinner. Craig knows the perfect spot down a dark alley, and I'm sure this is a bad idea. Eventually, we find the diamond in the rough, La Dolce Vita, and enter through a picturesque garden. We have our pick of tables draped with red and white checkered cloths. The waiter exuberantly presents us with menus offering such a variety of dishes, it's hard to choose. Dave buys the first round of drinks, while Arun sits happily on the table banging a spoon on an overturned bowl accompanied by Devi singing along. Jack rolls his eyes at their childish behavior.

After a long, laughter-filled meal, Dave and I load up like pack mules. Jack, exhausted, gives up his aspirations of being the "big kid," and climbs on Craig's back. We hail a taxi for one last ride back across the bridge to our side of town.

Once my sleep-heavy, rag doll children are tucked in bed, I wrap up in a scratchy yak wool blanket and tiptoe out to the terrace to gaze at Swayambhu off in the distance, like the flicker of a candle, glowing bright on the hilltop. I wish upon elusive stars for us all to get what we need.

Jack has a new box. Yes, a box. The best box ever! When our neighbor moved in, she discarded the wooden packing crate on the patio for the gardener to carry off, but before he had a chance, Jack commandeered it, enlisting Dinesh to help him drag it to the side of our house like a puppy with a too-big bone. He spends countless hours in his secret hideout—No Girls Allowed! Luckily, the most secret thing he's up to is reading the *Hardy Boys*. I call him in for dinner, and he shouts back from behind the towel-turned-magic-curtain that covers the doorway, "But I'm getting to a really good part!" I love it.

The series of cats he's created for the art portion of his home-schooling program are amazing. His use of color and texture, utilizing any found material possible—cereal boxes, cellophane packaging, discarded textile remnants from the tailor—is inspiring. I had to draw the line at "organic" (i.e. dead animal) matter after seeing the spark in his eye as we passed a deceased rat in the alley, "Mom, look at his fur!" My favorite cat is the one made of black construction paper with a plastic pink nose, blue fabric eyes, and aluminum foil whiskers. I adore the cardboard cheetah with shiny, black, plastic-bag spots. With such creativity flowing, it's easy to let the book-work slide.

It's as if Jack has become a teenage boy overnight. He eats all the time but stays as thin as Gandhi on a hunger strike. I can't ignore the fact he's growing; the sleeves of his counterfeit Snoopy pajamas I bought when we first arrived are already two inches above his wrists. "All right Jack, I've had just about enough of this," I bark at him, employing one of my father's favorite lines: "Stop growing right now!" He finds my mock discipline hilarious.

Then there's my little Tasmanian Devi—I wonder if I will ever sleep again. Yesterday afternoon, Jack was snacking on a bag of broad beans, then gave Devi the leftovers, which she heartily consumed. She was up wailing and moaning with what I guessed was an epic tummy ache, confirmed by the enormous poop she displayed proudly this morning. Clearly, she has no internal regulation to signal when she's had enough to eat, so she will eat until it's gone. Those tiny little locks on the kitchen cabinets just might come in handy after all.

Night terrors continue to rock her dream world, and at times, I give up trying to comfort her, which tears me apart. Watching my little zombie girl stare blankly into the night, exhausted from fighting me, is beyond heart wrenching. As she screams and thrashes, I feel like I'm watching someone drown, unable to convince her I'm there to help. I've padded the walls around her bed with pillows to prevent self-inflicted injury during her epileptic-like fits and bought another foam mattress for the floor as a safety net for when she inevitably falls out of bed. I wake to her caged-animal shrieks and move to the end of the bed to watch her, making sure she doesn't hurt herself or pull out her hair like she did when we first met. I think back to the first pictures the agency emailed to me; I'd attributed her sparse, patchy hair to malnutrition, but now, I've come to a different conclusion.

The hope that comes with the promise of spring wakes me up in the night, and I feel too warm under all those layers; I'm surprised to see no frost on the windows in the morning. As the days grow longer, so does my patience, and with new flowers blooming every day, it's easier to see beauty amid the chaos.

With the house to himself, Dave invites Nora, Craig, and me over for dinner and drinks while his host is Stateside. At the last minute, Nora calls to bow out, engrossed in preparations for her upcoming trip to Everest Base Camp, thereby leaving me alone to drink whiskey with the boys.

After a modest dinner prepared by the *didis*, Craig and I make ourselves comfortable in the sitting room, while Dave fetches glasses and a bottle of Teacher's Scotch Whisky. "The Teacher is in," he proclaims. As Craig laments the trials of being a professor, and Dave vents about his never-ending Embassy ordeal, I drink up the good company and too much whiskey. I share the story of a rock-climbing trip, long before single momhood and am reminded to call and check on the kids. All is well, and I tell Dinesh I'll be home in about an hour. Without Nora there to keep him in check, Craig is especially flirty, and after several rounds of drinks and a dwindling grip on sobriety, he moves closer to me on the couch, casually putting a hand on my knee. I briefly question his intentions, but knowing his lack of boundaries, and naturally charming demeanor, I think little of it. I'm sure his teasing will go nowhere until Dave gets up to answer the phone, and Craig slides his hand up my thigh, inside my skirt.

"Finally, we have some time alone," he sighs and leans in close, smiling dangerously.

"This is pretty alright," I reply, trying to sound sexy, but being so out of practice, I have no idea how.

Then, to my surprise, we're sloppy kissing. My mind races, shocked by this turn of events. I get the sense we're being watched and start to giggle. We come up for air to see Dave standing over us, grinning. "So, do you two wanna room or what?" Before I can say anything, Craig blurts out, "Sure!" He takes me by the hand and leads me up an endless staircase to a part of the cavernous house I didn't even know existed. Passion takes hold and inhibitions drop as we wiggle out of clothes and crash naked on the bed.

I'm spinning, still stunned to be kissing this man I'd refused to even fantasize about. At long last, "we" are happening. I drift off to sleep in his arms, feeling like a secret wish has come true.

Way too much later, I startle awake, like I have slept through my alarm and realize it has been much more than an hour since I phoned Dinesh to check in. Craig is out cold, so I untangle myself from his lead-like limbs and pull a blanket around me, then I shuffle through the darkness, groping for a light switch. I'm so disoriented, I give up and try to wake Craig from his man coma.

"Craig . . . Craig! I have to get home," I plead, shaking him by the shoulder.

"Huh, what?" he mumbles.

"The kids are with Dinesh. I have to get home," I repeat, but he looks at me like I'm a lunatic.

"Oh, you're not getting home tonight; all the taxis have stopped running, and I know I can't walk," he concludes. "Come on, just get that sexy ass back in bed," he takes my arm, pulling me toward him, reaching inside my blanket. I reluctantly move away and stumble into the pitch-black hallway to try to figure out how I got to this room. I'm sure Dinesh is worried, and I try not to panic. I feel like poor Pi, trapped in the lifeboat, with Craig as my tiger. Even if I could find the courage to walk all the way home alone, it's so dark, I don't even know where my clothes are, much less how to get out of this giant house.

I step out to the terrace and take a deep breath of the cool night air, hoping to clear my whiskey-clouded mind. I try to relax and convince myself this isn't so bad, but with every irresponsible heartbeat, all I can think of is my children and how I'm failing at being a "good mom." Then, I hear Arun crying from somewhere in the house and thank him for his role as accomplice to get me out of here.

"Dave! Dave!" I call, and suddenly he is there in the darkness, Arun in his arms.

"What's wrong? Are you okay?"

"I've gotta get home," I wail.

"It's *way* too late . . . you can't walk alone."

I feel utterly defeated. "Will you call Dinesh for me? Tell him I'm sick and can't come home?" Which doesn't feel too far from the truth.

"Sure, Kate. What's the number?"

I'm amazed I can remember it, and, soon enough, I hear Dave on the phone, covering for me. I feel like a teenager out past curfew. Miserable, I slide to the cold marble floor, shaking like a scared street puppy, and roll up in a ball.

It's still dark when I wake again; my hip and shoulder ache from sleeping on the chilly marble floor. I abandon my self-imposed punishment and return to the scene of my folly, the forbidden bed where Craig is snoring. He wakes enough to gently take my hand. I allow the comfort of companionship and slip back into bed. Craig pulls me close and I sweep my hair aside, so he doesn't smell the street in it. As he dozes off, nuzzling into my neck, I wonder what the light of day will bring.

The pale rays of dawn creep through the gauzy curtains and I slide out from under Craig's arm, pulling a blanket with me to tiptoe downstairs for a glass of water I hope will wash away my sins of the night before. After surveying the pantry and finding nothing appealing, I return to our room and sit softly on the side of the bed to disassemble the heap of clothes on the floor, sorting into piles of his and hers. I pull on my tank top and flowery undies as Craig wakes up. "What's going on," he asks.

"Nothing," I whisper, hoping he'll go back to sleep so I can make a quick getaway.

"What's this all about?" he grins, pulling playfully at my top. I shrug and look away, still unable to believe I'm here with him. I'm painfully self-conscious about how I must look, not to mention smell. But he just smiles the same smile that got me in this mess to begin with. I melt as he lifts my shirt over my head, kisses me along my ribs, and moves toward my embarrassing bud of a pot belly. He tastes my skin as he slips off my flowers. I tremble as he moves next to me, holding me close.

We lie in the warm morning sunlight, my head on his chest, listening to his heart beat.

"Are you going to tell Nora about this," I ask, feeling childish, worrying she will be upset.

"No way. I think we should figure things out first."

"Yeah, it seems like she wouldn't like us being together, but I don't understand why," I trail off, afraid of saying too much.

"You're right. So, we don't talk to Nora about this, booga booga?"

"Okay. Booga booga." And there, the spell of secrecy is cast. Our night together no longer feels awkward, and I trust Craig's suggestion that we figure out our relationship before sharing it with Nora. In the light of morning, he shows me that he still wants me, and my insecurities fall away. I had come to the other side of the world to find this man, once a boy who went to my rival high school. Some of us do things the hard way, I guess.

Bidding our host good day, Craig and I walk up the footpath with me on his arm, still wanting to be close before we have to hide signs of anything more than friendship in front of Nora, or, more importantly, Jack. More than once, he'd mentioned what a good dad Craig would make, always on the lookout for the missing man in both of our lives. Though Craig and I usually prefer to walk, we catch a taxi, stopping at Craig's place first. He gives me a lingering kiss and says he'll see me soon, leaving me filled with hope and butterflies.

When I get home, no one is there. I call Dinesh's house, and Leena tells me they are on the way over. I shrink a little more, imagining them with two more bodies to squeeze into their tiny sleeping quarters. When I hear them arrive, I see Dinesh is visibly concerned, and I feel like a total jackass.

"Madam, I was so worried! I am afraid someone has taken off with you in taxi. I don't know how to call Dave. I don't know what to do."

I apologize profusely and blame my delinquency on street vendor's food rather than admitting to losing my head over a man. I'm ashamed of my web of lies and want nothing more than to slink into a hole, but I settle for a much-needed shower instead.

Dave calls around noon to see if I want to meet up at Summit, and I'm relieved to get out of the house.

At lunch, Nora wants all the details of the previous night, and

I can barely I hold it together, subtly glaring at Dave. He's already been directed to keep all details to himself, the booga booga pact now extending to him as well. Of what we disclose, Nora finds hilarious, focusing on my unfortunate "illness" and Dave finding me lost in a cavern of his house.

"You're lucky you had Dinesh to save your ass," she jeers, and Dave laughs all the harder at my little secret. I just hope Craig doesn't show up. As much as I want to see him, clearly, I can't be trusted.

Thankfully, Nora is easily redirected when I ask about her upcoming travel plans. Since the Maoists have called another cease fire, she's excited to get out of the Valley for a trekking adventure.

"Birendra has it all worked out for us, the gear, the porters, the guesthouses; all I have to do is show up!" She grins ear to ear.

"Well, I *still* can't believe you're going to leave me to fend for myself with my mother coming," I wail, dreading my impending guest. Though I've looked forward to the idea of my mother's visit, as it draws closer, I'm overwhelmed with anxiety at all she will undoubtedly find lacking in my life. While she thinks she's being supportive, she has a tendency to focus on my shortcomings, unable to applaud any achievements, as if any praise will go to my head.

"Dave will be here, and Janelle. I bet she's great with Moms!" Nora encourages while Dave shakes his head, refusing any involvement.

"Don't look at me, I have my hands full," he justifies as Arun does his best to knock over any beverage still standing on the table.

"I guess I'll have to count on Jack to pull me through. Maybe he'll be so fabulous she won't notice my Tasmanian Devi," I sigh. So far, my mother has been deaf to anything that could be amiss with Devi. She declares that I can't blame everything on Devi being adopted, convinced she's just fine. "Please, don't leave me!" I beg Nora one last time.

"There are mountains to climb, and men to conquer, my friend, sorry!"

And I wonder, with Nora away, what will happen with the man whose dangerous smile has conquered me.

With Nora trekking her way to Everest Base Camp, Tessa still in the Netherlands, and Christina back in Paris, Dave inherits the role of BFF, which he seems delighted to take on as a welcome distraction from his endless wait. Since we both have little people in our lives, it's not necessary to leave the kids home so I can have private girl-time. We arrange kid-friendly outings and frequent the fabulous Japanese restaurant Café U, complete with a jungle gym, slide, swings, and toys galore. The owners have a little girl about Devi's age, who makes herself scarce when we arrive, rather than risk life and limb for time with the toys.

As BFF, and keeper of my great secret, Dave is privy to all my relationship woes. "I just can't believe he would do this," I lament, replaying the last conversation I'd had with Craig when he'd stopped by to talk. He kindly explained he wasn't looking for a relationship and blamed our night together on too much to drink—an excuse I hadn't heard since college. Then he asked if we could still be friends. Shocked, and moreover disgusted, I told him I would have to think about things, then turned away before he could see me cry. My heart needed me to stay away from him and his mixed messages.

"Well, Kate, I hate to say it, but maybe Craig's just being a guy," Dave suggests bluntly.

"Just *being a guy*? What does that mean?"

"Oh, I don't know. I think guys just see these things differently. He probably thought you were up for a night of fun, no strings attached." He juggles a wiggly Arun on his lap.

"Seriously? Do I really seem like a freewheeling, no strings attached kind of gal?" I glance down to find Devi pulling the heads off dolls from a basket.

"Hey, I'm not saying that's what *I* think, just offering a guy's perspective." He lowers Arun to the floor to assist Devi with her decapitation project. "Look, what's done is done, lesson learned."

"Yeah. I guess I was just hoping for more," I fill another cup of green tea from the ceramic pitcher.

"Aren't we all," Dave sighs as he stares off into the distance, no doubt thinking about his life and his marriage on hold.

We enjoy our lunch, lingering until Devi and Arun make it clear naptime is imminent. We load up our bundles into baby backpacks, alternately cinching each other's straps, and agree to talk later in the day as we head in opposite directions. The rhythmic crunch of my sandals on the gravel road lulls Devi to sleep almost immediately, and her grip on my ponytail loosens enough for me to turn my head freely. Jack opted to stay home to spend time in his box, and I can't help but question how all this box time has become "normal."

I enter the compound to find mud splattered everywhere—the gate, the walls, the guard house. Then I spot miniature muddy footprints leading up the steps and around the side of the house to the kitchen door.

"No, *Didi!* No!" Jack squeals, accompanied by Leena's tinkling giggle. I peek around the corner of the house with trepidation to see Jack caked from head to toe with mud, *lots* of mud, like something out of a *Swamp Thing* movie; Leena is unceremoniously spraying him down with the hose. They are in their own little world, and I don't want to wake Devi, so I slip inside the front door just as the battle cry of a second almost eight-year-old rings out. Sarresh's flip-flop feet run past on the wall behind the house, followed by Leena's ferocious scolding and a triumphant cheer from Jack, now able to escape his captor and elude cleanliness. What on earth is going on?

I scamper upstairs to unload my bundle, giving thanks she is exhausted enough to continue sleeping.

A range of screams and squawks is followed by the slamming of the door below. Back downstairs, I find Leena washing her muddy hands and muttering in frustration.

"Leena?"

"Oh, Madam! Jackie, *dedi badmas!*" she exclaims. *Badmas* means naughty, in a funny, clever way.

Gradually, through Eng-pali, mime, and the obvious evidence, I understand that after a clandestine trip to Laxmi dairy just before lunch, Jack and Sarresh were sent to help the gardener and subsequently got into a mud war. No one, certainly not the gardener who is barely more than a boy himself, was going to interrupt their mischievous fun. This was just the latest in a long line of derelict adventures. Sarresh, the son of a Brahmin, and Jack, a white American, immune from any caste label, are quite an unstoppable team. They've been busy cashing in all sorts of neighborhood favors, from candy at the tea shop to extra kite string from the traveling vendor. There is little to exploit here in one of the most impoverished countries in the world, but for these two, the fun is in the conquest.

Leena apologizes repeatedly, clearly worried that I'm upset, like when I found Jack lighting small fires on the roof while she was managing a Devi tantrum in the playroom. But this scene is so comical, I don't have it in me to be angry; all I can do is laugh. Leena watches as I lock the doors and take a box of juice out of the fridge, pouring two big glasses. I then motion for her to follow me, past the snoozing Devi, onto the terrace. I set the juice on the wide railing and pull up two wicker chairs as Leena quizzically looks on. I offer her a seat where we have a perfect view of the continuing mud war. She's shocked by my easygoing demeanor because she's used to my stricter-than-strict ways. I'm always after Jack to do homework, practice violin, or pick up after himself. Hesitantly, she joins me to watch the scene, and we can't hold back our laughter. We watch the boys wrestle as they rub mud in each other's hair and destroy clothes and nearby flowers. The poor gardener has abandoned his post. Eventually, Sarresh's mother descends the back steps, snapping and stomping, her point clearly made. Sarresh cowers and follows her back up to his house. Fun over.

At last, someone else is the "bad mom."

Maybe I didn't wash my hands well enough. Maybe I opened my mouth the tiniest bit in the shower. Maybe that glass of fresh lemon soda wasn't so fresh. Whatever it was, now I'm sick, sicker than sick, and scared.

It hits me in the night like a vice crushing my skull, waking me and demanding something I can't comprehend. My head feels like a bowling ball perched on my toothpick neck. I take a sip of water hoping to quench the fire behind my eyes, only to be rocked by waves of nausea. I stumble to the bathroom just in time to lose last night's fabulous five-star dinner from Chez Caroline. I'd been out with Dave and Janelle when I started to feel a little off, but I'd thought the chills were due to the cool night air and had wrapped up in Janelle's *pashmina*. Now I know it's something much worse.

Between rounds of heaving, I make my way to the bedroom to grab my pillow and blanket, then return to the bathroom, afraid of venturing too far from the toilet. I collapse on the floor, the cold marble a welcome relief against my fiery skin. Through the night, I shake with chills, my teeth chattering so loudly I'm sure I'll wake the children. I drift off only to startle awake and heave again and again until my ribs ache. My strength evaporates, forcing me to lay my head on the toilet seat, and I'm thankful for Leena's diligent housekeeping. As the sun comes up, light filters through the smoky glass shower windows, and I crawl back to bed. Almost instantly, Devi perches next to me, chanting, "Devi hungee, Devi hungee." The rhythmic pats on her belly upend my world.

"Jack, please, take Devi down for some cereal," I beg.

"What, Mom?" Bleary-eyed Jack rolls over to face me.

"Devi hungee," she repeats.

"Please, Jackie . . ." I start to spin again, and dry-heave into the towel I brought from the bathroom as a security blanket.

Jack pushes back the covers and groans, stretching. As he sits up and looks at me, his eyes grow wide.

"Mommy! Are you okay?" he cries, jumping out of bed, putting his hand to my forehead. "Mom! You're on fire!"

"It's okay Jack, I just don't feel very good. How about helping get Devi's day started?" I whisper, panting under the effort of speech.

"Um, okay," he agrees with a puzzled expression. He's never seen his unstoppable Mom like this before. "Do you need anything?" he asks, concern pinched between his big brown eyes.

As I shake my head "no" my brain sloshes in my skull and the bed becomes a violent amusement park ride.

I listen to them rustling around in the kitchen.

"You stay here. I'll be right back," Jack says sternly, then the kitchen door slams shut, and I hear his little sandals slap the concrete as he runs to the back steps. I hope he's not fetching the landlord, but there's no calling him back. I struggle to remain conscious, but the sunlight is so painful, I cover my eyes. As I spin, I see Devi drifting in an ocean of clouds and try to reach out to her, calling her name, but my cries fall silent and she floats away. I wake up, soaking wet, feeling panicked as my heart races like a scared rabbit. Dinesh is standing over me, brows knitted in worry. Leena is right behind him, with Devi perched on her hip, gnawing on a biscuit.

"Madam, Madam," Dinesh calls to me, but I'm far away, unable to focus in the bright, blurry world. I'm vaguely aware of the Nepali voices around me, but I'm helpless to communicate and sink into the darkness again. Sometime later, I wake to Leena gently holding a wet rag on my forehead and nervously stroking my arm. There are voices downstairs, now coming up and into the room. Dinesh has enlisted Dave in the rescue effort, and when I open my eyes, I'm struck by a lightning bolt of sunshine.

"Kate, are you in there?" Dave asks, gingerly putting his hand to my cheek.

"She's on fire. We gotta get her to the clinic. Good work, Dinesh." He lifts me from the bed, as Leena smoothes my wet, matted hair from my face.

Then I'm in a taxi, my head banging on the window with each bump until Dave shifts me to his lap, simultaneously instructing the driver, "*Chitto! Chitto! Madam tati ramro chaina.* (Fast! Fast! She is not good)."

A blur later we are at the international clinic. Dave sits on the edge of his chair, elbows on knees, hands clasped in palpable concern.

"This is the karma I deserve for lying to Dinesh about being sick that night I was with Craig," I mumble, barely coherent.

Dave chuckles at my feeble attempt to lighten the mood. "With all that goes on in this crazy world, I hardly think the Gods have time to punish you for having a good time."

The doctor appears, and I willingly offer my arm for blood draws, then start to spin again. Dave answers all the questions I can't quite grasp; the voices around me morph into the monotone of the teacher from *Peanuts*. With help from a nurse, I stumble into the bathroom to drip-drop a teensy urine sample, feeling the fire from inside me through the plastic cup.

The paper sheet crumples under me, sounding like an avalanche, as I shift to find a position that doesn't make my entire body ache. I can't shake the smell of vomit and finally realize it is in the links of my watch, leftover from when I passed out the night before with my head on my arm.

The doctor eventually returns to report he's ruled out typhoid and several strains of hepatitis. Meningococcal meningitis is a possibility, though remote, and Japanese encephalitis unlikely, since it's carried by mosquitoes not yet hatched in our mountain climate. He disconnects my IV and sends me home with medication for the fever and a handful of hydration salts with instructions to push fluids slowly to avoid more vomiting, then says he will call to check in the next day. Back in the taxi, having lost any concern for Dave's personal space, I collapse in his lap.

Dave enlists the help of the gate guard to carry me up the steps, then Leena takes over and gets me to bed, where I drift in and out of consciousness for the next three days. Dinesh spends the nights on the tiny wicker sofa, refusing to leave me alone with the children. By day, Leena makes countless trips up and down the steps to check on me and keeps the kids busy downstairs in the playroom or outside in the garden. I'm barely aware of her coming and going and wake only slightly to the welcome feel of the cool rag on my head and help to the toilet. Dave checks in often, bringing Janelle for a second opinion, and reassures Jack that I'll be fine. My logical, bent-on-independence brain rails briefly at all the help, only to drift back to *Wizard of Oz* dreamscapes looking for the yellow brick road, floating away in a hot air balloon only to see

Jack and Devi being left behind. Nighttime brings relief; the house is finally dark, still and quiet, absent the sunlight blasting through the floor to ceiling windows that has tortured me.

By the fourth day, I can hold my head up without assistance and eat a small piece of toast, much to Dinesh's delight. Slowly, slowly I'm able to sit up. When Dave brings miso soup from Café U, I ask what day it is and am disturbed to realize that my mother will be arriving in two days.

The day after the fever finally breaks, all I want is to take a shower. Before I can finish, I have to sit down as the world spins, and by the time I dry off, I'm ready to get back in bed, thoroughly exhausted. My mother arrives tomorrow.

While she has boldly asserted that she knows what she's doing, having traveled all over the world, I'd tried to explain to her that Nepal is different, but she pooh-poohed my concerns saying, "I've been to Mexico. That's a third world country." I bit my tongue and refrained from reminding her that she has only been there for a few hours when her cruise ship docked to allow passengers to go shopping. She'll find out soon enough. Now that she's almost here, I'm anxious, feeling responsible for her comfort, physical as well as mental. Even on my best day, my mother is a challenge, and in my weakened state, I don't know if I can even make it to the airport. Dave offers to pick her up, but I fear this would be a poor start to her visit. If she knows I'm sick, she'll arrive in a state of panic, worried for my health. If I don't disclose my illness, she'll be disgusted that I sent a stranger to pick her up. Unwilling to gamble with something as fragile as a jetlagged mother in culture shock, I decide I have to go.

Barely down the lane in the private car Dave hired for us, I have to lie down. Thankful for the spacious backseat, I quickly fall asleep.

"Mommy, Mommy! It's time to get Grandma!" Jack pats my shoulder with excitement, waking me as we pull into the airport.

Too weak to carry Devi, I take her left hand and Jack takes her right; between us we're able to keep her in tow as we inch through a stockade full of waiting people. Devi pulls at my skirt, anxious in the jostling crowd. I take a deep breath and lift her up, then feel the world start to spin as I prop her on the metal barricade. Her legs dangle over the banner that Jack has worked tirelessly on with decorations of balloons, stars, GRAMMA in big letters, and, of course, cows. It feels good to be the ones holding the sign, instead of looking for it. Just when I think I'm going to have to sit down on the filthy concrete before I pass out, she appears, juggling luggage and looking lost.

"Gramma! Gramma!" Jack squeals like a groupie. Relief floods her face as I wave her over to a break in the barrier and direct her porter to come with us to the car. She stops for hugs and kisses, busily asking questions that have clearly been brewing over the last twenty-eight hours of flight, and then come the tears. I know she is a jetlagged puddle of exhausted emotion, so I take her arm and lead her to the waiting car. Devi climbs onto my back to escape the chaos as Jack takes Gramma's other hand and keeps us going in the right direction. With luggage loaded and the porter tipped, I realize how much my life has changed since our arrival months ago. Now, Kathmandu is home, and I'm excited to share it.

"You picked a great day to arrive, it's *Holi*," I say with as much enthusiasm as I can muster when we see a group of young men in the street intent on sharing their colorful holiday joy.

Holi, a significant Hindu holiday, is celebrated with drink, raucous fun, and loads of color *everywhere*. In the hotter climate of India, the festival of *Holi*, and the splashing of colored water is a reminder of the coming monsoon season, and the promise of cooler days ahead. Foreigners are a favorite target, and our driver is quick to avoid the young men angling to surround our car.

"Oh, I see," Gramma says with fear in her eyes as she watches the scenes of poverty and squalor pass by. "Do you live near here?"

The crack in her voice tells me she's worried, and I know my job has begun. "Not too far, just across the river . . ." I trail off. I know she isn't hearing me, overwhelmed by the sight of dirty, shoeless children and mangy street dogs.

As we enter our neighborhood, she relaxes a bit. Then, when we arrive home, she is surprised by how *tall* the house is. I'd described the Inca steps, and sent pictures, but actually seeing them makes it real for her. I focus on staying balanced while supporting my less than agile mother, and when we finally reach the top and step inside, I collapse while Jack shows her around the house. Leena, seeing the color drain from my face, hands me a glass of water laced with hydration salts to bring me back to life. After the tour and some brief chit chat, I confess I'm not feeling well and need to lie down.

"Oh, that's fine!" Gramma smiles with a southern drawl, her face glowing with excitement. "I need to get unpacked anyway."

"We don't have a closet or dressers, but Jack will bring you some baskets and hangers," I offer and disappear.

When I wake up, it's dark outside. Jack tells me they tried to wake me, but I was "talking the crazy talk" again, so they left me alone. It takes me a minute to remember that, yes, my mother is here.

"Boy, you must've been sleepy! Did you have a good nap?" she asks.

"Yes, thanks. You had dinner?" I question, already knowing the answer, spotting the tray Dinesh has left for me with toast, miso and slices of mango.

"Oh yes, Jack said you didn't want to get up. That Durresh . . ."

"You mean Dinesh?"

"That's right. Dunush. He is just the sweetest thing! He made a delicious dinner of native food. Do you call it Nepala food?" she chatters happily, her southern charm ignited.

"Nepalese. Or Nepali."

"Nepali. Yeah, that sounds right. Anyway, it was just delicious! Is that how you eat every night?" she asks with enthusiasm, and I realize she's getting her second wind; it's morning for her, and I need it to be night.

"Mom, I'm excited you're here and I've been looking forward to telling you all about our world, but I really need to get the kids ready for bed." I try to let her down easy, not wanting her to think I'm avoiding the bonding time she's craving. I'm aware of how she might take my lack of attention, but all I can think about is being horizontal.

"Hey, I'm here on your schedule, so you just tell me what's going on. I don't want to throw off your routine or anything," she continues her bubbly babble.

"Can I stay up with Gramma just a little bit longer?" Jack pleads, and I agree. Anything to get me out of the room and back in bed.

The next morning, I wake to Jack's hot breath tickling my ear, whispering. "I'll handle Gramma, you rest."

Part way through breakfast, I make my way downstairs to an expectant audience. I purposely waited long enough for most of the breakfast dishes to be cleared in hopes of keeping my lingering nausea under control. I suggest a quiet day to allow Gramma to adjust, and mention lunch at Summit. I hide my hands as they start to shake, knowing if I share details of my recent illness, I'll be inviting a level of scrutiny I have no defenses to battle. My mother stringently questioned my decision to come to Nepal, and a mystery illness will only give her cause for an "I told you so" lecture. I have no resources to entertain her, so I hope she'll enjoy time with the kids and accept my absence without too many questions. I'm quickly running out of steam and have to get back to bed.

At Summit, when I order toast, claiming not to be hungry, I finally confess that I've been ill. "But I'm feeling much better," I insist. "I just need a few days to get my strength back." I'm met with skeptical looks from Gramma, as Jack not-so-subtly rolls his eyes.

Over the next several days my mother makes it easy, enjoying time with her grandchildren, letting Devi literally walk all over her, refusing to believe she needs to establish any boundaries. I'm too weak to care, still needing to nap twice a day. By the middle of her stay, I'm able to make it through the day resting only once, and we craft a list of sights to see in her remaining week: Boudha, Swayambhu, Patan and of course, shopping. I'm careful to select places where I think she'll feel safe as I watch her struggle to keep the jolt of Third World culture shock off her face.

A full moon falls during her stay, so Janelle and I take her to Boudha for the ceremonies. She is enchanted by the butterlamps, moved by the chanting monks, and terrified by the traffic. She is determined to wait for a break in the ceaseless train of taxis, so Janelle and I get on either side of her and force her to cross. Halfway into our effort, I look to see if she's okay and find her with her eyes squeezed shut.

On the day Jack and I take Gramma to Swayambhu, Leena distracts Devi with an outing to play with the big kids at her house. I've convinced Gramma that Devi is not a good tourist, and I know I'm in no shape to be her sherpa. While making a video for Gramma to take back to the States for Jack's class, we're shaken by an explosion. The Maoists have become active again since the ceasefire expired with the passage of *Holi*. Several *bandh* days had been called, conveniently at the beginning of my mother's stay when I still needed to be housebound. Since then, we've gone out for lunch at all our favorite restaurants, Dan Ran, Café U, and finally Roadhouse. When Devi's behavior began to rapidly deteriorate, my mother nearly paniced when I suggested that she and Jack take a separate taxi home. Instead, she ordered a second scoop of ice cream to pacify Devi and allow her to finish her meal. Luckily, Leena stepped in that afternoon as I crumpled, useless, on the bed, as Devi came to a screaming crash from her sugar high.

The day we spend at Durbar Square in Patan is lovely. We walk through the temples with a self-proclaimed guide, my mother delighting in all he has to tell. While I focus on finding places to sit and lean as I battle the spins, Jack poses on an elephant statue for his eager, camera-toting Gramma. As the afternoon wears on, and soldiers begin to patrol in earnest, I know it's time to put the camera away and head home. The last thing Gramma needs is to be caught up in a spontaneous demonstration while trying to catch every moment on film.

Finally, with gift list in hand, I take her out shopping, starting at Weaves and Blends, the best custom *pashmina* shop in town. The owner is a self-made woman, a rarity in Nepal, and I love to support her whenever possible. Her color combinations, textures, and high-quality craftsmanship is suitable for New York's Fashion Week. What my mother isn't able to buy off the rack, we special-order for me to bring back once Devi's adoption is complete.

For a little local flavor, I decide it'll be fun to walk from there to the carpet shops, just around the corner and down the road. Along our way, a mangy, matted street dog trots up to me, something our veterinarian, Dr. Devkota, regularly teases me about. He's convinced word of my compassion has spread among the street dogs, so if they need anything, they find me. This walking dirty mop is proof of his theory. Not wanting to disturb my on-the-edge mother, I try to ignore the dog, practically tripping over him, before realizing the magnitude of his plight—he has nylon twine tied around his neck, dragging it along behind him. I try remove it, but it's tangled in his matted fur and is cutting into the flesh of his throat. Forgetting my mother's comfort, I calmly tie the skittish dog up outside a rundown supermarket and tell her to watch him. I dismiss the look of horror on her face at being left alone on the street and dash inside, returning with a can of sardines. The pooch in peril is now my best friend forever.

"I need to make a detour by the vet," I announce as we start back down the street.

"Well, whose dog is it? Don't you think they'll be looking for it?" she asks, scampering along behind me.

"Mom, I don't think this dog belongs to anyone."

"Well, you know, it could have rabies," she cautions, hoping I'll abandon the mongrel.

"This will only take a minute."

Leading first the dog, then the mother, we head through one of the busiest traffic circles on our side of town. Making quite the spectacle, the locals can't help but stop and watch, some even point, hands covering laughing mouths. Dr. Devkota sees us over his newspaper and walks up to offer his hand in a gentle shake.

"*Namaste!* What do you have for me today, Madam?"

After introducing my mother, I explain that the dog followed me, and I noticed the twine growing into his neck.

"Oh, another one," he says, turning to my mother. "When I first meet Madam Saunders I tell her, Madam, there are 60,000 street dogs in Kathmandu, you can't help them all. And you know what she tells me?" Incapable of speech, my mother just shakes her head. "She says, 'well now there are only 59,999.'" He laughs at his own story. "Your daughter has a kind heart. We Nepalis can learn from this."

He takes the dog into the clinic and sedates him so his assistant can shave him and cut the twine from his oozing neck. "I believe this dog is purebred, maybe Llapso Apso, a Tibetan holy dog," he announces, shaking his head. "Most likely abandoned by expat family."

"Why would anyone do such a thing?" my mother gasps, clearly horrified.

"It is more common than you would think, Madam," Dr. Devkota replies. "This is why I work with animals. Their intentions are pure." Then he turns to me. "I'll keep the dog here for a while. His pedigree will make it easier to find a home for him. I have a colleague who recently lost his pet. I will see if he has interest."

With my good deed done for the day, I feel energized and ready to continue shopping, but we don't make it very far before my mother hits the wall. Whether it was the goat heads on the counter of the fly-infested butcher shop, or the street children begging in the square, or the suffering of the dog with the twine growing into his neck, my local tour has pushed my mother into full-blown culture shock. As the carpet vendors roll out one exquisite work after another, she's unable to make a decision. I help her choose, then haggle with the shopkeeper for a reasonable price and hail a taxi to take us home.

"Mom, are you okay?" I ask, concerned by her silence.

Now it's her turn to say, "I'm fine, just tired."

With only two nights left, our unofficial ambassador, Dinesh, insists we come to his home for dinner. I feel guilty he has spent his own money to feed my family, but he is proud to host us.

As we walk through the small, crooked metal gate into the courtyard outside Dinesh's flat, we are greeted by the ceaseless barking of a chained-up guard dog. My mother huddles behind me, clinging to Jack's hand for her own safety rather than as the protector she tries to portray. When we enter the small, dark hallway, she cringes at taking off her shoes, but politely complies. Bright and shining, Dinesh meets us at the door, eager to show us around, but the first room is so small, crammed with beds and packed with children that it's impossible to actually step inside. Jack and Devi tumble right in with their adopted family to roll on the floor and guzzle warm Coca Cola, the true sign that Gramma's visit is an event to celebrate. In the second room, we make ourselves comfortable on the sofa that doubles as Leena's brother's bed, while Dinesh helps her finish the last of the dinner details. Soon enough, we are ushered to the table for a bountiful, traditional Nepali dinner.

Watching my mother load chicken onto her pile of rice, I reflect on American-sized portions as Dinesh serves himself a sparse helping. The meal is so delicious, I can't stop thanking Dinesh and Leena for their hospitality, making us feel welcome in their home. My mother has presents from the States for all of them: a cookbook for Dinesh, wool for Leena, an avid knitter, books for the girls, and a soccer ball for the boys. She had all sorts of grand ideas of dresses and remote-control toys, but I reminded her that everything here is communal property, so she needed to bring gifts suitable for a wide range of ages and nothing that required batteries, which would create a financial burden. The eventual gift selections, while they bored my mother, thrill the children.

After polite conversation, when Dinesh gets up to make more tea, my mother grabs my arm, urgently whispering, "I need a bathroom, *now*." Seeing panic in her eyes, I know she's serious, and the "going native" experience needs to end here, bypassing the squat toilet.

"Dinesh, I'm afraid we need to go. My mother has to start packing," I say, not wanting to hurt his feelings by telling him she's ill. I try to gather the cracked-out-on-Coke-kids and dig through the pile of shoes in the dark doorway while my anxious mother does a subtle dance, crossing and uncrossing her legs. Finally, I'm able to peel the children away, and Dinesh insists on walking us home, sauntering along in no particular rush. Our house isn't far down the gravel lane, but I can tell by my mother's quick step, unceremoniously breaking away from the pack, that she's reached a crisis point. I send Jack running ahead, skeleton key in hand, ready to play superhero on the *Gramma Needs a Bathroom* mission. Dinesh and I slow our steps, no longer trying to keep up with her.

"Thank you again, Dinesh, for your kindness and generosity," I say, appreciating my *Dai*.

"Anything I can do for the Mommy," he replies sweetly, referring to my mother.

The last day of Gramma's visit is quiet as she soaks up the last of her time with her grandchildren. Her visit has gone by quickly, punctuated by afternoon naps and hilarious games of Uno by candlelight when the power is cut; it's near impossible to see the difference between the blue and green cards in the dark. She has showered the kids with First World toys and books featuring characters with blond hair and blue eyes. While I am grateful for her bountiful gifts, somehow, in our sparse playroom, they just feel like more stuff, something, I realize, we are happy without.

I borrow a bathroom scale from Dave's house to weigh the luggage filled with winter-wear that I'm sending back with her, trying to figure out how to make it all fit. Refusing my help, my mother insists on playing the weightlifter, heaving bag after bag onto the scale with her, straining to peek around the bulk to see the numbers register. While it's true that I feel like a wrung-out dishrag, she had spent most of the night making trips to the bathroom, plagued by the infamous traveler's diarrhea. Dinesh offers to help, but she stubbornly refuses, acting strangely agitated. Sweating profusely, she works herself into a frenzy and snaps at any suggestion I make to rearrange heavy items and balance the load.

Finally, her mental teapot boils over, "I just don't know how you can stand it! The filth, the noise, the terrible poverty everywhere! How in the world can you enjoy living here? This is the most horrible place I have ever been! I love you, but you're crazy to want to stay in this country. I can't wait to get out of here and never, ever come back!"

And there it is, how she really feels about my daughter's

homeland. She's tried to hide it, keeping up the masquerade with plastered-on Southern charm, when really, all along, she's been horrified and disgusted by our Shangri-La. As she continues to rant, I drift off, *Om Mani Peme Hum*, seeing her anger for what it is: fear. Our brave new world is full of things she has no hope of controlling—illness, poverty, violence—and that lack of control scares the daylights out of her. She's terrified of leaving her little chicks in this Third World nest where she is unable to keep them safe, but what she can't understand is that I *do* feel safe. As uncertain as our future is, I trust that what I'm doing is right and know, deep in my heart, that we will come out the other side intact.

I'm not bothered that my mother doesn't like where we live. Instead, I feel sad for her. She's come all this way and missed the big picture—in the face of unimaginable poverty, Dinesh and his family found a way to share what little they have with us and provide an example of how to find satisfaction in the joy of simply being together. They adopted us with a loyalty I never knew from my groovy grocery store employees, and I'm awed by their strength of spirit. Now, seeing that my mother has missed this piece of the puzzle, the best of all the sights to be seen, I'm broken-hearted. Like the ratty blanket I refused to give up as a child, I love Nepal with all my heart—garbage, street dogs and all. I refuse to allow what I find beautiful to be tainted by her harsh words. She will never see my Nepal, so all that's left to do is to let her go.

When Nora returns from her trek to Everest Base Camp, it seems like years have passed. While drinking in her tales of adventure in the Himals, I have trouble remembering all the stories I saved up to share with her. There is a silent tension between us when it comes to Craig, and my obvious disinterest in his company forces me to break my booga booga pact. So, as we stand in the mob, posing as a line, to renew our visas, I say the words no one wants to hear: "Nora, we need to talk."

"Well, it's about time. What in the world is going on? While I was in Everest, I kept wishing I would come back and everything would be normal again. Please, just tell me."

"That night at Dave's house? I slept with Craig," I stammer, and her face goes blank.

"You mean you had sex with him?" she squeezes out with a faint squeak at the end.

"Um, yeah," I look down, ashamed. The bumping and pushing of the crowd behind us doesn't make this any easier. I glance up to see the tightness around her lips, and realize, although I'd thought about telling her of my indiscretion a zillion times, I had no idea what her response would be. I reach over and lift her fake Dior sunglasses to try and read her expression.

"Well, now it all makes sense," is all she can get out.

"Really, it's fine. I just need a break, being around him is too hard," I try to summarize.

"Well, how did you leave things? I mean, what happened?" She's a flurry of anxious questions, clearly caught between her loyalty to her big brother and sticking up for her girlfriend.

I relay the course of events, from the first drinks to the "talk" a few days later. I babble and ramble, with far too many details (given her pained expression), but I'm a levee breaking.

"I am so sorry he did that to you," she finally says. "Ugh! what pathetic excuses! I wish you hadn't had to carry that alone."

"Well, I did tell Dave," I confess, glancing over to where he is waiting patiently, flipping through an outdated *Stardust* magazine. She looks confused. "I had no choice!" I try to lighten the mood. "Can you imagine me trying to talk to Leena about this?" She chuckles slightly. "Besides, he was there, he already knew what happened." The reality of my indiscretion registers on her face. "I'm so sorry, I just didn't know what to do." I shrink a little more.

Then Nora produces one of her wonderful tidbits of handed-down wisdom, "Well, like my mother always says, a problem shared is a problem halved," She smiles genuinely, then hugs me tight, releasing me from my self-imposed sanction.

"Oh, Nora. What will I do without you?" I choke into her

shoulder. "I didn't want this to be hard on you or uncomfortable with Craig."

"I'm just so pissed! How could he do this? And then say, 'I was so drunk.' What are we, in college or something?" She's visibly agitated.

"Nora, he's just a guy," I state simply, using Dave's line. I don't want her to see how much he hurt me.

"Oh, I'm going to get all kinds of New York on his ass!" she says, and I know she's back. The secret is out, and I am *so* relieved. We hand over our visa forms and passports for the last time together, then gather Dave and walk out into the hazy sunlight to hail a taxi.

April

April crept in quietly, like the Maoists, and then literally overnight, I woke up to a world unlike any in my previous life experience. I came to an odd appreciation for the extra rest brought on by my mystery illness, as if I'd been unconsciously gearing up for what was to come.

With Nora's departure looming, I mold my time to meet her busy schedule and accept an audience whenever she summons me, happy to be her faithful companion for "last" errands: last henna hair treatment, last trip to Thamel, last lunches at our favorite cafés. Discussion of my fall from grace with Craig remains off limits, like a contentious political topic. We have an unspoken agreement to let the conversation end where it began, in the visa office. After sharing nearly every thought and experience of our time together in Nepal, Craig becomes an uncomfortable silence that follows us everywhere like the stink of hidden trash heaps, out of sight but not out of mind. Fearing an uncomfortable conversation, I decide to bring Jack along for our last lunch at Erza Café, knowing Nora won't breathe a word of what had happened with Craig if Jack is at the table.

As Jack drops my hand to trot down a quiet section of the lane, I think back to when this same spot was scary and new. Knowing our time here is finite, just as that of our friends, makes my heart heavy. Tilting my head skyward, I drink in the perfume of jasmine blossoms overflowing the brick walls surrounding one compound after another. I can't imagine a more beautiful place, street dogs, garbage, goat droppings, and all. I'm sick at the thought of leaving Nepal and mentally touch the heartbreak to come.

Striding up the steps, I spot Nora through the front window of the café flipping through a Hindi fashion magazine, sunglasses perched atop her head. I take a deep breath and give thanks for whatever divine intervention brought us together, then vow to get through lunch without crying or begging her to stay. I'm terrified to be in this world without her and selfishly want her to hold my hand to the end. Realistically, with political tensions on the rise once again, I know she has to leave while she still can. Tessa will be returning, but it's unclear when. Food and petrol shortages are sending expats fleeing like rats from a sinking ship, and as much as she is ready to return and continue her various projects, uncertainty in the Valley is giving her reason for pause. Jonathan, too, is away on holiday in Thailand, and with revolution in the air, the terms of his contract with the British School are tenuous. Janelle has already left for the States, the final steps of her adoption finally complete just in time to escape the renewed political drama. And then there's Dave, perpetually stranded, caught in his own *Twilight Zone*. It feels as if all the players in my life are moving around like pieces in a game of chess, and I'm fearful of being the last one left on the board.

Nora is thrilled to see Jack, and any worry that our final lunch might be awkward evaporates like water sprayed on the dusty city streets. We laugh and reminisce, thinking of all the things Nora will do when she gets home: a hot shower and being able to let the water splash in her mouth, sleeping on an actual mattress, eating out anywhere without fear of gastric distress, doing laundry in a washing machine—all things I realize I'm more than willing to give up to stay on in the Kingdom indefinitely.

After lunch, the street is crowded with honking taxis and bleating goats; since we decide this is a terrible place to say goodbye, we stroll over to Summit. Jack continues home to check on Devi, leaving Nora and me to have some alone time. As we watch him skip down the drive, I notice Nora has tears in her eyes.

"I'm really going to miss you guys, you know that?" she whispers, wiping away tears with pretty pink fingernails, a memento of another "last," our trip to the House of Beauty.

"Well, we were really getting bored with you, so it's best you're on your way," I joke, trying to lighten the mood.

We giggle through our last pot of lemongrass tea, and then before I know it, the moment I've been dreading has come; it's really time for her to go. We hug each other like passengers in a lifeboat watching the Titanic go down, and I can't hold back any longer.

"Oh, Nora. What am I going to do without you?"

"You're going to play in the garden with your children and love Devi even when she's screaming in the night. You're going to eat the wonderful food our beloved Dinesh *Dai* makes and you're going to learn more Nepali from Leena, even if it isn't the language of Devi's village. You're going to email me every day, so I know you're okay. You'll make sure Dave doesn't go crazy waiting, and most of all, you're going keep your chin up. You can do this, I know you can," she instructs. "Even if I'm not here, you have to know, I'm always with you. I'm your biggest fan!" she says as tears stream down her cheeks.

All I can do is nod; the boulder-sized lump in my throat blocks all the last words I want to say, except the most important ones, "I love you, Nora. I never would have made it this far without you."

"Of course you would have, but it wouldn't have been nearly as fabulous," she teases. With love in her eyes, she backs away, slowly turning from me. She saunters down the drive, looking back over her shoulder with one last wave as she flashes her glamorous smile.

The Warden's Security Message is in my email again, but I hardly notice it, feeling like I can recite it word-for-word by now. A few details have changed, but the spirit of the letter remains the same: tensions are rising, keep a low profile, stay home. In spite of the *bandh*, Nora had been whisked away in an army truck early in the morning via a favor Craig called in from a friend whose father was a Royal Nepalese Army general.

I'd told her repeatedly that she would be much safer in a private vehicle marked TOURIST ONLY, but like a moth to the flame, Nora relished the dramatic departure. A generic group email from Craig reassured me that she made it to the airport and safely onto her plane, and that was all that mattered.

The word on the street is that things are about to get much worse. Maoists have come into the Valley in large numbers, bringing less-than-willing villagers with them for a push toward toppling the King for a chance at democracy. There is nothing to do but wait, watch, and pray.

While the political tension intensifies, I'm able to remain reasonably calm. After the multiple *bandh*s since our arrival, I question if this latest round of demonstrations will go anywhere. We're now on day three, and the streets are filled with political demonstrations and protests, along with a curfew imposed by the King and enforced by the Royal Nepalese Army.

Sitting in the middle of my bed gazing out to where the Himals, clouded by hazy pollution, should be, I try to relax. Before Janelle left for the states she taught me to knit and gave me her needles as well as a new hobby, and a break from my paperback novel marathon. I practice staying present as the needles click, but my mind wanders; I lose count of where I am, and I'm not experienced enough to know how to pick up or drop the necessary stitch to continue. I don't want to guess how many times my labor of love has been unraveled to nothing but a confused pile of yarn, so representative of my life right now, waiting for me to try, try again. If only it were this easy with Devi. I wish I could simply unravel her past and start over.

From the café behind us I hear Bob Marley wailing, "This morning, I woke up, in a curfew. Oh God, I was a prisoner too . . ." A chill comes over me, and I realize the lyrics I'd heard so many times before now mean something wholly different. The song, like so many other things taken for granted, will never be the same for me again. I wonder, how many other things from this time will haunt me, changing shape in my mind forever?

As evening falls, I step out to the terrace, anxious to know what is happening in the city around us. The phone lines have been cut for most of the day and into the night, so I'm completely disconnected. I've grown dependent on Dave as my main source of news since his host's daughter is married to a US Embassy security officer and is always in the know. The distant drumbeat of protests and black smoke signals from burning tires point to the activity beyond our compound walls. I repress the manic impulse to try to connect to email one more time to see if there is a message from the Embassy, but know the lines are still cut, and I work to convince myself that reality can wait for one more day.

I put the kids to bed and turn on the television, settling in to unwind for an evening of recycled American sitcoms. Quickly bored by the same episode of *Friends* I've seen a half dozen times since arriving in Nepal, I channel surf, pleasantly surprised to find the *BBC World News*. The images are typical; crowds shouting, scuffles and conflict, police arresting protestors in some small country somewhere. Then reality smacks me in the face—the report is coming from Kathmandu! Until this moment, I've remained somewhat aloof, shrugging off the violence I know is happening. So far, the conflict that has been ongoing for ten years has been without result. Now my walls of denial are crumbling like the mortar between the bricks surrounding me.

Heart racing, I furiously click through the channels, searching for a local news station. Garbled Nepali voices and a poor quality feed show horrific images of protestors being beaten and dragged away, a young girl sobbing and clinging to her mother, shots fired indiscriminately into a crowd, men with blood-soaked bandages around their heads, eyes gouged, hospitals overrun with victims of what is being termed *Janaandolan*, "The People's Movement." The hair stands up on the back of my neck, and I feel sick as I listen intently, desperate to decode the language describing what I'm seeing. The same disturbing images play again and again, and I begin to recognize neighborhoods, shuttered storefronts, the ever-present Ganesh watching from the background. Numb, I turn off the TV and walk out to the terrace to look down on the now dark and silent city, a surreal world evolving rapidly around me.

In the morning, I skim an email from the Embassy, announcing a town hall meeting for US citizens to be held at the Ambassador's residence. Before the phone lines are cut again, I call Dave. Although he is staying home with Arun, the others from his household have offered to pick me up on their way. I'm thankful for this life buoy to grasp in the churning sea of political instability. I put down the receiver and notice my hand is shaking. *Deep breaths*, I coach myself. *Om mani peme hum*.

As we speed through the city, I'm stunned by the signs of recent violence. Army troops are everywhere, and gun turrets have been erected where days ago there were street vendors. Burned out cars, piles of bricks, and remnants of tires litter the street. Clearly, this is not the same Nepal it was a week ago; it has become a war zone. We pull up outside the Ambassador's lavish mansion surrounded by extensive gardens and show our US-issued badges at the gate.

Inside the grounds, white chairs parade along the greener-than-green lawn awaiting our arrival, making it feel more like a wedding reception than a get-out-of-town hall meeting. I recognize some of my fellow expats standing in cliquish clumps chatting, all eager to hear what our mighty leader has to report. Finally, a patio door opens, and as the Ambassador emerges, I peek inside at what looks like an elaborate buffet, renewing the feeling of being invited to a perverse celebration. The Ambassador takes the microphone and briefs us on what we already know, but in terms that make it more real—words like, "political stalemate," "urban civil war," "total system collapse," and, finally, "evacuation." I get dizzy as the words swim through my brain and I squeeze my eyes tight to stop the tears. As I try to breathe, I wish this man would stop saying all the things I don't want to hear and magically turn into the Justice of the Peace in my fantasy wedding from a parallel universe. Distressed questions from the shocked group are followed by more disturbing information.

"All US citizens are encouraged to leave the country immediately. Failure to follow this directive may result in an inability for evacuation by US personnel if circumstances continue to deteriorate."

Once the talking points are thoroughly exhausted, my fellow expats pour out of the compound, anxious to get home before the demonstrations start and the curfew begins.

"Go ahead without me," I tell my ride. "I need to stop by Saleways and pick up a few things." They look at me crosswise, but simply caution me to be safe and hurry on their way.

Screwing up my courage, I approach the Ambassador before he can retreat into his safe house.

"Excuse me, Mr. Ambassador, I'm Kate Saunders," I offer, struggling to control my voice. "I'm here adopting my daughter, but our process isn't complete yet. I'm not sure what to do."

"Well, Ms. Saunders, as I stated, you need to return to the States as soon as possible and wait for your adoption to finalize, then come back once the political climate has become more stable. It may be quite some time before the Ministry is functional again, so waiting here until that time may become increasingly dangerous."

Fearing I will be offering too much information to definitely the wrong person, I try to be brief, but feel increasingly desperate, and crack under the pressure of his repeated party line. I fish a picture out of my bag of Jack and Devi laughing together.

"Well, you see sir, she's been living with us since September. What am I supposed to do? Drop her off at the orphanage on my way to the airport?"

Seeing the shock on his face, I know I've spilled every bean, let every cat out of any bag, shown every one of my cards. I've blown it for sure. He looks long at the picture, then takes me gently by the arm, and turns me away from the crowd, leaning in close, speaking quietly so no one else can hear.

"Absolutely not," he says, holding my gaze. "If Nepal is burning, we will get you out. Just get yourself and your kids to the airport, and we'll break out the visa machine. Make sure all your documents are in order—anything you can get your hands on to prove she's an orphan." Then, snapping back into character, he steps back while shaking my hand and says loudly enough for those nearby to hear, "So nice to meet you, Ms. Saunders. You take care." He is swarmed by his entourage and whisked from the now empty garden.

I am dumbfounded. This *really* is my life. And it is time to prepare for revolution.

I scamper across the street, away from the compound, as the crowds begin to build and soldiers fill the intersection above. Fearful of being caught in the crossfire as the official US vehicles emerge from their lair, I jump into a nearby taxi.

"Summit Hotel?" I request, ready to be home.

"No," the driver says flatly.

"No?!"

"No."

Now what? Defeated, I crawl out and huddle behind a tree to take stock of my situation. I dash across another street, away from the growing crowd, and hail a second taxi. Thankfully, rupees talk, and this driver is willing to speed away across the river, back to my neighborhood. I lean my head back on the seat and take a deep breath as we cross to the other side of Ratna Park, away from the raucous demonstrations. It's surreal watching the scenes buzz by in a blur: protestors, police, smoke, shouting. What would I give for a pair of ruby slippers. *There's no place like home, there's no place like home.* But right now, this *is* home.

In my best Nepali, I ask the driver to pretty please stop at Saleways. I know I should be content with the supplies we already have, but deep inside I feel I need something else, something intangible I'm frantically grasping for to make me feel safe. The only thing I can come up with is stockpiling more cereal. The driver sees the fear in my eyes as we dodge the crowds in front of the Nepal Bar Association and kindly complies.

"Yes, Madam, please hurry," he says as he pulls to the back door, out of sight of the crowds. The curfew is now in effect.

I'm shocked by how bare the shelves are; the staples I'm most in need of, like flour, sugar, and salt, are already long gone. I gather the few things left that make sense: cans of tuna, crackers, juice, cereal, and one of the few remaining bottles of Teacher's Scotch Whiskey. I hear Dave's voice in my head, "trust the Teacher" and smile for a moment. I dash for the checkout where they actually almost hurry to get me out the door. Back in the taxi, we are the only car on the road as we speed through the neighborhood. I've never seen the streets so empty—it's creepy. All the shops are shuttered with steel garage doors that display advertisements for paint, motorcycles, and Gem plasticware. The men playing card games on the corner are absent. I spot a little boy splashing through puddles, oblivious to the tension surrounding him. Turning off the main road and up our little lane, we scoot into the alley and out of sight. I hand the driver a wad of rupees, tipping him handsomely for his bravery, and quickly gather my bags. The ever-present gate guard ushers me in, looking both ways as I enter, cautious of the soldiers who are more often than not stationed only a few feet away. I scale the steps, which feel exponentially steeper today.

Leena sees me enter with the bags and holds back laughter as she unpacks boxes of cereal. "Jack, lots of cereal," I sigh.

She reassures me with laughter as light as her chiffon sari, "Yes Madam, Jackie like cereal."

"Much trouble, war in Nepal. Jack has cereal," I confess, knowing she can see the strain on my face. I trust she can identify with my longing to keep my children safe and fed, or maybe she's just used to the crazy American woman who can't get enough cereal.

```
Dear Friends and Family,
    First, I apologize for the group email.
In the interest of time, and imminent power
```

outages, a group email is a must, so everyone knows we are okay, although the country seems to be falling apart around us. We have been advised by the Embassy to make clear that any information shared is NOT FOR DISTRIBUTION TO THE MEDIA; this email is for private use only. For security reasons, please respect this request.

   We live in a relatively safe area, surrounded by NGOs and close to the UN headquarters, so lots of armed soldiers line the streets and there are several tanks around, I try to convince myself that their presence is keeping us safer. The stillness of the city is amazing, void of the usual unconsciously comforting sounds of taxis honking, vendors calling out their wares, people chatting in the markets, now all replaced by distant yelling of protestors, military helicopters and sirens. Even the street dogs seem to have taken the hint and are lying especially low. From our terrace I have a bird's eye view of the Valley and spot clouds of black smoke rising from burning tires, hints at where the heaviest activity is throughout the city.

   The days are all running together as the curfews continue. Is it day five now, or day six? I've lost count. We're thankful for what Jack calls the "secret passage" behind our house, the steep stone steps we climb to the back of the compound. At the top, I'm careful not to get caught up in the rusting barbed wire softened by the morning glories haphazardly twining around it, creating subtle beauty interwoven with a clear sign of danger. I gaze across the Valley toward Swayambhu, its golden spire twisting skyward, twinkling in the sunshine, with bands of colorful flags fluttering prayers on a whisper of spring breeze. Passing our landlord's house, I pause at the tall metal gate and listen carefully before peeking through to survey the street. Seeing most of the troops stationed at the bottom of the hill, I give Jack the "all clear" signal and he scampers up from his hiding place behind the goat shed to join me as we escape our little world inside the high compound walls. We hippity-hop across the lane playfully, holding hands, and trot down the drive to Summit, our oasis in this political powder keg. Breathing the intoxicating olfactory cocktail of jasmine, rose and iris in the extensive gardens, it's hard to remember where I am. The shuttle buses with FOREIGN TOURIST ONLY and BBC PRESS, simple paper tools to prevent a hailstorm of bricks from protestors, remind me. All around us is violence I have only ever seen on news clips. I am acutely aware that I have never been so close to anything like this, and now, it's just down the lane.

   We order fresh lemon soda and a banana split to share, and Jack jumps in the pool. He's shocked by the chill, but thrilled for the freedom, bobbing along, floating on his back, Batman mask in place, flippers flopping. I marvel at his seven-year-old bliss, unaware of the chaos surrounding us. My mind returns like a broken record to the startling images I've seen not only on the BBC, but local stations as well: police charging demonstrators with sticks and clubs, students at the teaching hospital walking out and joining the protest, Nepal Rastra Bank employees abandoning their posts forcing closure, protesting foreigners hauled off and jailed, artists reading poetry in a peaceful demonstration beaten and carried away, children dancing around the waves of protestors, as if this is just another festival. I've seen so many images like this on television, but now I recognize where it is happening, just down the road and across the bridge.

Am I afraid for our safety? Not really. I am scared, but not for myself or my children. I fear for all those who want "democracy" so much they are willing to give up their livelihoods, their businesses, their very lives. I respect the Nepali people beyond words. I get dizzy at the thought of what it takes to beat someone with a club, what that anger is that lies inside, sickeningly disturbed by what humans are capable of.

Civil servants are required to show up for work, in spite of the curfews. However, if they do go out, they are in danger of being shot on sight for failing to comply with this same curfew. If they're lucky, they will just be attacked and beaten for violating the Maoist-called strike. Nepal is at the top of the list for state sanctioned abuse and torture of civilians, holding a similar ranking for "disappearances." Additionally, it leads in the number of children injured or killed by explosive devices, most likely due to the number of child soldiers forcibly recruited by the Maoists, each family required to offer up one of their own. Twenty-five journalists have been jailed. Over 2000 people have been arrested for peacefully demonstrating just in the last week. Hundreds have been severely injured. The number of dead is unknown, due to reports stating that, after firing into a crowd, the Royal Nepalese Army quickly whisked away the bodies to prevent the number of casualties from being discovered.

There is uncertainty about what will happen next. It's clear that the situation is rapidly deteriorating, the entire system tottering toward collapse. Friday marks the Nepali New Year, and the King will be speaking, as per tradition. Much is riding on what he will say, and what posture he takes. The cast of characters involved includes

```
the King, the Seven Party Alliance, and
the Maoists, each with their own agenda,
so making any sort of prediction as to the
eventual outcome is impossible. The players
are too volatile.
    Don't pray for me, I have already been
blessed in this life beyond measure. Pray
for patience at the hands of those holding
the firearms. Pray for the Nepali people, who
don't have a tiny fraction of what we were
simply born into. But most importantly, give
thanks for what you have: clean water to
drink, electricity when you flip the switch,
24-hour grocery stores, a street without
tanks or soldiers with guns. Give thanks for
spring, and the flowers and the birds and
the butterflies. In your mind, see us out on
the terrace, kids riding bikes, cat sleeping
in the sunshine, and the Himals in the
background. Really, the weather is lovely.
    Love, Peace and Namasté,
    Kate
```

THUMP! My eyes pop open, startled awake by a bump in the night. Once I get my bearings, I remember, there's good reason to be afraid. I drift back to my dream, convincing myself all is well, and then *BANG!* There it is again. I slide out of bed and tiptoe past my sleeping children to reach for the door. I worry about the security of my laptop link to the outside world, then hesitate as gruesome flashes from the evening news burn in my brain. Suddenly, I'm not feeling so brave. *THUMP!* Sounds come from the kitchen door. I creep out to the terrace and look outside; nothing but quiet and moonlight. Trying to talk myself down, I trust our street dogs will alert me to any intruder, like the night not so long ago when I awoke to the sounds of people moving in the alley outside the bottom gate and peeked out to see their armed silhouettes, a clear sign that the Maoists were, in fact, infiltrating the Valley. The sight had sent me scrambling back to bed. Now, peering over the rail, I see little Kali, looking up at me loyally, ears tipped back as if she were leaning out the window of a moving vehicle. Stealthily, I move around the perimeter of my terrace tower. I hear a quiet whistle, not like someone whistling for a dog, something my Nepali neighbors laugh at me for doing, but this is a low, quiet, signal of a whistle, followed by rustling in the field behind the compound wall. Bewildered not only by where on the globe I'm standing, but what is happening around me, it's comforting to see Swayambhu in the distance, glittering like a Christmas tree ornament. I hop up onto the roof to look around the back of the compound from a theoretically safe distance. I glance around, still unable to detect anything, when suddenly, I see shadows moving in the garden behind the café. I duck behind the water tower and beg my heart not to beat so loudly, certain the bad guys can hear it. Screwing up my courage, I peek around again to see them. A couple of stick figure men with rags for clothes quietly, but determinedly, are pulling at vegetables and placing them in a burlap sack, and I understand. My "valuables" are nothing to them, what they need is *food*. I feel like a voyeur, observing yet another side of the human tragedy, and I almost wish I had left the kitchen door unlocked.

I slink back down the roof and slide into the bedroom. I glance at the clock, 3:51 AM. At least it's almost morning. Climbing into bed, it feels softer than ever and I wrap my blankets around me, like a velvet pouch protecting delicate jewelry. I feel blessed by all I have, and drift back to dreams of revolution.

The days slide together like gravy in mashed potatoes, something I was never fond of. Stories of the *Janaandolan* flood in: banks shutting down, fuel shortages, skyrocketing food costs. Rumors of dwindling supplies have become reality with the Maoist blockade of all the roads entering the Valley; trucks are lined up, but unable to deliver. Even life in the ivory tower is affected; the menu at Summit is now printed on a small chalkboard, based on what is still available. No lemon soda, no lemons. No *lassi*, no yogurt. No banana split, no bananas.

While the phone lines are up briefly, I call my mother to check in. She's surprisingly upbeat, my first signal that all is not well. I ask about Mimi, her work, her brothers, but her answers are short, quickly deteriorating to snappy, and I realize she's just trying to keep it together. Her best defense, denial, has her in a stranglehold. I quickly shift the conversation to funny stories about Jack and Devi, skipping over any information as to the reality of our situation, knowing it's more than she can handle. She is powerless against the truth of our world.

"I'll call again as soon as I can," I promise. "Don't let Mimi watch CNN." I hope she will take the hint as well.

Next, I check in with Dinesh. It's strange not seeing Leena and him since they are unable to venture to our house due to the curfews. He asks about our dwindling supply of propane, and I remind him of all the cereal, which elicits a chuckle, and we hesitantly say goodbye. I know he will do anything for us, so try not to let on how desperate I feel. I could never forgive myself if anything happened to him on the way to our place.

I try to watch *Seinfeld*, my latest cornerstone of normalcy, but just as George and Elaine are sitting down with the psychic, the signal goes bad, and I am left with a snowy news report from India. The ticker is flowing both ways, one left to right in English, the other right to left in Hindi. I flip channels past Bollywood and Hindi soap operas, and Jack wails from the kitchen table, forever marooned on Homework Island, "I can hear you watching TV up there!" I give up and debate whether it's too early to start drinking.

Lacking the will to ration my secret box of After Eight dinner mints any longer, I sneak up to Jack's favorite hideout on the roof to finish off the box and bypass the depression of watching them dwindle. Savoring them for as long as I can, toward the end, in the bottom of the box, I notice subtle movement of ants. Why hadn't the freeloading gecko that lives in the cabinet taken care of them? I wonder how many I have inadvertently eaten, then look out to the fluttering prayer flags of Swayambhu and wish them many happy rebirths.

I hear Sarresh, in his singsong whiney English, clearly learned from a cartoon, nagging the Swedish man on the terrace of the house behind us.

"Loook, I'm juuuumping! Loook! Loooook! I'm juuuuumping now!" Sarresh prods incessantly.

Finally, the man succumbs to the torment, snapping, "I don't really care to see you jumping."

Another adult's patience has worn thin, and I consider asking him to join me for a cocktail.

Day fourteen comes with rumors of growing protests that heat up an already volatile climate. The brief break in *bandh*s and curfews is a chance to get errands done since Leena is able to mind the children, and it's questionable when we'll be permitted to move freely about the city again. Dave calls; he needs to pick up paperwork to complete his appeal, and we both are due to renew our visas for the month of May, so we plan for him to stop by on the way into the city. I make a quick call to Rajkumar, still hoping I might collect documentation proving Devi's orphan status in the event of an evacuation. The sporadic phone service has made it difficult to get through to the orphanage, so I'm overjoyed when someone answers.

"Hello, Kate!" Rajkumar answers, surprisingly cheerful.

"*Namasté!* Is it possible I can come by and pick up those documents?"

"Ahh, yes. Can you come to the office tomorrow?"

"Well, I've heard there are to be more demonstrations tomorrow and . . ."

He cuts me off. "Can you come over now, then?"

"Yes, of course," I stammer, amazed by my stroke of luck. I gather up my rain jacket, umbrella, and a book, then triple check my mental to-do list: passports, paperwork, money, passport photos. Ugh! One more very necessary stop to add to the list.

I glance out the window to see Dave turning in, so dash out the door, pull up the hood of my jacket, and splash down the alley to the taxi.

"I'm sorry, Dave, I'm disorganized. I need to pick up documents at the orphanage, and I just remembered I'm out of passport photos. Maybe you should go on without me?"

Dave sighs and chuckles, "Well, you're not the only one. Thanks for reminding me, I need photos, too. No big deal, hop in."

We arrive at the orphanage just as Rajkumar is climbing on his motorbike to zoom out; he tells me through a muffled helmet that Amita has my documents ready and waiting. I thank him, bowing humbly, *namasté*, and jog up the steps where Amita hands me the papers right away. I'm convinced this is the fastest transaction in Nepali history.

When our two-minute photos take far more than two minutes, Dave gets nervous that our taxi is about to abandon us and stands guard having a smoke. Soon enough, the photo man presents me with a sheet of pictures, a row of four shots of each of us. As he slow-motion slices us apart, I toss him some rupees, and we are on our way again through the colossally congested streets to the visa office.

We step inside to a chaotically packed lobby, surrounded by a United Nations of fellow expats: a Chinese lady in worn sneakers and a silk dress, a noble monk sporting a fake Rolex, an anxious Indian woman chewing her blood red nails. I find an empty space at the counter and pull out my completed forms, much to Dave's amazement, especially after our stutter start. I reach across the counter for the stapler, affixing my photo to my form, and Jack's to his. A familiar clerk approaches to take my papers, then states sternly, "I must see your plane ticket."

Plane ticket? What? This has never been part of the drill in the past. "Excuse me?" I ask politely.

"Plane ticket," he repeats, obviously irritated. Then begins to mutter, then yell, alternating between Nepali and English, "Proof when you leave Nepal! Where plane ticket?!"

"Yes, I understand. But I have until the end of June. I cannot leave until I complete my adoption," I continue calmly, sure this is just a misunderstanding.

"No visa until you show plane ticket," he grumbles.

Suddenly, the spirit of New York Nora flows through me and I stand my ground. "Look, there are a lot of troubles in Nepal right now, so I WILL NOT confirm a plane ticket until my adoption paperwork is complete!" I rant, raising my voice, feeling the room start to spin.

The clerk glares at me, then submits, turning my paper over and pushing it across the counter. "You write statement that you leave Nepal by end of June."

Knowing I have won the battle, I gladly comply, as I notice, out of the corner of my eye, Dave subtly shifting away from me in hopes of not being associated with the Ugly American. I return the paper and move to the line for payment and take Dave's hint, ignoring him until he is through the paperwork gatekeeper.

With the hardest part over, we walk to the Women and Children Services office for Dave to acquire the next set of documents for his appeal. I tamp down the impulse to tease him and ask if they are real, not wanting rock his fragile boat. After waiting in the dismal office for a painful stretch of time, I pass Dave a note saying, "I need to go potty," which earns me a smile and a nod as he waits at silent attention for the man in the next room to address him. I step outside and locate the prominent Men's room, then search around and behind the building to see the decrepit door for the Ladies. I hesitantly step inside to find the toilet seat splashed with dirty water, obviously coming from the hole in the roof above. Not wanting to chance where the next pit stop might be, I turn to lock the door, only to discover it has no lock, not even a latch. Feeling exhausted, I shift my mindset and accept it for what it is, then put up my umbrella to shield me from the indoor rain and hover above the seat. In the midst of revolution, this was no time to be picky.

Eventually, Dave is granted an audience and emerges with the necessary documents to send to Delhi, further proving Arun to be a legitimate orphan. With errands complete, and no taxi in sight, we walk further into the city hoping to find somewhere open for lunch. It's surprising to see so many people milling about in polite afternoon picnics. Men huddle in familiar circles, playing cards and smoking stubby hand-rolled cigarettes, children engage in a Third-World version of King of the Hill on an abandoned oil drum, goats on tiptoe stretch to nibble tender leaves from the canopy of trees above, and female soldiers eat quietly with their children. It's all surreal, for everyone living life normally and staying present in the face of what is sure to erupt. One restaurant after another is closed, so we decide to head back to our side of town. We appreciate the freedom and enjoy walking rather than feeling inconvenienced. Then we hear shouts of protest in the distance. As we approach Narayanhiti Palace, the King's residence, we see a group of RNA soldiers clutching outdated firearms. We keep our distance, skirting the crowd that's growing in number and intensity, as we continue in the direction of the demonstration, unable to deny our curiosity. Dave snaps pictures furiously, but all I can do is watch. It's a party atmosphere, but the subject is deadly serious as the crowd chants in Nepali, "Time to bury the King!" RNA soldiers stand by, prepared to defend the Monarch inside, itchy trigger fingers at the ready. The excitement is palpable, and it's hard to keep walking; the impulse to stay and watch is contagious. As we approach the epicenter, the focus of attention comes into view, a statue of the King draped in red, a clear sign that his reign could soon come to a gruesome end.

Aware of how quickly peaceful demonstrations turn violent, we pull ourselves away and continue toward the bridge to our side of the river as the chanting voices fade behind us. We catch sight of a taxi willing to stop, safely away from the threat of angry protestors, and gladly rest after hours of traveling on foot.

Sad for our day of freedom and companionship to end, Dave pledges to keep me informed of any news from his Embassy source, and I, in turn, promise not to go any farther than Summit. We say our goodbyes, wish each other luck, and share in the discomfort of uncertainty.

Demonstrations ramp up with reports of hundreds of thousands of protestors defying the curfew and taking to the streets as the *Janaandolan* enters its sixteenth day. The dichotomy is striking. Jack and Devi ride their trikes on the terrace, and in the distance, streams of black smoke rise throughout the city while helicopters circle and distant shots ring out. Occasionally, military trucks rumble down our lane with loudspeakers blaring warnings of the mandatory curfew, demanding we stay indoors. It is an epic challenge to remain cool, and I can only hope intuitive Jack won't catch on to my fear. We only have a few days of propane left, so we lounge on the sunny terrace, picnicking on tuna, cheese, and crackers. We play countless games of UNO; Devi prefers to hide the cards in her dress, only to be amazed when her plot is foiled the moment she stands up and they all flutter to the ground like colorful cardboard butterflies. We read every book we own at least three times. We express our artistic sides in Ganesh coloring books and play pat-a-cake until my hands are sore from Devi's forceful slaps. By the end of the day, I'm exhausted, and with phone and power lines cut, I'm desperate for some news about what is happening around us.

Once Devi is off to sleep, and Jack is engrossed in *Tin Tin* comics, I ask the gate guard to keep an eye on the kids, then steal up the back steps and across the lane to Summit. I feel like a local defying the curfew, even though I'm just dashing across the lane in the dark. It's surprising to find the lounge buzzing with expats and journalists from the BBC and CNN. Finding friendly acquaintances, I settle down for a drink and listen to the chatter. Hard facts are difficult to come by since the news organizations have been denied curfew passes, so inside whispers have to suffice.

"I heard the King called back some of the political leaders who were in exile in India, then the moment they got off the plane to join in the supposed 'talks' they were arrested and taken away, who knows when we'll hear from them again . . ."

"Well, now that all the bankers have joined in, good luck getting any rupees to buy your way out. I heard the protestors are destroying the banks . . ."

"The human rights abuses are what trouble me. The UN High Commissioner was denied a curfew pass, so now they aren't even able to monitor the situation . . ."

"I heard the RNA opened fire on another group of protestors today when they tried to move toward the Royal Palace . . ."

"Did you hear about the young boy who was shot by the Maoists? He wanted to go back to check on his family, but they treated him as a deserter and fired on him as he tried to cross the river..."

"Too bad the Royal Brat isn't of any use, he's worse than the King! Starting bar fights with celebrities and thrashing his own best friend in that motorcycle wreck? At least the people seem to know he's worthless..."

"I'm worried about how this is starting to ripple into the rest of the region. Pakistan is getting nervous about India building up troops along the border to control Maoist activity..."

"Even when the markets are open, my staff can't afford to buy anything that's left, with inflation in double digits. I gave them a little extra this week, I can't stand the thought of their children going hungry..."

"I heard the Maoists are calling for the King's execution!"

"Time is definitely running out for the King. He needs to stop thinking about saving face and give the people what they want. He's deliberately delaying steps to resolve this crisis and the people know it. He's just making it worse for all of us thinking the people will still accept him as anything but a ceremonial figure. There's no way he'll retain any power when all this is over, he'll be lucky to stay in the Royal Palace and out of exile...."

Suddenly, I just want to be home, holding my kids tight and praying for all of this to be over. Having the paperwork on hand to prove Devi's orphan status is of little comfort once I realize we would have to get to the airport on foot, several miles through some of the most volatile areas of the city. Now, escape seems impossible. I thought the wait to file our paperwork at the CDO had been a challenge—I had no idea what might be ahead.

I quietly excuse myself from the escalating gossip session and walk down the Summit drive, ducking in the doorway of a shuttered tea stall as heat lightning slashes through the night sky. I quiet my mind, *Om Mani Peme Hum*, and take a deep breath to settle my nerves. I wait as the headlights of Army trucks filled with patrolling soldiers fade before cautiously sneaking across the road, only to find the landlord has bolted the gate, unintentionally preventing my re-entry. Hesitantly, I creep around the corner to look down the lane where I see a group of armed soldiers below. It is impossible to reach the bottom gate without being seen. Then, I hear the rumbling of oncoming trucks and know I don't have time to get back across the lane to the safety of Summit. I start to panic and scramble up the wall, my rock-climbing skills still intact as I wedge my fingers and sticky rubber sandals between the crumbling joints between the bricks. Frantically fighting my way up the compound wall, I traverse to the gate and swing over, hearing my skirt rip on the rusty barbed wire as I crash to the ground. It's a small price to pay to be back on the right side of the compound. The earth shudders as the truck lumbers by, its dusty draft billowing under the metal gate.

"Pick yourself up, dust yourself off, and start all over again..." a strangely cheery voice sing-songs in my head as I lay in the dirt shaking with fear. Then I look over to see Good Dog watching sleepily from the porch, hardly bothered by my nontraditional entrance. I tiptoe down the steps, counting them in the absence of a light, then feel the flatness of concrete at the bottom, and move through Jack's secret passage behind the house to slip in the kitchen door.

Jack is upstairs in front of the TV, watching *Johnny Quest* in Hindi. He barely notices me or my torn skirt as I catch a glimpse of the stream of blood running down my leg, an unconscious injury from the barbed wire. I feel as if I've been initiated into the People's Movement with the spilling of my own blood, as thunder in the distance warns of the coming storm.

Demonstrations continue the next day, despite the King's attempt at compromise by requesting the Seven Party Alliance nominate a candidate for Prime Minister, something he'd refused only a week ago. His ongoing missteps ignite the crowds, now chanting, "Not enough, not enough," and demanding deeper change after his insulting New Year's speech. He's offered no condolences for the countless demonstrators injured and killed;

instead, he praises his security forces for their restraint and a job well done. Clearly, he's lost touch with his constituency, failing to heed the suggestions of a special envoy sent from India to try to talk some sense into him, despite their familial ties. Even private audiences with Ambassadors from India, the US, and China are unable to produce a reasonable response. Protestors vow to march to the center of the capital and break through the security forces, right to the door of the Palace. My head spins thinking that Dave and I were there just days before; it feels like we've spent weeks behind our compound walls.

Before the daily curfew sets in, I take the kids to Summit to stretch their legs. The gardens become their jungle as they hide behind rocks and leap from bushes. Jack is a tiger, and Devi, his dedicated disciple, mimics everything he does. I chat with one of the hotel owners about how we feel cast in an Asian version of *Hotel Rwanda*, and wonder if we will end up drinking the pool water. We take advantage of Summit's propane and have lunch from the meager menu. When the helicopters begin to circle, it's the cue to go home. We take our places on the terrace to watch the show unfold once again. I feel disgusted by my role in all of this, on our white ringed terrace, more and more the ivory tower. Just down the road and across the bridge, the Nepali people are desperate for change. They are willing to risk their lives for democracy and the right to a representative government, something I was born into and have taken for granted. I have always voted, years of activism through Amnesty International made me profoundly aware of all those without that fundamental right. Unfortunately, I often bitterly saw my vote as a choice between the lesser of two evils, never having experienced just how evil the absence of democracy could be.

In the afternoon, Annie calls, much to my surprise (first, that the phone rang; second, that it was her). "I just heard the State Department has upgraded the current evacuation status from 'voluntary' to 'ordered.' Are you planning to leave?" she asks.

"Not yet. I can't leave Devi," I say somberly. "I'm set to wait it out and see what happens next."

"Well, if you decide to go, she can come back here with us. I won't leave the babies."

"Thanks for the offer, I'll be in touch."

Taking advantage of the working phone lines I call my mother, and give her as positive an update as I can manage, omitting as many details as possible without sounding secretive. I repeatedly call Deveshi Shrestha, the Minister of Women, Children and Social Welfare, in the unrealistic hope she will offer an impossible favor; namely, pushing my file through so we can get out of here. We'd met early in my stay, but her schedule was so demanding, we hadn't kept in touch. The phone rings endlessly, and I wonder if she has joined the demonstrations, given her past in political activism, or, more likely, if she has been jailed. Next, I send an email to the adoption agency in San Francisco, letting them know that while Annie has made me aware of the ordered departure, I have resolved to stay on, sticking with my promise to my little girl.

When I call Dave to check in, he's buzzing with excitement.

"I can see the Ring Road from here; it's filled with demonstrators who've been pouring in from outside the Valley all day! They're marching and chanting, no doubt intent on making their way to the palace. And get this, the soldiers are *standing down!* They're totally outnumbered in the face of the hundreds of thousands of protestors." He's breathless with all he has to report, it's nothing short of amazing. "There are so many people, I can't see the beginning or the end of the line of protestors."

"Wow, this is really happening."

"Yeah, it's really happening, and we're here to witness it."

"Well, thanks for the report. Stay safe and let me know if you have any more news." I get off the line in case his Embassy contact calls with an update. We don't even discuss the ordered departure; we both know leaving isn't an option.

After yet another picnic dinner with the kids on the terrace, I flip channels looking for an update. And then, like all the other nights in recent history, the power goes out, and so do I.

As the sun comes up, I wake with a familiar heaviness, knowing today is the big day, when the protestors will converge on the Palace. The sound of beeping surprises me, but I guess the curfew hasn't gone into effect. I get up with Devi, and while she digs into a bowl of cereal, I turn on my laptop, hoping phone lines haven't been cut yet. I'm shocked to see a flood of emails from the States asking about the celebrations. Celebrations?

I surf to *Kantipur Online*, my local news source, and find out, it's true! The King has called for the restoration of Parliament, a huge step in the right direction. The Maoists are satisfied and have released their stranglehold on the city which allows much needed supplies to flow in. Still, hesitant to believe the struggle is over, I wait for Dinesh to arrive and I ask him if the news is good.

"Yes, Madam," he replies in his familiar mantra, and I'm flooded with joyous relief.

I see an email from Dave asking if I want to meet for lunch, and I reply with an enthusiastic yes, my mouth already watering at thoughts of our favorite place, Dan Ran. We agree to meet at Pilgrim's, and I hustle out the door, giddy with freedom. The sun shines bright as the flowers dance in the breeze, and the beep beep of taxi horns is like the sweet aria of songbirds; the hustle and bustle of city life is choreographed like a Bollywood production. I spot a familiar taxi driver, and his ordinarily sweet grin has a whole different energy behind it today. I join him, smiling, a smile from within, a smile growing from the knowingness of a shared joy, the joy of the People's victory. It's as if the last few weeks were just a dream, and normalcy has returned. There are no more soldiers, no more guns, not even the "cute" mini tank. Passing by a pile of broken bricks, yesterday's arsenal, I hope the King can be trusted, I hope this peace will last.

I fall even more in love with Nepal—in love with our dirty, winding little street, with the men drinking tea in front of shops, with children spinning bike tires with sticks, and with the street dogs wandering lazily across the road. Hearing the familiar banter of the fruit vendors and customers haggling, I'm flooded with such a fondness for all that surrounds me I'm ready to burst with a contentment I've never known in America. My logical mind argues that it doesn't make sense to love a place so filthy and polluted, the lingering stench of the Bagmati River that would make a boys' high school locker room pleasant. Then it hits me: I feel safer, more comfortable, and at ease here than I ever have in the States. The chatter in the market makes more sense to me in a foreign language than any conversation I'd overheard in a stateside shopping mall. In spite of my skin color, I feel more coordinated with the people around me than I ever did in heels striding through Washington DC. My puzzle piece fits in this life, in a way I never felt I fit before. I spent so many years contorting myself to the American dream, only to realize, it just isn't *my* dream.

At Pilgrim's, Dave finds a wooden elephant with wheels and some blocks for Arun. I pick up the Narnia series for Jack and a woven, rainbow colored blanket for Devi. The manager, Balbir, is working, and I'm happy to see him after so many weeks. I'm warmed by his presence and touched that he is happy to see me, too. We chat about the sudden turn in the political state, and I sense he is much more savvy than I had previously given him credit for. He always struck me as intelligent, but I had yet to find many Nepalis outside of Birendra's Men's Club who were willing to talk politics. As I'm trying to grasp all he is sharing, I become distracted by a truck full of security forces rumbling by. Suddenly, I fear that all this jubilation is premature, that the masses have not been satiated, that they want more than the King has offered. But, then, we hear them, thousands of voices rolling down the road like thunder through a mountain canyon. Soon, we see the procession of people, waving flags, chanting and jumping, with unadulterated joy. My eyes flash to my friend, and I see his smile, that same smile from within, and he bobbles his head saying, "*Vijay Yatra*, Madam. They are celebrating."

Feeling drawn to the crowd, I float out the door to a scene like nothing I've ever witnessed. The people, so real, are overflowing with effervescent joy, like I'd seen in the taxi driver's face, multiplied by thousands. Just as I think they have come to an end, another wave flows through: women singing with children in tow, men beating drums and makeshift cymbals, a leader chanting, exuberantly echoed in victory. Dave snaps photos, but I just watch, overwhelmed by pure emotion. Tears of true joy flow, and I bow *namasté* as the crowd passes. I've never been so selflessly happy in my life; I never knew these feelings existed. This is a taste of nirvana. This is what they have been fighting for.

As we make our way up the road moving against the flow of the crowd, I consider joining them, but realize this has not been my fight, and now it's not my celebration. Sharing in the spoils would be shallow, since I've done nothing to help achieve their victory. I've only been a bystander, watching it unfold. And I consider, what would it take for me to give up all I had, close my business, leave my home and take to the streets? Rally to bring home troops from an unjust war? School shootings? Running out of gasoline? A president as crooked as the King? What would I be willing to risk my life to fight for?

Dave and I round the bend to the gates of Dan Ran for our own private celebration.

"Oh, look. They saved our table for us!" Dave laughs as we step into the empty garden.

"Yeah, I called ahead and made a reservation," I quip.

The smiling waiter brings us fresh lemon soda (hooray, lemons are back!), and we settle in for a long, childless lunch. The garden is less chaotic without our small counterparts, a welcome change after days of compound fever. We talk about Dave's anticipated timeline and my lack of one, what we will do when we get home, what we will miss, and what we won't. I confess my fear of not finding meaningful work upon return to our small town, feeling my aspirations expanding to a greater world community after so many years of hiding out in the mountain west. Still, the future feels very far away. Dave's appeal is still held up in Delhi, though the end of his review period is in sight. It's hard to believe he will really be leaving. He makes a list of people to invite to his going away party and I tease him about his last going away party, back in January, then seeing his weak smile, I realize maybe it's too soon for that joke.

On the way home, I stop in a little nursery to pick up a few flowers for the terrace. I spot some deep purple pansies, as the owner points out other options I should consider, and I bask in the oasis of rare and striking varieties I've never seen before. Then, unexpectedly, I come across columbine, one of my favorite native wildflowers of the mountain west. They are a lovely white, reminding me of my garden in the States, another special spot in my world.

"I have many more, if you would like to see them," the shop owner offers in excellent English.

I smile. "Where I come from, the columbines grow wild. This one is perfect." As I saunter out the gate and down the lane, I glance at my little flower and wonder if it will survive on our terrace, then realize, the columbines have adapted beautifully to living here, and so have I.

May

May brought summertime to the Valley, and Summit remained our favorite neighbor. Once Devi was down for her afternoon nap, Jack and I would slip through the secret passage, up the back stone steps, across the compound and out the gate to our sanctuary, the Summit swimming pool and gardens that were vibrantly coming to life. Jack and I enjoyed our time together, and then, when Devi woke up, Leena would bring her over to meet us, fresh and energized for the second part of her day.

With the Jandaalon victorious and the soldiers gone, the streets bustled with life, but for me, there was yet another delay. With the formation of a new parliament, all the ministers appointed by the King were sacked. As a result, all adoption files in the queue were placed on hold for further review, yet another chance for my house of cards to come tumbling down. I forced myself to remain optimistic.

Dave was still plodding through his appeal; the officials in Delhi continued to raise questions regarding some "grey areas." In the initial police report, Arun's mother had been reported dead, but since she was really an unwed girl who disappeared into the night, there was no gravesite to substantiate the story. I couldn't fathom how Dave was able to handle the pressure, so I tried to be supportive without asking too many questions. We communicated daily, often meeting for lunch in the garden of Café U. He was my surrogate best girlfriend, and I played the role of his stand-in wife, fetching extra formula or bringing over Devi's outgrown socks for the sprouting Arun. I was glad to sign up for any task, even if it was simply an exercise to distract myself from my own seemingly endless wait.

It is impossible to predict when Devi will fall apart, which creates an emotionally agonizing dynamic. We were having a wonderful morning playing together in the sun-drenched garden, watering flowers, and reading books. Then, as if a switch flipped, she starts to aggressively grab at pages, frantically yanking the book out of my hands and thrashing. I hurry to pick up the other books before she can make projectiles of them as she screams and stomps her chunky feet, ankle bracelets jingling. I reach out, calling to her, desperate to bring her back, but all I can do is toss the books aside and scoop her up as she flails and screeches, yanking at them with animal grunts and lunatic grabs. While I'm coming to understand her attachment issues and know that after a period of feeling close and connected, she rebels out of self-preservation, fearful of being left again, I struggle to accept this as just another facet of my traumatized little girl. Why can't she just trust me and love me back?

"Kitty! Kitty! *Namasté*, kitty! *Ama*, kitty! *Aaaama!* Kitty!" The otherwise sweet words are unwelcome at 2 a.m. Devi is wide awake, and having a lively discussion with Tenzing, our lovably independent cat, happily conversing in deep manly mews and a vibrant purr like a distant motor bike.

"Devi, go to sleep. Leave the kitty alone," I mumble and roll over. The nights are already getting hot, and I want to avoid coming to full consciousness in the sticky night air. I drift off again only to be awakened by the scream of a cat, followed by bizarre noises—neither dog, nor bird, nor human—accompanied by light thumps on the roof. I bolt out of bed and dash to the terrace but find no source for the sounds. Tenzing is gone.

The gate had been banging all night from the street dogs squeezing through to investigate the squawks and shouts of unfamiliar beasts. I peek over the edge of the terrace, as the screeches continue, moving through the trees, and wonder if we have been visited by the legendary monkey said to live on the Summit grounds, a mystery Jack tirelessly investigates.

In the morning, big old Bruce mraows on the back stoop for his breakfast and I open the door for the brute to lumber in and grace us with his musky presence. We have come to accept his intermittent visits, but the "gifts" (i.e. rats) he presents me, clearly concerned I'm not able to provide for my young, are less appealing. Our feline companions sit at the top of the urban food chain, unlike our Stateside mountain home populated by predators, so I haven't worried for their safety roaming at night, until now. Tenzing is still nowhere to be found.

After breakfast, I go out to the terrace and survey the scene of the crime. At first, it looks like nothing more than poor personal hygiene on the part of our resident felines, but on closer investigation, the clues become clear. This was not merely a lack of litter box etiquette; it looks like defecation under duress, with drops of blood peppering the scene.

Throughout the day we call out to Tenzing. Jack and Devi, with their thin little voices wailing for their beloved kitty, pace between the patches of sunlight among his favorite napping holes and hideouts. I'm secretly afraid his kitty cat karma has finally caught up with him and worry if we will ever see him again.

The next morning, our fabulous feline returns, proudly carrying a sewer rat. He is distraught when I deny entrance for him to feed his human young and loses his prize to Good Dog, the great opportunist. Jack scoops him up and brings him to me to examine. He has strange oozing cuts on his back, neck, and chest, which we liberally pack with our dwindling supply of Jesus in a Tube (aka Neosporin). His appetite is still intact, and he gulps down outrageously expensive kibble to make up for yesterday's lost meals.

Later, by the Summit pool, we hear that a troop of monkeys came through the neighborhood in the night and my assumption of there being few predators is debunked. Veterans of the Valley agree it is quite possible they could have grabbed our cat, probably turning him loose once he started to put up a fight. Imagining our cat being carried off by monkeys strangely fits in this bizarro world. At least they weren't *flying* monkeys.

Devi and I climb up the back steps for a stroll in the Summit garden when Sarresh materializes as we pass his house.

"Someone died there last night," he points to a room in the downstairs flat where usually the sound of a television blares. Today the door is padlocked, the shutters closed.

"What happened?" I ask, startled.

"My best *Didi* died," he states, matter-of-fact.

"Was she sick?"

"No, just dead."

"Was she old?" I inquire, thinking of our adopted Hindu grandmother who insists on telling me stories no matter how much I shake my head, unable to understand.

"Oh, no. She is sick for long time and dies," he replies in his usual sing-song voice, accompanied by a strange, detached smile.

"I'm so sorry," I sigh, grasping to understand the grieving process of this smiling child. "Jack is home if you want to play."

"Okay!" he shouts and skips past the outdoor kitchen toward our house. I'm sure Jack, currently exiled on Homework Island, will be thrilled for the interruption.

Glancing at the padlocked door, I think of a younger woman I'd seen on the patio of the landlord's house, always sullen, never returning a *namasté* much less a smile, lazily sitting on a stool, picking at her split ends. It never occurred to me her melancholy might be the result of illness, and I wonder if it could have been something easily treated in a Western country. I remember the pretty little white goat Jack wanted to save from sacrifice. Had it been killed for her? I guess the offering to whatever Gods they were hoping to appease didn't work.

Devi and I step through the gate to cross the gravely road, but she still avoids holding my hand, although she knows this is the rule. Finally, she relents with a little less resistance, and I convince myself it's a sign of improvement as she swings and pulls our way to the pool.

We picnic in the shade and look at books as her little belly gurgles. Before boredom sets in, I take her to an outdoor bathroom stall to change into swim clothes. She proudly pulls her things out of her turtle backpack, laying them out on the bench, just like *Ama*. I peel off her sticky sundress as she splashes in the shower puddles, grinning and giggling, looking up to me for approval. *Good grief, she's cute!*

We sit by the pool, dangling our legs, when Jack joins us, trying to convince me that his homework is complete. Although I'm skeptical, I don't want to interrupt my outing with Devi to go home and check, so I let it slide.

"Jump to me Devi! Come on, jump!" becomes my mantra for the day.

Thrilled to be the focus of my attention, Devi is ready to burst with bubbly giggles. She watches Jack, Godlike bronze from the sun, golden locks flowing behind him, diving and swimming under water. Not ready to fully emulate him, she settles for jumping from the side into my waiting arms again and again.

"Yay, Devi! Good jump! You're so big and brave!" I cheer enthusiastically.

With each jump, a little more trust grows, building, building, one jump at a time. Then suddenly, she changes the game, she won't jump, and I guess she's had enough, but I don't know why. I've been careful not to let her face go under, intimately aware she's not keen on that, still wrestling to simply wash her face; but still she won't jump.

"Go, *Ama!* Go, go," she repeats while standing on the side of the pool, waving me away with her chubby arms in fluorescent orange water-wings squeezed on like Michelin Man muscles.

"Okay, Devi. I'm going to swim a little, and then come right back," I can't understand what she wants, but she's so insistent, I comply, feeling the familiar dig of rejection. Taking slow, deliberate strokes across the pool, I lazily roll over in a flip turn, spinning like an aquatic ballerina. I surface to see her bobbing along, legs kicking like she's running in place, eyes crinkled shut in an enormous grin, a Cheshire cat in day-glo floaties. Quickly, I swim over, afraid she's slipped in, only to be denied. I feel like a washed-up lifeguard.

"No, *Ama!* Devi wimming!" she gleefully announces, and off she goes, casting me aside like an unnecessary flotation device. I swim alongside her, aware she has to tire out sometime, and I don't want her to panic. As she moves through her own private ocean, she occasionally reaches out to grab my fingers, using me to pull her along, or maybe for a little secret reassurance, but for the most part, she just keeps kicking. *At last! An acceptable outlet for all that kicking!* She's so proud of her independence, I give her space and let her do it herself. Then, when she drifts a little too far away, and I see the tiniest hint of fear, she allows herself to reach out for me, and I am always there. As we swim back and forth and back again, I see something shift in her, just ever so slightly—she knows she needs me. She has to have me. What if I abandon her? But I don't. My teenage lifeguard self reincarnates.

I wonder, *is she starting to believe she can trust me?* We've found a place where she truly needs me. She reaches out and lets me rescue her.

Then comes the hangover—her persistent instinct to reject me, to push me away with everything she has and refuse anything I offer. Now I'm the one drowning in the destructive aftermath of connection. The fallout is like clouds rolling in, an impossibly oppressive and gloomy concrete-grey sky. I struggle to embrace the clouds as part of the process, wrapping myself in them like a fluffy down comforter of denial, but I just feel damp and hollow.

Logically, I get it. Really, I do. She felt close and allowed herself to become dependent on me, so now she has to push me away. Still, I feel defeated. Deflated. I plead with her, and she sticks out her tongue and laughs, wearing away at my patience until I come undone and yell at her. Her eyes go vacant as she checks out—then comes the creepy smile, an instinctual response to keep the bigger beast from eating her alive. I take deep breaths, count to ten, then twenty, feeling frightened by how fast my heart is beating, banging out of my chest, exploding in my head. How can such a small person elicit such a strong reaction? Why can't I have the limitless patience I strive for? And when I finally do lose it, why does she look so satisfied? As if this explosion is what she needed all along, to get her hit of endorphins. I hate being in this place with her, feeling her jagged chewed fingernails scrape raw the tender flesh of my internal Madonna. I want to run to the Summit garden and lie down in one of the perfectly manicured flower beds and dissolve into the rich, coffee ground earth. *Om Mani Peme What?* My heart cracks at the thought of her finding comfort in my anger instead of cuddles and lullabies. *What happened to her?* Things I don't want to imagine.

I wake in the night to her standing by my bed with the creepy smile. I reach out to her, to bring her under the covers with me, but she grunts and pulls away. There is a storm coming, inside and out. Lightning flashes in the windows behind her as thunder rumbles in the foothills.

"Devi, get in bed. It's sleeping time," I whisper, trying not to wake Jack, but only my zombie girl is present.

I usher her to the bathroom, searching for a logical reason behind this midnight wake-up call. I ask her to tell me when she's done on the potty and fall back in bed as flashes of lightning illuminate the room. I hear her little feet smacking the marble floor in the bathroom and go in to check on her and am met with the creepy smile. I lift her off the potty to see she's done nothing and ignore the grin, afraid if I acknowledge it, her head will start spinning.

"Hop in bed, it's time for sleeping. See how dark it is outside? It's nighttime. Time for sleeping." I direct as kindly as possible and drape the covers over her, then tiptoe back to bed. I listen to the rustle of her feet under the sheets, and I know she is incapable of sleep. She's gone away to her secret world, and I don't know the password. I can't comfort her, I can't even *find* her, how can I possibly protect her from what she sees when she closes her eyes?

The night is punctuated by cries and wails, whines and moans. I call out to her, desperate to reassure her, "It's okay, Devi. Go back to sleep." I fight every instinct I have to touch her, knowing my hand will be a fire-hot dagger in her distorted sensory manual.

"Devi, you're okay, go back to sleep," I soothe, and she answers with a high-pitched yelp, followed by violent thrashing and labored breathing, then suddenly she's quiet. I roll over and bury my head as the torture of her night terror assailants infects me. The thunder rumbles in long, low groans and rain taps on the terrace. *Wash all of this away*, I pray, *just wash her pain away.*

Morning comes, and I get up to try again, sitting patiently at the table while she eats her cereal, helping when elusive flakes float out of reach at the bottom of the bowl. She toddles into the playroom and I sit down to check my email only to hear a crash. I go in to find she is channeling the Tasmanian Devil once again, scattering doll dishes and puzzle pieces everywhere.

I calmly begin to straighten up. "Devi, let's be nice with our toys, *bastadi, bastadi*," I say, but I turn to see she's gone. In the other room, she spills my tea while tapping away on my laptop (the no-est of no no's), standing in a puddle of urine on my chair.

"What are you doing?!" I shriek, and I feel myself failing her, incapable of seeing the flattery in her imitation. She screeches like a wild animal and falls limp, refusing to walk to the "time out" spot, so I sweep up her noodle body and deposit her next to the door.

"You stay here and wait for *Didi*," I command, but her switch has flipped. Her eyes are vacant as she nervously plays with her toes, mouth slightly open, as if she's in awe of what has just happened.

Heady with blown circuits, I put as much space between us as possible, going into the bathroom and shutting the door. I slide down onto the cool marble floor and start to cry. I have failed again, and the day has only just begun.

Leena gives me time to regroup, and I struggle to the surface to try again, remaining dedicated to time in the Summit garden with Devi. A soft breeze blows, freeing blossoms from the Jacaranda trees. Lavender tissue paper butterfly blessings from above float gently groundward, enticing me to slip into a world of my own as I watch Devi joyfully skip and dance, spinning as they fall around her. My eyes flutter, and I slip away, over the Himals, into the sea, drifting in an ocean of nothingness. In my mind I see her bobbing nearby, orange floaties as a signal flare, waiting to be rescued, and my heart aches, knowing I can't reach her.

If she were a drowning man, I could save her, my lifeguard training manual rattles through my head. "When approaching a drowning victim, one must always be cautious as the victim may panic and attack. All the reassurance you give, 'I am here to help you,' may not be enough to keep the victim from lunging and grasping, desperate to stay afloat. Always keep a considerable distance from the victim and assess the situation before attempting rescue. If the victim begins to panic, dive below and swiftly approach from behind. Once immobilized, if the victim begins to thrash, allow them to roll, but do not lose your grip. If necessary, release the victim and quickly move away. It is essential to preserve your own energy. Allow the victim to tire themselves out and when they begin to lose vital energy and go under, attempt another rescue."

I took my lifesaving test on a six foot, two-hundred-pound man in a lake. Compared to this, that was easy. With Devi, I am lost. I'm watching her drown, waiting for her to tire enough to allow herself to be rescued. But I'm afraid she will always outlast me. I feel helpless and realize I am the one exhausted, and desperate for rescue.

As the days tick by, so does Dave's clock, counting down to the deadline for a decision from Delhi. Calling on congressmen, senators, and eventually a spook secured by his faithful brother, a visa is granted, and Dave and Arun are finally going home to an anxiously waiting Melissa. With only the final exit interview at the Consulate to go, Dave, like Nora, has a list of final to-dos, and I'm happy for the distraction from my own little bundle of disaster. I feel like a junkie, strung out on Devi and her rare, but blissful hits of trust.

Marooned in the Himalayan Kingdom for six months, Dave's finances are strained, but a whole tribe of supportive friends and family are enthusiastically awaiting their return to the States, with welcome home parties and baby showers. During a long, rainy afternoon with "The Teacher," we come up with the idea for a house party where loyal fans of his epic adoption can purchase Nepali wares, offsetting the bottomless pit of expenses. A shopping trip legends are made of is in the works.

Everywhere we go, it's assumed Dave and I are a couple, so we fully embody our roles: Dave, the bedraggled husband toting his wife's endless purchases, beaten down with demands for more rupees, shaking his head in defeat, and me, the impatiently pushy wife eager to acquire everything in sight for a mock list of friends and relations, snapping at him when he says no to clandestinely elicit the sympathy of the male shopkeepers. We argue, I throw a fit, he silently begs the vendor with sad rolling eyes, and the bartering starts. Rather than tangle with me, especially once I begin to haggle in Nepali, the shopkeepers quickly relent, and we walk away with great deals.

In our neighborhood, we gather handmade ceramic soap dishes and incense burners, locally-crafted note cards and Ganesh coloring books, all the while practicing and refining our show before stepping up our game in Thamel. There, we move swiftly from one vendor to the next, loading up on boiled wool slippers, brass Buddhas, armloads of incense, handcrafted handbags, fluffy *pashmina* shawls, seemingly silver jewelry and finally, iconic embroidered t-shirts in a rainbow of colors proclaiming YAK YAK YAK with the namesake proudly displayed. Thinking back to my first shopping trip with Christina, I'm amazed at how much has changed in my world; the chaotic market is no longer overwhelming me. At the end of the day, Dave treats me to Dan Ran and we unwind from the epic shopping trip. "You even intimidated me," Dave confesses, "and we were on the same team!"

I try not to grasp at my last days with Dave; instead I live vicariously through his anticipated return to Melissa and their life in the States. The kids and I attend his going away party at Café U, all of us happy for a night out with friends. I'm sadly surprised that Annie doesn't come, and even more surprised that Rajkumar does, along with Mr. Rana, the owner of the orphanage, and Amita, his daughter. They are genuinely happy for Dave and can see his bond with Arun, who is smearing his Daddy's face with sticky rice. We dance while the kids play toy instruments— and everyone is joyous that the process is finally complete—bittersweet relief in the air.

The next morning, I'm happy to assist with the packing challenge, and play with Arun, realizing how much I'll miss his squirmy baby games. Dave shuffles and smashes, weighs and repacks. Overflowing with mixed emotions, I insist on seeing them off at the airport the following morning and hire a car from Summit to ferry us and their voluminous luggage. As Dave schlepps the bags out, I hold tight to Arun, preventing his last chance to topple down the steps or pinch fingers in a door.

Glancing around the pile of luggage, I ask Dave, "Is your diaper bag ready?"

"Well, yeah, I have some diapers in my backpack," he replies, and I remember, he's never traveled with a baby.

Quickly, I start looking around, gathering and washing baby bottles, prepping them with powdered formula so he will only need to add water. I find some faux Tupperware and pack them with distant relatives of cheerios, pretzels, and goldfish crackers. Rustling through the pantry, I find the kin of Ziploc bags and stuff them with wet wipes and rags, saving a few empty ones for unanticipated messes. Diving into the duffle bag containing toys, I pull out a few new ones to capture Arun's attention. I then wrestle out two more changes of clothes and pajamas, and a few board books, cramming it all into Dave's backpack, and tossing his bulky fleece aside. Finally, I pull out Arun's favorite blanket, holding it up to smell his baby-ness one last time, and simultaneously wipe away my tears, feeling our goodbye coming.

"Kate, we gotta go!" Dave shouts from the door. I swing the backpack over my shoulder, scoop up Arun, and drag the oversized duffle behind me.

Driving through the city feels different, seeing it through Dave's departing eyes. He clicks away with the camera, snapping up images of his last sights, and me smiling with Arun, propped in my lap. He bursts into laughter and I look behind me to see his muse: two men riding a motorbike with a goat slung crosswise between them, a perfect ending to his otherworldly journey.

We pull up at the Embassy, and Dave runs in to collect Arun's waiting visa, while I pace outside juggling the squirmy baby and giving him last minute instructions. "Now Arun, you have to be a good boy for Daddy on the plane. He really doesn't know what he's doing, so help him out and sleep a lot. I put all your favorite things in the backpack, so you have plenty of books and toys to play with, but don't take them all out at once or you'll be bored later. Look around, Little Buddy, this is your homeland, so don't forget it. You have a wonderful Mommy to go home to, so be sweet to her and give her lots of kisses." He grabs my face and stares deeply into my eyes, nuzzling my cheek with sticky lips, the best baby kiss ever.

Dave dashes out and motions to the car, making it clear I should be inside and ready to go. We hop in and zip off, the long-awaited documents in his hand.

"So, Kate, have you and Nora been keeping in touch?" Dave asks as he stuffs the paperwork in a pocket of his backpack.

"Well, yeah, on and off. She's busy looking for an apartment and a job, but I'm sure we'll stay in touch. She's looking forward to visiting us when we get back to the States."

"I'm just asking because, well, I'm not that good at communicating, you know, once I get back home and into my life again. It's nothing personal, I just know myself. I've met a lot of really wonderful people when I've traveled, but I'm not that good at staying in touch. I just thought you should know," he says gently, and it feels like he's breaking up with me. I look away, trying to hide my confused emotions.

"Hey," he says, putting a hand on my knee, "I can't thank you enough for being my wife; really, I couldn't have done it without you."

I feel his sincerity and take his hand, squeezing it tight. "It was my pleasure, really," and now tears start to roll down my cheeks, drip-dropping on Arun's head.

We hold hands in silence the rest of the way to the airport, watching the city fly by. He has been what I can only imagine a brother to be, listening to my Craig drama, counseling me when I feel I've failed Devi time and again, reminding me how brilliant Jack is in spite of his refusal to do schoolwork. I can't picture my life here without him and force myself to smile, knowing he is going home to Melissa and their beautiful house in the woods.

We pull into the airport and as a porter unloads the luggage, I speed-talk instructions about the contents of the backpack, but realize he isn't hearing me in his flurry of excitement. The moment has come to say goodbye, and I fight to let go as I hand Arun over to his daddy. I kiss his sticky cheek, and he makes one last grab at my shiny, dangling earring. I look Dave squarely in the eye, "You know, I couldn't have gotten through the last few months without you either." I try not to cry again. "At least let me know you got home okay?"

"Oh, Kate, of course I will," he says, pulling me into a bear hug, squishing Arun between us. "You're going to be fine. You're a great mom, and Jack and Devi are lucky to have you. Keep on keeping on! You'll be heading out of here before you know it."

I nod and smile, letting him go. "You better hurry up, or you'll miss your plane and then who knows how long you'll be stuck here."

"Hey, you stay out of trouble!" Dave shouts over his shoulder as he turns to go, disappearing into the sea of people.

I climb into the car, and when we return to Summit, I tip the driver a thousand rupee note, a final salute to Dave and our ongoing joke of affluence. I walk down the lane and ask Ganesh to watch over them, to grant them a joyful reunion with Melissa, and that they all sleep through the night. I slip down the alley to our big metal gate and look up to the terrace to see a smiling Devi, smashing her face between the ornate plaster rungs. "*Aaaaammma!*" she calls out, turning to run and meet me, mimicking Jack. I am home, where I belong, and I feel blessed.

As the summer heat sets in, I trade my afternoon walk for time out in the cool morning air, meeting Birendra for a trip to Swayambhu and an urban trek up the 365 steps to the temple complex. Birendra is great fun and has a never-ending positive outlook on life, and am awed by the peace that flows through him. But like the conversations with my mother, I stop talking to him about what might be lurking in Devi's past. I can't decide if he is trying to hide some awful truth about his Motherland and its archaic cultural attitude toward women, or if he just doesn't know, but his repeated response drives me crazy.

"She's just a little girl," he insists, smiling. "She will forget her past and be fine."

I feel such guilt not being able to get through to Devi; when he casually dismisses her issues, it makes my head spin. So, we stick to happier topics, like what Prince Jack is up to, or if either of us have heard from Nora. Birendra has an arsenal of hilarious stories of wild times with the men he's introduced me to. His friends are a true blessing. They have carried him through the death of his wife and now faithfully keep him company in her devastating absence.

On the way home one morning, I ask Birendra to drop me at the bottom of the hill, just over the bridge. I cut through the market to pick up some mangos, deliciously ripe with the season, and tiny bananas, just Devi's size. I pause, gently petting the doomed goats, sending them love as they stand patiently tied to the vendor's shack. The man, proudly displaying gum and cigarettes gives me an odd look, so I wish the bleating goats many happy rebirths and walk on. Passing an abandoned and crumbing house, I move through the back path by the trash heap, then step into the street to walk up the hill to our house, sitting proudly at attention, its red roof signaling my refuge ahead. I spot a group of orange crush clad *saddhus*, essentially beggars with a cause, and I duck down our lane and out of sight. I'd been intrigued by these holy men when we first arrived, imagining the insight and clairvoyance they must have. So devoted to their spirituality they take a vow of poverty, and depend on others for support as they follow their path to enlightenment. They always smile kindly, enthusiastically greeting Jack and me on the street, rambling unintelligible praises as they tweak and pat Jack's still chubby cheeks. Often, I see them in the alley from our terrace and always allow Jack to run down and offer them a portion of the unending supply of fried rice Leena keeps on hand, and, on a good day, extra pastry or guava as well.

As I turn down the alley, I'm surprised to see the group of *saddhus* grumbling around our gate, checking out the donations in each other's small silver buckets, like children comparing Halloween candy. As I approach, they recognize me as the lady from the terrace and part like a tangerine sea, revealing a man in black at their epicenter. Up to this point, I'd only seen them in jailhouse orange robes, with iconic, bundled white hair and unkempt scraggly beards.

As I move toward the gate, The Man in Black notices me and begins bowing, *namasté*, as do the rest of his posse, and I return the sentiment, smiling. As I reach up for the latch, The Man in Black begins to make hand motions vaguely reminiscent of a Catholic priest, motioning to his not-so-empty bucket and making gestures of eating.

"Yes," I say, pointing to our house, "From us." Then I realize, he wants more. I shake my head, "Sorry." Up to this point, upturned, empty palms had been enough to get me off the hook in the never-ending dance with disadvantaged locals, but not so with this guy. He drops some sort of magic bean, possibly made of resin, in my hand, and by giving me something, he now has a legitimate reason for increased expectations of support for his livelihood. As I continue to shake my head, saying, "I have nothing more," he speaks kindly, smiling and gesturing grandly, pointing to his black robes, in a show of his obvious importance. Then, to my complete and utter shock, as if to prove his point, he opens the folds of his robe like the curtains surrounding the Great and Powerful Oz, to show me something of supreme significance, something no amount of counsel from any guidebook or even ever-so-wise-on-all-things-Nepal Christina could have prepared me for. He is totally naked (which makes sense, black is a hot color) insisting on explaining all the "accessories" attached to his "member." I feel my face flush in prudish shock as I stumble into the gate, tripping over my own feet.

"No. . . . Thank you" are the only words I'm able to utter, clanging the gate shut like a rude suburbanite on a Jehovah's Witness, but he continues chattering away on the other side as I scamper up the steps.

Later, at the pool, catching up with Tessa, who had returned a few days before, I try to explain what I'd experienced. She rolls with laughter as I recall the disturbing sight: a tight fitting ring, some sort of chain and maybe some bells? I was hoping she would have some deep spiritual insight as to the significance of all of his "jewelry" (and I use that term loosely), to explain my encounter with the local religioso, but she just laughs at my naïveté. I finally give up and accept this as yet another unpredictable, unforgettable quirk of Nepal.

"Mommy! You have to *see* this!" Jack squeals. "Come 'ere! Come 'ere! Look!"

A line of ants streams across the kitchen floor, rushing out from the darkness under the sink, likely from the sewer, the home of all things freaky. Their organization and strong work ethic are a force worthy of respect as they trek up the wall and out the window. Leena stands ready with a can of something deadly, her mission deterred by Jack.

"Mommy look how hard they're working. We can't just *kill* them; they're only doing their job." His big brown eyes plead with me to institute some justice before Leena starts her killing spree.

"Jack, they're just ants. We can't have them living in our kitchen. There are lots of ants in the world."

"MOM!" Jack interrupts, disturbed by my lack of empathy. "They have just as much right to be here as we do. They deserve to live a happy life, too."

"You're right, Jack, but are you willing to make sure they don't get into the food? We can't have ants in the cabinets; it's just not sanitary." I hope the magnitude of this project will dissuade him.

"I will, I will, I will!" Jack hops up and down, careful not to squish his new colony of friends. "No, *Didi*. No killing," he states sternly, wagging his finger.

"Okay, Madam," Leena bobbles and puts the can away, clearly amazed by the latest directive from the crazy American lady.

I trot downstairs to take Devi out for our daily stroll in the Summit gardens and find Jack behind the house where he has crafted a trail of crumbs from leftover rolls to direct the ant exodus and lead them to safety, up the neighboring wall and into the adjacent garden. I stifle my impulse to send him to Homework Island and count this as an earth science lesson. At least he isn't lighting matches on the roof.

As Devi drags me from one garden to the next, demanding I smell every flower she selects, I try to imagine what our life will be like back in the US. Dave's departure has made me acutely aware that my time in suspended animation will eventually come to an end. With new ministers selected, files are starting to move through the queue again. Thoughts of our Stateside home now make me anxious, rather than offering comfort. As challenging as life here can be, we've made it our home. Acknowledging that the support system I have here will be absent in the States rattles me. What will I do with Devi once we get back and have no one else to help me care for her? Will she be able to handle preschool? Where will I find a job? Around and around my monkey mind jumps from one branch of anxiety to another.

With the slim chance of our adoption process being completed by June, I had been worried about my visa expiring, but surprisingly, Annie has finally come through by connecting me with a lawyer to help secure a visa to explore a business opportunity. While preparing my proposal, the prospect of staying in my adopted country flitters in my heart, and I dream of making this new world our permanent home. Still, I have things to take care of back in the States, especially my faithful dogs and aging tomcat.

Our stroll begins to take on a hint of dysfunction as Devi's movements become more erratic, her energy frenetic, and I steer us toward home. When she realizes where we're going, she employs her latest protest tactic, the noodle body, so I scoop her up and toss her over my shoulder like a sack of potatoes. She screeches, beating my back with her tiny fists, chunky legs kicking the air as I tilt my head to avoid being struck. I'm no longer self-conscious about what the locals think of my parenting style. Logic and reasoning are wasted on my little Tasmanian Devi.

Inside the compound walls, I plunk her down and let her rage with only the gate guard and the gardener as audience, now unfazed by her meltdowns. I sit patiently at the bottom of the steps until she tires, then ask, "Are you ready for lunch?" Lunch—the magic word. We briefly battle over holding hands while scaling the steep steps, but she runs out of steam, and, motivated by banana-mango salad, complies.

Jack, still managing his insect exodus, looks up long enough to tell me Tessa called while we were out. We have plans to meet up in the afternoon to discuss a project to care for the brick kiln donkeys, cast out when they cease to be useful. They are like large, ornery street dogs, and have become a nuisance by digging through garbage for sustenance.

I return the call and Tessa is frantic. "I need a favor," she gasps. "A dog was hit by a motorbike in Kumaripati. Can you pick it up and bring it to the animal treatment center?"

"Of course!"

I trot over to Summit to hire a private car, armed with a load of towels to cover the seats. I'd laughed out loud when she suggested that I hop on Dr. Devkota's motorbike for the trip over, and even louder when she insisted that I wouldn't have to drive, just hold the dog. When I arrive at the vet clinic, the disabled dog is bandaged and sedated, a heartbreaking sight, but the bleeding has stopped and the leg is set. The assistant gently places the poor mongrel in the back seat with me, chuckling as I cradle the dog's head in my lap, unaffected by his stench.

Thankfully, the driver speaks fluent English, so directions are easy to communicate. As I gaze out the window toward the lush, rolling foothills, the car slows to a crawl to dodge a crowd of women in the road, waving their arms. I ask the driver to stop.

Shifting the slumbering dog's head out of my lap, I jump out, lured by the frantic, crying women. At the center of the crowd, a man holds a little girl, maybe Devi's age, and I see she is turning a sickening grey-blue. The women are trying to flag down a taxi, but none will stop. The drivers know the residents of this painfully impoverished area are unable to pay their fare.

I dash to the man and check the child's mouth, doing a finger sweep for foreign objects as her eyes roll back in her head and she goes limp. We shuffle her to the hood of the car as I put my fingers to her neck, feeling her rapid pulse while I look, listen, and feel for breath. Finding none, I tilt her head to open her airway and show the man how to pinch her nose and give her a baby breath, seeing her chest rise ever so slightly. He watches intently and repeats the action as the women around us wail and cry. My driver is in the road, flagging down a taxi, nearly throwing his body in front of it. I push through the women to grab my handbag, pulling out a thousand rupee note and shoving it in my driver's hand.

"Tell him to take them to a hospital, fast!" I direct as the man scoops up the baby and dives into the backseat. We are enveloped in a cloud of dust as they peel out. I look around to the crowd of crying women, holding each other in dismay. I have no language to convey my condolence, all that is left for me to do is to get back in my own car and deliver my canine package.

The scene is so shocking, I'm overwhelmed with grief for these women. There is no 911 service, if they even have a phone, and I question whether emergency aid is available, and what hospital is nearby. I caress the broken dog's velvety muzzle for comfort as empathetic tears fall.

"The baby will be fine, Madam. It was good of you to stop," the driver says, looking at me in the rearview mirror.

All I can do is nod, knowing, even if I had any words for what has just transpired, they would come out in choked sobs.

We are met at the gate of the animal care center by kind staff who take charge of my canine companion while the director shows me around the shelter. I've wanted to visit for quite some time, but now I feel numb, and the tour is just a blur. After spending a respectful amount of time, I excuse myself, wanting to be home, close to my small humans. On the way back, we pass the previously chaotic scene, now quiet, and I suppress the urge to ask the driver to stop and inquire about the outcome. Somehow, not knowing feels safer for my spirit than hearing that the little girl died.

At home, my little people are on the terrace waiting with exuberant cries, "Mommy!" and *"Ama!"* followed by a stampede to meet me at the front door.

Jack reports that the ant parade is over, but he'll make sure any others that got lost along the way will find their friends and family. Devi plops into my lap and begins playing with my necklace, and I can't help trying to hold her a little closer. She squirms, my closeness making her uncomfortable, so I let her go, but the ache of wanting to heal her invisible injuries remains.

"Okay, Madam?" Leena implores, sensing a shift in me. I just nod, there are no words in our Eng-pali dictionary to explain what transpired on my outing. I'll tell Dinesh about it later while he does the dinner dishes, and the burden of translating will be on him, once again.

We head over to Summit and order chips and *lassi* to be served by the pool. In the garden, I hear familiar voices and turn to see Steve and Lisa, with baby Indra in a front pack, head drooped to the side sleeping sweetly. They are back to complete the second part of their adoption and take their baby home. The dark clouds from earlier in the day lift, and my grief dissipates at the sight of the joyous little family.

After watching one little girl possibly lost, here was another one found. In this place of pain, tragedy, and immeasurable suffering there is also compassion, beauty, and abundant love. I promise myself to remember the love, and take it home with me to hold tight, to give me a little more patience, a little more strength. I feel blessed to have more time in the Himalayan Kingdom to emulate all these lessons, to carefully pack them away and carry them home with us.

With the monsoon rains come liquid blessings from above and the purification of everything around us: the air, the sky, the dusty rooftops. The streets are rinsed free of the grit and grime of daily life, and I wish to be washed clean of my endless frustrations with Devi.

Jack and I have taken to spending time in the damp, furniture-less bedroom where we store our empty suitcases and stash gifts for loved ones back in the States. It's also a safe zone for Jack to keep his things out of busy little hands and regain some of the space he's lost, both mentally and physically, to the little girl who now seems to be running, and in more dramatic moments, ruining, his life. While Devi is in the kitchen with Leena waiting for lunch, hanging on her apron with one chubby hand, munching on a *bapa* in the other, Jack and I steal away to his private chamber and work on puzzles as the afternoon rain blows in. We feel the storm clouds starting to build, the humidity rising and the light becoming dim. Jack is restless, feeling the electricity in the air.

"Mommy, I give up. All these blues look the same," he whines in frustration.

"Why don't you go check in with *Didi* and see if lunch is ready?" I suggest. "I'll be in just as soon as I can find where this teensy flower goes, see? I think it's part of her dress." I squint at the piece tweezered in my fingers, comparing it to the lid of the box.

Jack shakes his head. "Mom, you're hopeless! You really think you're going to find that tiny flower? I'll see you in about ten hours!" He trots out of the room.

Eventually, finding the satisfying click of puzzle pieces connecting, I stand up and stretch my back, tired from hunching over the thousand-plus pieces scattered on the indoor-outdoor carpeting. Walking out of the glorified storage space, I see Leena anxiously looking out the front windows.

"Madam, I go? Lunch ready, rain coming," she chirps in her shy, bird-song voice as she glances at the charcoal-purple sky.

"Of course! Yes, yes. Go before it rains," I agree.

Leena gratefully dashes out, and within minutes the torrent comes with crashing thunder and lightning. I scamper around the house cranking the windows shut. As the pounding rain gives way to a soft, steady pitter-pat, I notice the house is a little too quiet, devoid of any sibling squabble. Every parent knows, silence is rarely a good sign.

Looking around, I find the loft surprisingly empty. I expected to find Jack and Devi channel surfing with the volume down, a somewhat successful trick Jack has employed to sneak cartoon time. My second guess is that they are jumping from bed to bed, but that room is empty, too, except for a trail of discarded clothing leading to the terrace.

And then I find them, buck-naked in the pouring rain, having a blast. The terrace has become a Slip-N-Slide and they splash and tackle each other with glee. Finally, I clearly see, Devi *really is* better off with us. We are her family now, and judging by her gut-jiggling laughter, I know she is truly happy, at least in this moment, all the way through. And for now, that is enough.

June

Like waking between dreams, May drifted into June and I found myself largely absorbed in other people's lives. Dave's departure left me lonely, but I was soon distracted by the arrivals of Steve and Lisa, then Carrie, another adoptive mom-to-be. She'd emailed to share the news that our files were approved, and we had entered the queue at the CDO within days of each other. Although the agency she was working with had no in-country facilitator, they seemed to have a better grasp on Nepali adoption happenings than Annie, and I was glad for the connection via Carrie. Upon hearing that we were nearing the finish line, I was surprised by my reaction; I felt absolutely sick.

To confirm Carrie's information was accurate, I emailed my file number to her facilitator, Jacob, since I hadn't heard anything from Annie or my agency. Lately, I had more information than they did and had unexpectedly slipped into the role of their informant. Faster than any response I ever received from Annie, Jacob replied. It turned out, the approvals Carrie celebrated fell short of my file by four. They had approved up to 1495; my file was number 1499. I was secretly relieved to have a little more time in refuge.

Over the next few days, emails flashed back and forth with anxiously excited families soon to be on their second trip to Nepal, finally able to bring their children "home." Their questions were endless: How long do we need to be there? Where should we stay? Should we bring diapers? I'd become the expert and had almost all the answers. All but the big one: What will it be like once we have our baby? Luckily, no one asked this point-blank, even though it was the biggest question on everyone's mind. Instead, we focused on culturally-appropriate attire, sleeveless versus spaghetti strap; what the weather is like, hot or really hot; and, of course, when will the documents be ready.

It's wonderful to see Steve and Lisa again. They have a definite plan of action and are ready to go, but seem to forget where they are, and all the planning in the world is powerless against the flow of Nepali time. Annie tells them they can't go to Children's Home without her, putting them off because she's "very busy." I offer to take them, but since Indra is still living at Annie's, they don't want to create any issues. When they finally do hear from Annie, the news isn't good. Their file is stuck due to a stalemate between the agency and the orphanage over a past due debt. True to form, Steve and Lisa move through the obstacle with patience and grace and soon have little Indra's visa in their hands.

The night before they leave, we meet at Summit for celebratory cocktails, and they share the play-by-play of their Embassy interview. I'm relieved to hear there are no questions about where Indra has been living while her file was in the queue. Devi's file stated she was living at Children's Home, but when we first arrived, I'd divulged to the US Consulate that she was living with me, so now I worry there could be an investigation if the inconsistency is discovered. Luckily, Steve and Lisa report their interview focused on who had been paid, when, and how much. These are questions I can easily answer.

They thank me repeatedly for helping them stay connected to

their little one, especially during the *Janaandolan*, a scary time for all of us. I'd gone to Annie's several times to take pictures, sending them via email. I couldn't imagine how painful it was for Indra's babyhood to be passing by all too quickly without them. Somehow, knowing I was here looking out for her in some small way had made their wait a little more bearable since Annie had been so unresponsive. Once they return home, I'm flooded with pictures of their little bundle surrounded by friends and loved ones. The beauty of their happily-ever-after is touching.

On a whim, I stop by Children's Home with Devi on our way to the grocery store. I've avoided taking her to the orphanage, fearful of triggering painful memories, but I know that Rajkumar and Amita want to see her. Over the many visits I've had with Rajkumar, stories have slowly leaked out, like tea from the crack in my ceramic mug. I now know that while Devi was at the orphanage, she refused to eat, and they thought she might be deaf because she failed to respond or communicate in any way with anyone. It hurt my heart to imagine my catatonic little girl there.

As we walk down the alley toward the orphanage, I pause to ask Ganesh once more for a little help and envision any obstacles crumbling before us. Stepping inside, I'm curious to see if Devi recognizes this place, but not wanting to risk upsetting her, I go straight up to the office. Amita and Rajkumar are delighted to see us and fawn over Devi, tweaking her cheeks and speaking softly in Nepali. They remark at how healthy she looks, how much of her hair has grown in, and especially how big she has gotten, squeezing her chubby legs. As I sit down on the sofa, hoping the last of the springs will hold up, I feel her legs clamp around me, and she buries her face in my shoulder. I can only imagine the movie that might be playing in her head. I drink my tea too quickly, burning my tongue, in hopes of leaving before Devi melts down. But first, Rajkumar has some business to discuss.

Like so many of my experiences in Nepal, things are not

quite going according to plan. When the notice was placed in the newspaper for Devi's family to claim her, she and Arun had been pictured together. Now, the original, and *only* acceptable copy of the clipping is missing, possibly with Dave, or at the Embassy, or in Delhi, or lost somewhere along the way. My heart sinks at the thought of yet another hurdle, but something has shifted in me. I don't fall apart!

"I'll email Dave and see if he has it," I suggest. No drama, no freaking out, no tears.

As Devi starts to squirm, her pincher claws hard at work along my neckline, I bid Amita and Rajkumar *suva din*, good afternoon, and trot back down the steps, Devi bouncing on my hip. She seems unfazed, as if she has no idea the significance of this place, and that's fine by me.

I continually question just what it is about this chaotic culture that I love so much, but now it's coming clear: the total lack of control. Maybe this change in attitude really is the Nepali way. Letting the little stuff slide, knowing ultimately that we're never in control. What I have been thinking of as utter chaos has morphed into a new kind of trust that what is to be, will be. Here, a colossal, American-style hissy fit is futile. No adult temper tantrum will change the process, nor will a threatening phone call from a high-priced lawyer, or a political connection. We Americans are ill-equipped to manage in this "archaic" Third World government. In the midst of our judgment of other lesser countries and their second-rate systems, we are the ones who are powerless. All we can do is sit and wait, something we just aren't very good at.

Om. Mani. Peme. Hum.

Although Carrie is a bundle of nerves, she's sweet and funny, with bright eyes and flaming red hair. She's making the trip with her sister, a mother of three, since her husband needs to stay home and work. Carrie's agency suggested a very different approach to the advice I'd been given about how best to integrate her new daughter. She was told to go to the orphanage, pick up her child, leave, and don't go back. I don't want to challenge her agency, but I worry that this could be a very bad idea. And it is.

Soon after arriving, Carrie and her sister set off for the orphanage to pick up little Priya, now almost two. While I understand her desire to be with her little one as soon as possible, the day they have planned sends a chill down my spine. It scares me to imagine how it will feel for the pixie-like girl who has no idea where she's being taken or what's going on. She hasn't learned any English yet, and Carrie doesn't speak any Nepali. Meanwhile, Carrie's sister, disturbed by Third World conditions, insists they take Priya immediately to the doctor for multiple vaccinations. Upon returning to Summit, they give her a bath, an experience which, from what Carrie reports, is traumatic at best. That's when she calls me.

"She just won't stop crying. I don't know what to do!"

"Try giving her some *dal bhat*," I suggest, hoping the familiar meal will provide her some comfort. "I'll bring Devi over and maybe that'll distract her," I further offer, hearing Priya howling in the background.

When we arrive, the poor babe is sitting in the middle of the floor, exhausted from screaming and whimpering like a wounded street puppy. Devi gets to work attempting to break all the toys and totally ignores her new "friend." Carrie is a wreck. She feels terrible for not making Priya's transition more gradual and wonders if she should take her back to the orphanage and try again tomorrow.

"It'll be okay, Carrie. What's done is done. Just try to move forward and repair the damage," I reassure her as her sister rolls her eyes, clearly bothered by this incorrigible child. I give her a hug and the last of our chamomile tea with hopes it will settle all of their nerves.

While Carrie has come fantastically prepared, she too has found herself in a Nepali trap. Just as she arrived to complete her process, the Minister responsible for signing off on the adoption decrees departed for a holiday in India until the following week. Although her file has been approved, it still isn't signed. So, to help pass the wait, I play hostess and invite Priya and her over to explore the books and puzzles in our playroom. With no siblings of my own, it's hard for me to understand the hold Carrie's sister has on her, so I try to dispel some of her misguided teachings.

"You know, kids like ours are very different from biological children," I offer gently. "Really, they can be night and day from your nieces and nephews. With Jack, I thought I was Super Mom, but with Devi, it's totally different. Trust me, Priya's fits have nothing to do with you or your lack of parenting experience. They don't mean she's a bad kid, or that you're a bad mom, you both just need time to adjust and get to know each other. You have been dreaming of her, but she's had no way to prepare for her new life with you."

"My sister keeps telling me to put her in 'time out,'" she sighs, "but that doesn't work."

"I have no doubt your sister is a great parent," I agree, "but she has no idea about parenting kids with attachment issues. A saint wouldn't know what to do with what our girls can throw at us. I hate to say it, but time out will probably only make your situation worse."

I draw more comparisons using Jack and Devi as living examples and offer her my mini-library of books on attachment. When it's time for her sister to leave, rather than asking her to extend her stay while she waits for the final signatures, Carrie happily sees her off, and the resulting freedom proves to be a wonderful relief. I understand her fear of being alone with this little stranger, but assure her that she can do it, and as days go by, she becomes *Ama* to little Priya, on their own terms and in their own time.

Just when I think we've discovered all that Summit has to offer, Jack finds one last prize. As usual, once Devi is down for her nap, Jack and I head for the pool. Stricken with puppy love, Jack does his best to impress a cute little girl, but she's determined to ignore him. Once her father gets out of the water to relax in the shade, as her little sister bobs along in the shallow end, Jack slowly wins her attention and they soon develop a friendship.

Federico is from Italy and a perfect stay-at-home dad, working as a private consultant, while his lovely wife Astrid, from Norway, is a tireless force within UNICEF. They adopted their two daughters, Isabel and Sofie, several years ago while stationed in Zambia. They understand the adoption game all too well, and we instantly become inseparable. They live just around the corner from Summit, and the path between our houses is soon well-traveled with Jack and Isabel trekking back and forth, trailed by their tiny sisters trying to keep up, and faithful *didis* in tow. While our little tribe plays in the gardens, the grown-ups have time to drink, laugh, and in Astrid's case, chain smoke. Federico and I mercilessly harass her about it, plugging our noses, mock gagging and coughing. She takes it all in stride and is quick to point out our shortcomings as well, namely, Federico's terrible driving and my pathetic hippie wardrobe.

After my cherished American friendships, Federico and Astrid are a fresh breath of cultured European air. They are so worldly, so refined, and their gourmet, home-cooked meals make it hard to believe I'm still in Kathmandu. As soon as they realized the culinary limitations of their local help, Federico began making dinner for the family most nights, and insists that my clan join them. I'm amazed by what he's able to concoct with ingredients I didn't even know could be found in the city. I always offer to help, but usually end up perched on a stool sipping wine and asking philosophical and ethical questions, since I'm sure he has all of life's answers. Astrid eventually stumbles in from work, always glad for the company and a legitimate distraction from the piles of paperwork that weigh her down. They're pros at living abroad and share fantastic stories of their adventures, particularly while in Africa; their experiences make the *Janaandolan* seem like a tea party.

I'm especially impressed by their stamina and dedication to exploring Nepal. They have their own car (a luxury in the Valley) shipped from their previous post which makes day trips easy. Jack is always a welcome addition on their outings since his presence seems to break up squabbling between the sisters, and he ends up seeing more sites than I do. The outings are too stimulating for

Devi, so we usually stay behind and enjoy quiet time together. Jack always brings some little trinket back for each of us, a practice Federico finds touching.

At Federico and Astrid's urging, I agree to tag along to a birthday party Jack has been invited to. We hop in for a ride with Federico and their kids, in spite of the tales of his terrifying driving, and Astrid agrees to meet us after putting in a few hours of work at the office.

When we pull up to the valet at our destination, I know right away I'm out of my element. The home of the birthday girl, near UN headquarters, is an exquisite old mansion restored for expat use. Jack, Isabel, and Sofie immediately disappear into the bustling crowd of children while Devi, already overwhelmed, grabs fistfuls of my skirt. Federico seems to know everyone, and I try not to cling to him like Devi does me. I feel like a pathetic country bumpkin and push our crudely wrapped gift to the back of the mountain of extravagant presents. I try to blend in and move through the crowd with Devi on my hip as demure waiters float about offering dainty hors d'oeuvres and champagne in plastic flutes. I attempt to mingle but can't help noticing the fashionista women looking down their perfect, surgically-enhanced noses at me as if questioning who let me in; they're clearly horrified by the wild animal child now swinging from my arm.

Soon enough, I give up and take Devi outside to the private playground, in spite of it being over-run by screaming children fighting over toys and rides. The game area is a free-for-all, and I am an unwelcome adult in this land of spoiled children.

On the swings, two princesses are comparing notes: "Oh yeah? Well *I'm* going to Indonesia!" one little girl brags. "Well, *I've* already been there. *I'm* going to Thailand; the beaches are better there." The other little girl one-ups. I can't bear to listen to this whiney banter, so we move on.

The monkey bars are less popular, so I hold Devi as she swings rung-to-rung, back and forth, again and again. The moment I get distracted and look away, she tries on her own and immediately plummets to the ground. Remarkably, she gets up and comes to me crying, even allowing me to pick her up for comfort, a huge stepping stone in our rocky river of trust.

The clouds build quickly in the afternoon heat and soon the rain begins, giving me an excuse to leave as the party moves indoors. The thought of being trapped inside this museum-like home stuffed with all that worldliness is too much for me, and I prepare to take a soggy walk home with Devi. Luckily, Federico and Astrid are ready to leave as well, and they drop us off at our gate. We scamper up the steps into the peace of home to settle down for an afternoon nap, the rain tapping a sweet lullaby.

Then the screaming starts.

Waking in terror, Devi is inconsolable, raging from the moment her eyes open. After going through my list of ineffective remedies: holding her, singing to her, patting her on the back, and even attempting to distract her by getting Jack to comically jump on the bed, I give up and let her scream. I don't know what else to do.

These screaming episodes have become more frequent, but as much as I try, I'm unable to find a direct correlation to anything concrete. Today, I'm certain it's sensory overload, but there have been other, routine days that produce the same post-nap result. Dinesh and Leena are off for the day, so I take her downstairs and she sits on the floor wailing while I prepare our snack-style dinner. There's no way we can go to Summit.

We sit down to eat, but she waves the food away and continues to scream until she sees the meal is almost over; then she stuffs some crackers in her mouth, panicked that they are almost gone. My ears ring in the welcome silence.

The hysteria seems to have passed, so Jack offers to take her into the playroom while I clean up the dinner dishes, but almost immediately the crashing and thrashing start. I drop the dishes as more screaming ensues, but now it's *Jack*. When I get to the door, Devi has him on his back, ferociously choking him, determined to do some damage. Now I'm the one screaming as I fight to pull her off of him. His face is ghostly white, his lips already turning blue. I plunk Devi aside and scoop Jack up, slamming the door behind me, abandoning her, something I've promised never to do. I know she is too small to reach the doorknob, but I don't care. My nerves are worn raw, and I'm beyond furious.

Dishes crash and hurled objects thud against the door, accompanied by howls of rage.

"Are you okay, Buddy?" I look into Jack's eyes, frantic as he coughs and fights to breathe. "Are you okay?"

His tears of fear, frustration, physical and emotional pain, soak the front of my shirt as I hold him tight.

"Why is she like this Mommy? Why does she want to hurt me?" He croaks between sobs, his spirit as injured as his body.

"I don't know, little bear, I wish I did." I rock him back and forth, stroking his back.

Finally, as Jack calms down, so do the sounds coming from the playroom, and I feel able to face Devi again. I know in my heart she doesn't know what she's doing, but I'm totally unprepared for what I find.

Every toy we own is strewn about the room, and a book is torn to pieces at her feet. When I recognize it as *Little Elephant Goes Home*, our only book with a character of Asian descent, I lose it, dropping to the floor in defeat to gather the pieces.

"Devi! How could you do this?" I yell, which prompts her to start screaming once again. Before she can resume throwing things, as she kicks and hits, I carry her up to the bedroom and firmly set her on her bed.

"Stay here," I order and go into the bathroom to splash water on my face, trying to cool down while she explodes with more screaming. Desperate to fix *something* tangible, I grab a diaper, but when I kneel down and put my hand on the bed, it's soaked; she's peed all over it. I shift her to the floor and drag her bed and blankets out to the terrace where I will the rain to wash away not just the urine, but the entire day. Watching intently, Devi shrieks in terror, but at this point, I'm done. On the periphery of my mind I know she is scared and out of control, but so am I, and in this moment, I have nothing left for her. I try to breathe, wet with sweat, my dress clinging to me, my heart pounding in my ears. She is still screaming. *Breathe deep, breathe deep.* I tip my face up to the sky and feel the rain pelt me.

"Please," I beg, sending prayers to any God or Goddess, government entity or psychiatric institute, "please, just make this all go away."

Finally cooling down in the rain, I feel my heartbeat slow, and my breath becomes more even. I look back toward the bedroom to see Devi standing at the window, terrified. She is just as desperate for this bad run to end, and now she is shadowed by Jack. He watches helplessly, shocked by what his mother has become. *This isn't good*, whispers a little voice inside me.

What do I do?

I look over the edge of the terrace at our peaceful garden and take a few more breaths, aware my behavior is under scrutiny, aching not to further fail them. Finally calm, I walk inside and take Devi's hand. Her diaper is on; Jack must have done it, forgiving her much faster than I have. I lead her to the playroom and show her the book.

"I am very angry that you ruined your book." I say as calmly as I'm able. The playroom is trashed from her waves of toddler rage. I quietly place the toys, books, and puzzles back on the shelves, then right the tiny kitchen and stack the dishes, replacing the plastic food as Devi watches through zombie eyes. I've made a practice of having her help me clean up after one of these fits, but I just can't handle another fight. At least this is something I *can* fix.

I take her back upstairs to where her bamboo bed sits naked. "Because you peed in your bed, you don't have your elephant blanket to sleep with." I pull out one of the thick winter blankets for a makeshift mattress, eager for this day to be over. "Devi, lie down." She doesn't move. "Devi. Lie. Down." Still no response, just a cold, defiant stare. I pick her up and lay her down, and, as if on cue, she begins to scream again. All I can do is drape a sheet over her, turn on *Midnight with Mozart*, and leave the room. I have no reserves left.

I find Jack on the sofa reading a *Tin Tin* comic and sit down at the table with the remains of the book Devi had torn up and my dwindling roll of First-World tape. Why couldn't I have just stayed calm and done this with her? Shown her that even though she was out of control and angry, that I could be steady and stable, a point of calm in her storm. Instead, I showed her how scary I can be. I met her rage with an intensity of my own, making her feel even more frightened and alone. I proved that I am not to be trusted, just like all the others before me. Tonight, I continued her suffering rather than providing refuge from it.

As I piece the book back together, I see the story in a new light and realize how fitting it is that Devi chose this book to destroy. A little girl goes to preschool and takes home a baby elephant, but the elephant is very sad and screams at the girl that she is not his mommy. Eventually, the little girl sees how unhappy the baby elephant is and takes him back to school so he and his mommy can be reunited. I feel like a fool. How could I have missed this parallel to our own lives? I'd been blinded by the thrill of finding a book with a cute little Asian girl, wanting her to have something to relate to, not seeing past the surface. How could I have even read this book to her? I am ashamed by my own ignorance.

I tiptoe into the bedroom to find her sprawled halfway off her bed and kneel down to lift her up to me. She anxiously throws her arms around my neck, grasping tightly. I may be scary, but I'm all she has now, and she isn't letting me go. I lie down on my bed with her, feeling her weight on my chest, and breathe deeply into her, trying to infuse her with the love I *really do* have for her. I have to find a way to shift my frustration so I can remain patient and calm instead of reacting to her. As the moon comes up to shine through the gauzy curtains onto her exquisitely beautiful face, I promise to try again tomorrow.

When morning peeks in, I sneak out of the bedroom to check my email, hoping for answers to all of life's problems. I find a message from a mother I'd connected with in an online chat group for parents of children struggling with attachment issues; her daughter had been diagnosed with Reactive Attachment Disorder. She's checking in, sweetly asking how I'm holding up. I appreciate the support, even if it is from far away. She goes on to proselytize, telling me that now, that since her five-year-old daughter has accepted Jesus as her savior, she is cured. Well, that's one approach.

Another email is from a child therapist a friend from the States recommended, responding to a lengthy email I'd sent pleading for help. She offers vague suggestions, nothing I'm not already familiar with, but at least I know there's someone I can talk to when we return to the US, even though she can't help me now. What *do* I need?

I need to run far far away and figure this out, like when I used to pack up and go climbing for weeks on end, telling no one where I was or when I would be back, just me, alone, on the side of a mountain. I need a retreat, time to work on all of this, time to find the answers. But now I have kids—where would that leave them? I think back to a conversation with Jack's father when he was planning a trip to Africa for six months, giving in to his gypsy ways and desire for travel. I had tried to help him understand he couldn't have a relationship with Jack if he kept leaving him. Then I realize, every time I lose my cool, I leave Devi. I am *already* in retreat, I have been for ten months, and maybe this is the best kind of retreat, completely unintentional, unplanned, and unscripted. I know I can do this; I have two little gurus on site who are willing to give me all the practice at patience I could possibly require, forcing me to face lessons I never realized I needed to learn, like the one about anger last night.

Walking through the morning mist, the dew melting off the grass, I offer Ganesh a stick of sweet incense and ask for help as I renew my dedication to taking things one day at a time; I begin with mindfully breathing in patience and exuding loving kindness. I am Devi's *Ama* now, I am all she has, and I long to be worthy of the gift the Kingdom of Nepal has bestowed upon me. I will make myself worthy of her.

Jack watches me intently from time to time when I meditate, asking about the prayers I say under my breath when offering incense to Ganesh. He's comfortable with his own *Om Mani Peme Hum* mantras while moving around the stupa at Boudha, spinning prayer wheels, imagining his good wishes going out like ripples in a pond all around the world, but every day he has more questions than I have answers. He's intrigued by the little boy monks we see in their tiny burgundy robes, huddled around piles of offerings on full moon nights at Boudha or Swayambhu. He's entranced by the chanting, the bells, the gongs, and especially by the goose-like bellowing of giant conch shells. His questions are surprisingly sophisticated, and I share with him my own reasons for appreciating Buddhist ways and explain why I find them comforting.

Back at home, he always attended Buddhist teachings with me, sitting quietly, not even taking out coloring books to entertain himself. When he was three, Jigme Tromge Rinpoche came for a visit, and while we all stood bowing as he entered, he recognized something in Jack, and approached, taking his head in his hands and bowing to him, touching forehead to forehead, then later giving him his first string of prayer beads.

"I think I should stay here," Jack announces while we are out walking. "I could live at the monastery and learn how to do the right things to end suffering and my heart can be at peace."

Hearing these words from my seven-year-old, his big, brown eyes pleading to stay in his new home, I know it's time to request an audience with Choki Nyma Rinpoche, the presiding abbot of the White Monastery, conveniently situated behind Boudha. After attending his teachings, I'd learned that the Rinpoche held audiences for followers to come forward and ask for help, advice, and blessings. I can't fathom leaving Jack in Kathmandu, but his desire is so strong, he needs instruction from someone with more authority than me. The clarity Choki Nyma Rinpoche may offer could be invaluable. My secret hope is that he will advise Jack to go back to the States and return to study at the monastery after he has graduated from high school, a milestone far enough away that I can be comfortable.

On the way to Boudha, Jack is a flurry of questions: What will it be like? Where will we sit? Can he ask questions? What kind of questions? As we come closer to the *stupa*, the attire of the women in the streets shifts to that of traditional Tibet, and my heart feels light. They are so beautiful, their facial features so much like my little girl, I wonder about her elusive past. My eyes tear up thinking of how incredibly blessed we all are to have found each other. Not just to fulfill something inside me, or to rescue her, but for Jack to have a sibling, a relationship I never experienced.

We walk past the main gate to the *stupa* and duck down a footpath to wind through to the inner life of Boudha. Jack reaches for me and by the dampness of his little hand, I know he's nervous.

"You've got nothing to worry about, Buddy. Don't be scared."

"Oh, I'm not scared," he replies thoughtfully. "I just don't think I've ever been this excited about anything before, *ever*. I can't decide which question to ask first."

"I'm sure it'll come out the right way. Rinpoche is used to helping people figure things out," I offer, then leave him to his thoughts.

I lead him into the *stupa*, and we walk in a circle as we spin prayer wheels and set our intention as the multicolored flags flutter in the summer breeze. Then we slip down a side alley, passing vendors and partially clothed, dust-covered children, and take the path to the monastery. A few people sit patiently on benches outside closed doors, and I approach a woman in Western dress to make sure we are in the right place, then take a seat. Jack nervously swings his feet under the bench.

Soon, Choki Nyma Rinpoche ascends the stairs and nods acknowledgement to the waiting group as we bow respectfully, hands folded in *namasté* prayer greeting, then he disappears behind the closed doors to prepare for his audience. We wait to be summoned, then find seats on floor cushions in the long narrow hall adorned with *thankas* (silk banners) picturing a host of deities. Rinpoche presides over us on his burgundy velvet chair with spirals of gold ornately decorating the back, surrounded by vases of flowers. Jack sits at attention and stops fiddling with his prayer beads that gleam like pearls around his neck.

The first man recognized is trying to get home to his family. Rinpoche blesses his journey and offers him guidance, touching his forehead, and placing a colorful, braided string around his neck for protection. The next man has an ill child; he too is blessed, along with a sacred string of his own. Several others come forward, but my Nepali is not advanced enough to know what's transpiring. Then, finally, it's Jack's turn.

As he walks forward to make his offering of incense and oranges, bowing respectfully, Rinpoche gestures for me to approach as well. I sit slightly behind, and to the side of Jack.

"Well little one, what brings you to me today?" Rinpoche asks, leaning forward inquisitively.

"I want to come live in the monastery and learn how to be a good person," Jack states clearly, sitting up proudly.

"Oh, huh, huh, I see!" Rinpoche chuckles, looking past him to me as I smile humbly. "Well, young man, I think you are already good person, or you would not be here today. Tell me about these beads you are wearing."

Jack tells him the story of meeting Jigme Tromge Rinpoche, and I am amazed at how vividly he remembers the event. Rinpoche has a good laugh at his telling of the story, encouraging him by asking questions along the way. Jack answers with wisdom and insight I didn't know he had.

"So, what brings you to Kathmandu?" Rinpoche inquires, clearly enjoying his time with Jack.

"Me and my mom came here to find my little sister. She was in an orphanage, but now she lives with us."

"And how do you like having a little sister?"

"It's mostly good, but sometimes, like when she takes my toys, when I try to get them back, she screams and hits. But I don't hit her back, she's still too little."

This elicits more chuckles from the jovial abbot. "Well, it is good you are patient with her. She will be glad later."

"Can't I just come live here with you instead?" Jack pleads, getting to the heart of the matter.

"What I believe you need is not time in monastery, but go into world and share kindness already in you heart. Will you make me promise? To be good little boy?"

"Oh yes, anything!" Jack squeals.

"When people come to me, wanting to do good things in the world, one thing they do is take Bodhisattva vow. This is promise to not harm any other sentient being, to end suffering and causes of suffering any way possible. Can you do that?"

Jack agrees, nodding so fervently I am afraid his head is going to pop off.

"And Mommy, do you pledge to help you boy uphold this vow?"

I nod respectfully, bowing deeply, hands folded *namasté*.

Then Rinpoche motions for Jack to rise and move closer, asking him to repeat the words of the vow. Jack presses his hands together in prayer, making a promise I have no doubt he will uphold. "May I attain Buddhahood for the benefit of all sentient beings," and Rinpoche sprinkles water over his head, reciting a blessing in Tibetan. It is as if I can see golden glitter hovering around Jack's head as he glows from the inside out.

> Shantideva said this about the Bodhisattva vow:
> May I be the protector to those without protection,
> A leader for those who journey,
> And a boat, a bridge, a passage
> For those desiring the further shore.
> May the pain of every living creature
> Be completely cleared away.
> May I be the doctor and the medicine
> And may I be the nurse
> For all sick beings in the world
> Until everyone is healed.

As I come out of my own waking dream, I start to tear up as I bow to Rinpoche, so thankful for him, for this opportunity, for this *stupa*, for this country.

"All these fancy thing not necessary," the Rinpoche continues, gesturing around his adorned prayer room. "Bodhichitta live in you heart; you take everywhere you go. You do not need monastery to be good boy. You already good boy. Take you good heart into world and do good things for benefit of all sentient beings."

He hands Jack a card with his new Tibetan name on it, Kunpen Sangpo, and places another magical string around Jack's neck as well as mine, blessing us on our journey. We rise and bow deeply, thanking him repeatedly for his kindness and support. I can't think of a time that I've felt so proud of my sweet little boy, quickly becoming a young man.

Once we reach the back gate of the *stupa*, Jack is off, glowing as he skips through Boudha, spinning prayer wheels and singing out *Om Mani Peme Hum!* After getting a bite to eat, we start out the main gate to drop some rupees in the collection box, but before we reach it, Jack stops to admire a wooden door with an ornate tiger painted on it. Noticing him eyeing the piece, the shopkeeper comes out to chat, but there is no way we can take home a souvenir of this size, so I play aloof, and look at postcards in the next stall down.

"Mom! He said I can have it!" Jack bounces up.

"Well of course he said that, but I'm the one that has to pay for it. Come on, let's go," I reply cynically.

"But Mom! He said I could have it!" He argues, and seeing the doubt in my eyes, grabs my hand and pulls me over to the shopkeeper. "Mom, this is Nirad."

"Nice to meet you," I offer, taking the man's grungy hand. "I appreciate you offering this beautiful door to my son, but we will be going back to the United States soon and have already purchased many souvenirs."

"Oh, Madam, it would give me great pleasure to give this gift to your son on such an auspicious day. He is a special boy, born in the Year of the Tiger, and this door should be with him," Nirad replies steadily, explaining the symbols painted alongside the tiger and how they are of benefit to my young boy. "If this one is not to your liking, I have a warehouse not far from here. I will have my assistant take you and you may select anything you like."

"You are very kind, but I don't want to trouble you," I say, ashamed for doubting his good intentions.

"Madam, it is no trouble! please." He motions for his assistant, not much more than a boy himself, to take us down to the warehouse.

We enter the dark, dank building to find we are surrounded by pieces of people's homes, brought from war-torn Tibet. Doors, kitchen-sized cabinets, armoires, and trunks depicting dragons, Gods and Goddesses, auspicious symbols, and many more tigers, no two the same. We snoop around, squeezing through the tiny rows, fishing through piles, amazed by all there is to explore.

"I just want the one at the shop," Jack finally concludes. Nirad, clearly in awe of Jack, is committed to giving him this beautiful and incredibly heavy gift. He muscles the Hobbit-sized door out the front gate, haggling with the driver as I drop a thousand rupee note in the collection box, wishing Dave were here to see this spectacle. Nirad and the driver wrestle the ancient door through the hatchback of the taxi and onto the back seat. I smash myself in next to it, letting Jack jump into the front seat with the driver, knowing he will always remember this magical day as we bump along. He touches his beads, still hung faithfully around his neck.

"Mom! Look!"

He points to a group of kids by the side of the road throwing rocks at a street puppy as they kick and chase it. I groan and roll my eyes, sad for the little pup.

"Mom! I made a promise!" Jack cries out, as if he's the one in pain.

"*Rook nus!*" I command, directing the driver to stop. "Jack, you wait here." I hop out as the children corner the tiny pup. I shoo them away, "*Badmas!*"

The pup is terrified, shaking and injured. Without a second thought, I scoop her up as she ineffectively nips at my hand and cuddle her to my chest, plopping back in the taxi as the driver looks disgusted by my new souvenir. "*Jao, jao,*" I direct him, ignoring his disapproval, though the sewer stench coming from her is overwhelming. With my head hanging out the window, I remind myself, all we need is a little soap and water, the remedy to all of Kathmandu's ills.

At home, our gate guard handles the door as I hand the taxi driver another thousand rupee note, making him glad he picked up the crazy Americans, the door, and the stinky pup.

Leena is unfazed as I stride upstairs to give our latest rescue her first bath. Devi clambers up behind me, excited to meet the new family member. As I turn on the water, the ball of fur and bones, which up to this point had been scared stiff, starts to wiggle and protest. Devi kneels down and stokes her head, offering words of advice, "*Bastadi, bastadi,*" gently, gently. As I dip the pup underwater, her coat parts, and I'm horrified to see that she is *covered* in ticks. They are packed in her ears, covering her belly, and even in between her tiny toes. I take a peek at her gums and they are nearly white, lacking enough blood to make them pink. I pull the ticks off furiously, only for Jack to rebuke me.

"You're killing them!" he shouts, watching them slosh down the drain, "they're sentient beings!" Seeing the serious look in his eye, I resort to getting the sewer off her first and deal with the ticks later.

Jar in hand, Jack joins me on the terrace to help finish the job. As I pull off a tick, I drop it in the jar, and he slaps the lid over the top, careful not to let any of his blood-sucking friends escape. I agree to let him take the ticks to the trash heap down the alley when we're done, the only acceptable place I can think of. Devi continues to softly stroke the pup's muzzle, and I'm taken aback by her compassion. Before long, our new canine companion stops wiggling, closes her eyes, and drops off to sleep. I've never seen so many ticks on one dog, not even on the strays from the reservation back home. We stop counting at a hundred.

July

As June slid into July, Carrie and Priya left, but three other families were in a mad dash to the finish line at the Consulate. Though our files had been approved at the same time, it was now first come, first served, and I was happy to let them go ahead. No demand for speedy service, or mental pushing and shoving, would get anyone anywhere. Nepal moved at its own pace without regard for American plans, and on my extended timeline, a day or two made no difference at all.

After watching Steve and Lisa move through their final process with grace and ease, I felt cautiously optimistic that I knew what to expect. As a result, I had no intention of asking Annie for anything, believing, at this point, she would only slow me down. While I was beyond relieved to get word from Rajkumar that my file had been signed, I still had to wait to be summoned to the Ministry to collect the final documents.

I plotted out the tasks I had to complete on the calendar like a roadmap. Signing the final papers and collecting Devi's travel document issued by the Kingdom of Nepal would complete the paperwork on the Nepali side. Then, I would submit this packet to the American Consulate for review, take Devi to the doctor for a health certificate, arrange for my exit interview, and, providing there was no further investigation, pick up Devi's visa. The agency advised this process would take at least two weeks, but I knew I couldn't count on anything. Even Steve and Lisa had to wait several days for their file to be approved by the Consulate, and they had done everything by the book. While anxiety over leaving brewed inside me, I still had plenty to do before vacating our Nepali home, and first on the list was booking our flight back to the States.

After picking up the packet required for the Embassy, I reluctantly stop by the Thai Airways office. The tickets I'd purchased for Jack and me have an open return date, so I need to make a tentative booking. I begin to worry as I watch the space between the agent's eyebrows wrinkle while she taps at her keyboard.

"I am sorry, Madam," she concludes, "all flights out of Kathmandu are booked through July *and* August. Many people are traveling on holiday before the new school term begins; there are no seats currently available. Something will probably open up," she smiles in an attempt to reassure me, but her bobblehead response tells me what this really means: we could be here until September. Kathmandu continues to feel like the darkly romantic Hotel California. While I love our adopted home, knowing I can't leave is unnerving. I try not to panic, but I feel like an animal in a trap. Returning to the States after the school year has already started will make our transition back to American life considerably more difficult and stressful.

Once home, I email Christina to update her on our timeline. She's trying to get back to the Valley before we leave but is unsure about her travel dates as well. Of course, she has one last gem of advice: upgrade. It's likely there will be availability in business class, plus, the seats are far more comfortable, and our baggage allowance will increase. Now that our departure is in motion, I walk over to Summit and make a reservation for us to stay a few days at the end of July, just before we leave.

Everything is lining up, and I feel sick. Sick at the coming upheaval in Devi's delicate world. Sick at leaving our home and Nepali family. Sick at the thought of returning to a community devoid of my Devi-wise support system. But for now, I take a deep breath and remember, I have to keep my eyes on the prize, a visa for Devi.

Then the call finally comes. "Hello, Madam?" A cheerful voice sing-songs when I pick up.

"Yes. Hello Rajkumar."

"Can you please come to my office? It is time . . . to sign . . . your papers." He says slow and deliberate, knowing this is the call I've been waiting for.

"Now?"

"You are too busy?" he jokes.

"I'll be right there!"

"Madam!" he catches me before I hang up. "Don't forget to bring Miss Devi with you," he says, not missing the opportunity to tease me.

"I couldn't forget *her!*" I cheer and skip into the bedroom to change clothes. I have nothing "special" to wear on this most special day of all, so I choose the dress I have practically lived in, modestly long and flowing with tiny flowers on a baby blue background. Then I find something sweet for Devi, a pretty pink sundress, her favorite color, and wrangle her from the garden where she is helping Leena pick flowers for the table. Clean and dressed, we stop by to offer incense to our most auspicious neighbor, Ganesh, then hail a taxi to the orphanage.

I slip off my shoes and step through the doorway with less trepidation and fear of a screaming meltdown from Devi. Now I know, she holds her trauma in, rather than letting it run down her face like I'm prone to do. She will save her freak out for when we are safely home. In the office, Rajkumar gives me the necessary paperwork and directions to the Ministry office, and we shuffle back out to catch another taxi. Devi's legs clamp around my waist as her crab claws go to work along my neckline.

The day is already hot, and my back is wet with sweat as we

honk our way downtown. We swerve through the roundabout to enter the government complex of gleaming white buildings, a prime target for Maoists bombings in months past. As we pass the vacant gun turret, I'm thankful for the three-month ceasefire the Maoists have agreed to in hopes of gaining seats in the new Ministry.

I follow Rajkumar's directions to the first office and step up to a giant desk with a tiny man behind it.

"I'm here to sign my adoption decree," I say, offering him my paperwork. He looks me up and down before taking our passport photos and affixing them here and there. I offer him the expected rupees and he gruffly hands me a receipt, then takes my packet to the next desk, which is awkwardly crammed into a short hallway that leads to an enormous, carved wooden door. In a low voice, he presents my documents to presumably the next man in the hierarchy, gesturing toward me, frown still in place. The second man smiles and nods, then stands up and takes my packet behind the closed door.

"Wait here," the frowning man gestures toward a vintage faux-leather couch.

I pull out Devi's favorite board books and read quietly as her anxiety grows. The minutes tick by in slow motion. Finally, the heavy wooden door opens, and we are summoned inside. We take our seats before another man who appears to be at the top of the bureaucratic food chain. He flips through our file, asking questions to verify the information within, then crosschecks my passport, while smiling warmly at Devi. Eventually, he puts his stamp and signature in all the right places, then hands the packet back to me.

"Continue on Madam, around the corner and up the steps," he directs.

As we walk out of the office, Devi sweetly requests, "Potty, *Ama*," crossing her legs uncomfortably. This simple communication is a miracle in itself, and the search for a bathroom trumps any legalities. Knowing a women's room will be hard to come by, I settle for the men's and quickly duck into the filthy, dank closet of a bathroom, careful not to slip on the slimy wet floor. I hoist Devi onto the edge of a urinal so she can relieve herself, grateful she misses my sandal in her urgency. Once she has done her business, yet another miracle, we skip the "wash your hands" part of the process. I'm sure we will be more germ-infested after touching the grimy sink fixtures, so we wipe our hands on the tail of my dress.

As we make our way up the creaky staircase, I remind Ganesh we are still here, hoping he hasn't forgotten our mission. We are at the Nepali finish line, only steps away from being mother and daughter for real, on paper, forever and always. The office we are looking for is ridiculously overcrowded with filing cabinets for partitions that create cramped cubicles. As we squeeze inside, a man's head pops out from behind a stack of boxes; he's the only one here. I step over and around an inconveniently placed sofa to present him our packet of paperwork, to his apparent displeasure, while Devi attempts to scale my leg, uncomfortable in this new room. I can feel her stimulation threshold peaking.

"Wait, please," he directs, pointing to the sofa. And there we sit, and sit, and sit, and sit, reading all of our books twice more. Devi is starting to check out, chewing at her fingers and pulling her hair when she isn't pinching me. Knowing she's about to blow, we stroll outside and down the walkway, back and forth, back and forth, checking in periodically. I peek around the filing cabinet to find the man in the cubicle doing absolutely nothing. At one point he's leisurely eating his lunch and sipping tea. Next, I find him jovially chatting on the phone. Later, I'm convinced he's *actually* counting paper clips. Our paperwork hasn't even moved. Eventually, I'm able to get Devi to lie down with her head in my lap, and she allows me to stroke her sweaty back, something she has grown to enjoy. She drifts off to sleep and rolls over. Beads of sweat dot her nose, her mouth slightly ajar with exhaustion, one eye suspiciously half open, vigilantly watching for bad guys. Smoothing her hair from her face, I'm taken aback by just how incredibly beautiful she is, and again, I can't help but wonder, where is her *ama*? I ache, thinking of her mother unable to see her grow up; she has changed so much just since we met. I can't fathom giving up a child, trusting a stranger you've never met to keep her safe and healthy, to teach her how to do the dishes, how to sew a button, to help her get ready for her first date. Devi and I are looking at a lifetime together, but today her mother, the woman who gave birth to her, will be officially erased from her life forever. How can I find joy in her mother's loss?

"Madam?" The man's head pokes out from around a filing cabinet, shaking me from my trance.

"Yes?" I jerk upright, afraid he has seen my intimate thoughts.

"Please, come," he commands, waving me back.

I struggle to gather Devi, hoping not to wake her, but she startles and grasps at my neck frantically, nearly choking me.

"It's okay," I whisper. "We're still in the office."

She jerks back to look me squarely in the eyes, holding my face in her hands, studying me carefully, then, realizing I'm a safe person, she wraps her arms around me again, burying her head in my neck. I squeeze us between filing cabinets, so we are wedged in front of the desk. The man goes through the documents one by one, explaining what each is, verifying that I have signed in all of the places he points out. Then, he gets to the final page and reads me the statement I must swear to uphold. I promise to keep Devi well-fed, educated, adequately clothed, free of disease, and finally, that I will not use her as a servant or sell her. I blink past my shock and agree to all stipulations, my head spinning that this is really happening. He hands me a pen, and the moment I have been waiting for, dreaming of, is finally here. I will my hand to stop shaking and sign my name. I look to the Nepali calendar on the wall, but without a magic decoder ring, I have to ask the Gregorian date.

"It is the fourth of July," the man says.

Of course it is. I smile through my tears, and thank the little man, forgetting the tortuous wait, and he actually smiles back. He can see how much I love this sweaty little girl hanging around my neck though she refuses to look at him. He shuffles my papers and secures them in an envelope. "Take these to the American Consulate. You are now her mother. *Namasté*." I bow to him awkwardly, with an anxious Devi clinging to me, determined not to be left behind. And that is it. In the all-seeing eyes of the Kingdom of

Nepal, we are now officially mother and daughter, *Om Mani Peme Hum*. It's time to celebrate!

On the way home, we stop off at my favorite handicrafts shop for something to remember this special day. Devi chooses a handmade cloth doll, a grandma, with silver grey yarn hair swept up in a bun and a jeweled *tika* on her forehead. She's wearing a burgundy flowered sari with black sandals on her toeless feet and has red and gold bangles on her stuffed arms. Devi hugs her close and I think of her mother and her grandmother, wishing they could see her crinkled eyes smile. We step back out and into the traffic to walk up the hill to Summit for a banana split celebration. Along the way, we stop off at a tea stall to call my mother. It's the middle of the night on her side of the world, but I don't hesitate to wake her up and share the good news.

"You're officially a Grandma!" I sing into the crackly phone after her groggy hello.

"Oh Kate! That's just wonderful. I didn't think it would ever happen!" I can hear happy tears in her voice.

"Me either. It sure does feel good."

"Now you can just come home. I'm sure you can't wait!"

But I can wait. I've fallen in love with Nepal, and I can't stand the thought of leaving. I chuckle to myself, thinking I must have Stockholm Syndrome, now in love with what once felt like my captor.

After finishing our treat, Devi babbles to her grandma doll and I sink into the sofa cushions under a waterfall of relief. Although Devi isn't aware of just how special the day is, it doesn't matter. I know, and I will remember it for both of us. We've made it through, and now she really is my little girl, to have and to hold, from this day forward.

We return home and I tell an expectant Leena the good news, and she hugs me joyously, then heads home for the day. While the kids bounce off Devi's sugar buzz, I float out to the terrace to look down on the city. I want to memorize every part of it and never forget this magical time in the Himalayan Kingdom.

We continue to celebrate at the Roadhouse Café with the best pizza our side of the Bagmati. Once we are stuffed with pizza and still more ice cream, we taxi home and I get the kids in bed, then make myself a cup of tea and settle down for the evening. Now that I am on the other side of the wait, I feel confident making one last post to the online adoption group for Nepal. Annie had advised me to keep a low profile because the group was monitored by the Embassy, as well as by the Nepali officials. However, I've found so many fired up criticisms of the Nepali adoption process, the travel warnings, stories of trials and tribulations, cheers of support, heartbreaks and happy endings, that now, so close to the end, I'm ready to chime in with a perspective of my own.

Stand in the Traffic

```
Hello All!
    Today I officially became my daughter's
Ama! Almost exactly one year from the date of
referral, ten months after arriving in Nepal,
five months after signing at the CDO, and one
Janaandolan later. For the first time, sitting
in that run-down, crowded concrete block
office, sweat running down my back, beading
on my upper lip, my sleeping daughter's damp
head in my lap, I could really, honestly, say,
I would do it all again, and I think most
(dare I say all?) of us would.
    From my perspective, the issues that
prolong adoption in Nepal have been the
result of misconceptions, misleading
information or outright mistakes by Western
adoption agencies, not Nepal. Other times,
problems arise out of the nosy neighbor
mentality of the US Embassy. Yes, there is
political instability. Yes, there are delays.
Yes, at times the Ministry doesn't give a
hoot about us or our anxiety over bringing
our children "home." But we are guests in
their country, taking their children away
because they lack the resources to care for
```

them. In a culture where saving face is often of critical importance, I have to imagine, this must hit a nerve.

We come to adoption wanting a child, sometimes desperately. While we may cloak our desire in altruism, ultimately, this choice is to fill something we feel is missing in our lives, a precious child. We cannot allow our longing for that little bundle of joy to translate into anger at Nepal, our child's birth country. Placing all those feelings, bound up in a ferocious little package, on the doorstep of Nepal, is of no benefit to anyone, ever. We know the difficulties of adopting from Nepal at the outset, and if we weren't advised of these issues from the beginning, then those feelings should be let loose on the agency that misled you, not the people of Nepal.

I don't want to get on some spiritual soapbox, but my time in Nepal has been one of the most deeply profound experiences of my life, which I give great thanks for. I've come to realize what I really need in life. I see the power of compassion, and PATIENCE! Don't get me wrong, I do get frustrated (like while waiting at the orphanage this morning before going to the Ministry and watching my daughter shape-shift into a scared rabbit), but what does all that frustration do for me? Nothing. It doesn't make the time go faster, and really, it doesn't feel good either; for me, or my daughter.

We can come to this experience with a "hurry hurry, rush rush!" American mentality and be endlessly frustrated and anxious. Or, we can try really, really hard to trust that it will all work out in the end. This can be the most difficult lesson of trust we ever have, almost as difficult as crossing the street in Nepal, child in arms with chaotically disorganized laneless traffic rushing by on either side, horns honking and fumes billowing around us.

By our nature we always want to know the answer, and we want to know it right now! Is it black or white, up or down, left or right, July or August? Pursuing adoption in Nepal, we hand over the power of all these answers to a tiny country on the other side of the world. The answers are not clear. The process is anything but a straight line. The hardest place to be is in the middle, surrendering to the not-knowingness. Stand in the traffic and know you will get across.

My heartfelt thoughts go out to all of you. Whether you have gotten through to the other side, or are still waiting, look to your child, whether in the flesh or just to the tattered picture you carry with you wherever you go, and trust. This is what we ask of these little people when we bring them into our lives, we have to practice a bit of it ourselves.

Namasté,
Kate (still) in Kathmandu

With all of the tasks on the Nepali side complete, now it's time to tend to the requirements of the US Embassy. The first thing on the list is an official medical exam for Devi's health certificate. I know her short and traumatic history with doctors will create anxiety and distress, but since I'm mandated to use the physician assigned by the Embassy, rather than her familiar doctor, I have no choice but to swallow hard and move forward with board books and snacks in hand.

In a cramped, third-floor office, packed wall-to-wall with Nepalis of all ages exhibiting a wide array of conditions, we wait for the dreaded exam. I'm the focus of attention, being the only non-Nepali in the room, whiter than white in spite of my summer tan. Trying not to feel like an animal in the zoo, I convince myself everyone is just looking at beautiful Devi and gaze out the window and across the river, almost able to see our little house on the hill.

As the hours pass, Devi becomes less and less compliant, refusing to look at her books, throwing snacks on the floor or at me, and rolling around on the filthy tile under the plastic chairs. I feel the others staring, silently judging my obviously terrible parenting skills. I try to pick her up and pace around the office, "You're okay, we'll be done soon," I whisper, but she'll have none of it. She scratches at my face and bucks to be put down, freeing her to further terrorize the other patients, whacking them with magazines and stomping on their feet. I start to gather our things to go, surrendering to the reality I will have to try again another day, when finally, a nurse calls out, "Saunders." We shuffle into the privacy of an exam room where the shiny instruments only intensify Devi's fears.

I'd hoped the doctor, a Nepali with experience dealing with orphans, would be able to shed some light on my endless list of questions about Devi, like how old she actually is, or what the mysterious water blisters are that come up on her hands from time to time. But he is in no mood for talking, oblivious to everything but the form he has to fill out.

"Remove her clothing," he commands, and I know this is not going to go well. I wrestle her clothes off and he roughly pokes and prods her, trying to force her to open her mouth, a battle he soon loses, and shoots a disapproving frown at me.

"She hasn't had good experiences with doctors," I offer meekly. "Maybe if you are patient . . ."

But he can't hear me and continues to treat her like livestock. She starts to wail, low and quiet at first, looking to me for help, her bottom lip quivering, but as he continues to grab and squeeze, she lets loose with full on screams of terror. He steps away, shaking his head, making notes in her chart.

"What vaccines would you like?" he asks, as if all is well.

"None, thank you, we'll take care of that once we're back in the States." There's no way I'm letting this man stick a needle in her, besides, in a land of no refrigeration, I don't trust the effectiveness of anything he wants to inject her with. We would be going from a world saturated with frightening health conditions to one laden with hand sanitizer; I was willing to take the chance. I try to redress my frenzied little monster, desperate to get out of there, and sign forms with one hand, while preventing her from hitting me with the other. I'm crushed, feeling like she's lost all trust in me for bringing her to this terrible place.

"We're all done. Time to go home," I reassure her, but it's way too late. Her circuits are blown. She looks right through me as tearless, inconsolable wails pierce the concrete office. I pull her onto my hip, shuffling papers and pulling out rupees to toss to the receptionist on the way out. I know I'm living up to the expectations of everyone waiting in the office—the belief that foreigners are not suitable for Nepali children. Out on the street, I purchase a marigold garland to distract Devi, asking her to hold it for me. She settles down and politely plucks off every petal, leaving a tangerine trail behind us.

When we go to the Embassy for our exit interview, surprisingly, Devi is a gem. I don't know if it's the time of day, the improved environment, or the choice of snacks, and I don't care. I'm thankful for the timeliness of our visit, absent of the epic wait I've grown accustomed to; clearly the stars are aligned in our favor. The Consular officer, who usually does the interviews, and who also seems to have it out for Annie, or anyone connected to her, is nowhere to be seen. Instead, we meet with a polite smiling young man who is clearly taken with Devi and her charms, in spite of her rearranging a few items on his desk. It feels more like an afternoon chat than the anxiety-filled interview I had been dreading. No questions are asked about where Devi has been living, just who I paid and when, all easily answered with the detailed list I prepared ahead of time.

With the interview complete, Devi and I skip down the steps and head home for dinner. I stop myself from counting how many dinners we have left.

As our last days tick down, my to-do list continues to grow. There is the pile of donations for the orphanage: books, puzzles and outgrown clothes. With so many children there, our meager toys will only cause strife, so those go to the Café U play area, along with our chicken shack street dog, Kali. After seeing how sweet she was with their daughter, the owners gladly agree to give her shelter and all the Japanese food scraps she can eat. It gives me peace of mind knowing she will be well taken care of, extending her loyalty to her new family. All of the plants I've accumulated are shuttled over to Federico and Astrid's terrace before they leave on holiday. I can't help but tear up over goodbye cocktails, telling them the story of the goat planter with the missing ear, my gift for Jack after his tragic meeting with the pretty white sacrificial goat. Housewares are sold and distributed to incoming expats, Dinesh and Leena humbly refusing my repeated offers of everything, but gratefully accepting Jack and Devi's bikes.

With Devi's sleep being such a point of concern, I have a crate built to ship her bamboo bed back to the States, as well as Jack's prized Tibetan door. The modest tailor-made fall wardrobes for the kids, corduroy pants for Jack and velour dresses for Devi, fill in the nooks and crannies of the crate along with incense burners, tea cups, and my prized Tibetan carpet.

Jack and I decide it's best for our cat Tenzing to stay in his native land, knowing we will never satisfy his love of catching sewer rats in our mountain home populated by predators. A kind, single man is looking for a feline friend, so Tenzing goes to his new home. Bruce will be on his own, something he is clearly capable of. Tessa takes Squeaky to live at the orphanage she volunteers at, but unfortunately, poor Pete, our parrot, died in captivity, despite my best avian husbandry efforts.

I managed to find homes for the dozen or so street puppies that flowed through our compound over the months with help from not only Dr. Devkota, but also Jack's violin teacher. But now,

I'm challenged with a lame pup. While healthy, she is irreparably injured, most likely due to repeated kicks, an all too common Nepali approach to dealing with unwanted dogs. She drags her front paw, turning it under, and has worn a hole in the top of it.

"Madam, the leg has nerve damage, she has no feeling in it, so it will continue to drag." Dr. Devkota advises me. "The infection is not responding to antibiotics, and if left untreated, it will fester, and the bacteria will enter her bloodstream. She will die a slow and painful death unless we amputate."

While I understand it's necessary, I hate the idea of the vet amputating the disfigured limb, knowing she will be near impossible to find a home for. The sad truth is that female dogs are as undervalued as female children, and one that is seen as damaged, even more so. I accept that in addition to upgrading all of our plane tickets, I need to buy one more for our little pup.

I decide to have the procedure done sooner rather than later, giving her time to heal before the long flight home. Sitting in the vet clinic with a shower curtain used to divide the office and exam room, I feel queasy at the thought of what's happening on the other side. I hear our little pup whimper as she wakes too early from the anesthetic, Dr. Devkota still sawing at her leg with a length of wire. I try not to second-guess my choice to have the surgery done here and remind myself of the vet's unquestionable ability. I sit patiently, breathing deep, sipping my cup of tea, while empathetic tears roll down my cheeks, then look out the front door in time to see the zoo elephant out for his daily walk. I think of Ganesh and ask for his help with my little canine friend. Eventually, Dr. Devkota emerges from behind the plastic curtain.

"She will be fine. You have made a good decision," he says, offering me the dismembered limb wrapped in newspaper. Seeing the look of shock on my face he quickly asks, "Would you like for me to dispose of it?"

Swallowing hard, I answer, "No, I can take care of it," and think of a place in the garden where a little piece of her will stay in her homeland. The alternative would be for it to end up in a trash pile on the side of the road to be scavenged by other dogs and street children.

Skipping a taxi, I opt to walk home, glad for the opportunity to follow one of my favorite routes. I daydream of days gone by as I pass questionable cafés, Nora's old flat, the nursery I frequent, the tea stall where we first met Bruce. Eyeing all the places soldiers were once stationed, I see that Nepal has changed before me, just as Jack, Devi and I have changed. I've gone from being terrified of getting lost in the maze of city streets to knowing them intimately. Nepal will never be the same, and neither will I.

At home, Jack and Devi greet me with jubilant cries, eager to see the sleeping pup in Devi's outgrown baby sling. I put her on the bed Jack has made of sofa cushions, towels, and one of his dirty t-shirts in hopes that his smell will bring her comfort as she recovers.

My vigil is soon interrupted by the phone ringing. It's the Embassy. Devi's visa has been issued! No requests for further information, no investigation. We are free to leave Nepal.

No longer feeling the need to act on impulse and rush straight to the Embassy, I stick to my original plan for the day and look forward to spending time with one of my favorite people, Zenji, a gentleman from Tibet who operates a carpet factory on the outskirts of town. We slowly became friends over cups of tea after I wandered into his showroom, amazed by the beauty and craftsmanship surrounding me. I loved spending afternoons listening to stories of his childhood in Tibet, so when I told him we would be leaving the country soon, he made a generous offer to take me to his carpet factory for a tour. It's an opportunity I can't pass up.

With the drowsy puppy back in the sling, I kiss the kids and go to meet Zenji at his showroom. We drive past the Ring Road and into the countryside, stopping for *bapas* along the way for the children of the carpet makers he provides work and housing for, also Tibetan refugees. When we pull up to the building, Zenji looks around cautiously, then hustles me inside. He explains that there are still pockets of Maoists hiding nearby, and if they see him with a Westerner, they're sure to come looking for a "donation," a polite term for extortion.

Leading me from one part of the building to the next, he

explains everything in detail, from how the raw wool is processed, to where it is dyed and spun. Then, finally, we enter the largest of the rooms, filled with more than a dozen looms of various sizes, strung with carpets in all stages of completion. Happy, giggling children are everywhere, some of the women nurse their babies while taking a break from their immaculate work. I am in awe of the beauty, the family atmosphere, the honest work; all made possible through the perseverance and bravery of this one noble man. He addresses each of them, as well as their children, handing out biscuits with a fatherly smile, and introduces me as a friend. We retire to his office and its breathtaking view of the glowing emerald valley with the Himals in the background and share cups of the best tea I've ever had. As Zenji speaks softly, full of grace, I expect him to start levitating, and I drink in his wisdom. He patiently answers all of my questions, helping me to see another world view. I marvel at his ability to forgive and remain compassionate after living through the loss of family, home, and country. When the puppy wakes up, and pokes her head out of the sling, Zenji smiles with delight praising me for my kindness, a compliment I feel warm my heart. I confess we haven't named her, not planning to keep her until I realized how difficult it will be to find her a suitable home. I tell him how she was found on Buddha's birthday and ask if he has any suggestions. Eventually "Norbu" is chosen, a Tibetan name meaning "precious gem."

Then, like being shaken awake from a dream, Zenji spots something in the distance and rises to investigate further, his brows knitting in concern. I realize the sweeping view is not just for aesthetics.

With the same grace he carries through all of his tasks, Zenji announces it is time to go. If his vehicle is spotted, we will be expecting visitors, none of whom will be very friendly. As he tells his guards in hushed tones what he has seen on the horizon, I climb into the truck and he bolts the front entrance, apologizing for our hasty departure. Suddenly, I understand, the political tension is nowhere near over.

After bouncing back down the road without incident and

returning to town, it's painful parting ways, and I wish I had all day to simply be in his presence. I bid him farewell, promising to return. I catch a taxi to my next stop downtown to visit a woman, Carroll, who has started a company called Wild Earth, specializing in handmade soaps, salves, and lotions. I became interested in her enterprise when exploring business ventures for my visa, and although we are on our way out, meeting her is a must since I'm still secretly hoping to find a reason to stay on in the Himalayan Kingdom.

After wandering around three different Ganesh statues, I finally come upon the one that leads to the compound housing the company headquarters. I'm greeted warmly and shown around the beautifully renovated old mansion turned soap factory, the rooms smelling of sweet herbs. I'm impressed by the organization, its founder agelessly graceful and kind. She employs a staff of Nepali women, each operating a different part of the business. She is truly selfless, keeping her own salary minimal, and turning any profit back to the business to develop new products, thereby creating more jobs for more women. This empowers them not only to support their families, more importantly, it offers them the priceless gift of knowledge and improved self-worth. I feel myself melting into this world, dreaming up an extension to our life in Nepal, but there are responsibilities waiting for me back in the States. I snap back to reality and remember my next stop; it's time to retrieve the treasured visa for Devi.

As I leave through the lush garden and walk down the quiet neighborhood lane, I pause to ask Ganesh to help me find my way back here.

Finally, I'm on my way to pick up Devi's visa. As I wait to hear the rupees shuffle and spit out of the ATM for my final payment to the Embassy, I'm struck by a sound wholly out of place on the busy street, ducks quacking. I spin around to see the source and spot the pair of them, bound at the feet, unceremoniously hanging over the handlebars of a motorbike. The sight is hilarious (maybe not so much for the inverted ducks), but one I know I won't see once we return to the other side of the world. I thank the ducks for the comic relief and wish them many happy rebirths.

After so many months of waiting, this last step feels anti-climactic. I simply walk up to the window and state my business. Still, I'm energized, as much by the company that I've kept throughout the day because of this final adoption errand. As the woman behind the window shuffles papers, she can't help but notice my squirming bundle and leans over the counter for a peek, clearly expecting to see a baby. I pull the cloth back to reveal a furry face, and she smiles.

"Do I need a visa for this one?" I joke, feeling giddy that this is my last trip to the Consulate.

On the way home, I stop off at the vet to have Norbu's surgery site checked and redressed. Dr. Devkota reassures me all is well and presents me with a hard-to-come-by crate for her to fly home in. "You are giving her a life she will never have in Nepal." He smiles, and I wish he could come with us, too.

I hurry home for a traditional meal of *dal bhat* and *tsog* with the kids, only to dash back out again for one final errand, to meet a *Thangka* painter whose work I've seen hanging in Summit. I'm hesitant to purchase anything else, conscious of conserving funds to cushion the blow of returning to a First-World economy, but a traditional painting will remind us of where we became a family.

The artist's shop is in the Patan tourist district, a tiny space with a low roof, made darker by the afternoon rain and fading evening light. I'm astounded by the intricate paintings I'd once thought looked cartoonish, now appearing dignified and traditional. There are scenes of city and village life, an array of Buddhas, and other Hindu gods and goddesses. I'm drawn to so many but choose one that depicts scenes at sites throughout Nepal, many of which we've visited—Swayambhu, Boudha, Pokhara—as well as others I long to see—Chitwan, Varanassi, and, over the mountains, Lhasa.

By the time I'm ready to leave the tiny shop, it's getting dark.

"Madam, you should not walk alone," the painter cautions, "I will take you on my motorbike." Up until now, I've declined endless offers of two wheeled transportation, terrified of the chaotic traffic, determined not to chance leaving my children motherless. I'd been haunted by memories of a friend just out of high school who was killed one night on his way home from a party, driving much too fast on his motorcycle. The mere thought of climbing on one of these death machines is a painful reminder, but this is not suburban Virginia, and this demure artist has not been out late playing beer pong. I silence my fear and climb on, respectfully side-saddle.

As we buzz through the still wet streets, the cool wind whirls my hair, and I feel free. Free from the fear of losing my little girl to some bureaucratic nightmare, free from anxiety over political instability, free from emails filled with inquiries about when we would be "home" and what I will do for work once we get there. I'd been holding all these fears for so long, and now, I let the wind release them, watching them dissolve, like the red powder blessings sprinkled on Ganesh, washing away with the rain.

Disappointed when the ride is over and we pull into the alley, I realize how unhappily married to worse case scenarios I've been. Now, we are free to move on and live our lives. I hop off the bike and thank the painter for more than his work of art and the ride home.

Sneaking up the steps is easy without the boisterous greeting of Kali, and I feel our lives here emptying out, like the bedrooms stripped of books and toys. As I tiptoe past the door, I see the kids through the picture window inside the near vacant playroom. Jack is sitting on a blanket on the floor, with Devi parked right beside him, listening intently as he reads, the bandaged puppy sleeping faithfully by her side. He is her big brother, all knowing, powerful, and fearless. And she is his little sister, bratty, bossy, cute, and almost cuddly. I feel how they *really do* love each other. I brought my young son half way around the world to find a little girl, and now we are going home a family.

Once I get first Devi, then Jack, off to bed, I sit down to try to make sense of my magical day. I'm too exhausted to find the words to paint a picture for family and friends, unable to sum it all up in a way that will do my experiences justice. I don't know how to convey my love for this filthy, crowded, don't-drink-the-water, Third World city to my stateside cheerleaders, especially my mother. All they can imagine is how happy I must be to come "home." None of them will understand my desperate longing to stay. Finally, I come up with this:

A Day in the Life

5:00 am:	Wake up for a morning cup of tea on the terrace and marvel at the cotton-candy-pink Himals.
6:30 am:	Write a note to Jack and tiptoe out to take the street puppy to the vet to have her foreleg amputated (irreparably damaged from being kicked by a stupid human).
8:00 am:	Cry in vet office, have a cup of tea.
9:00 am:	Go home with crying puppy.
9:30 am:	Receive a call from the Embassy, Devi's visa has been issued.
9:31 am:	Do a dance of joy.
10:00 am:	Meet Zenji for a tour of his Tibetan carpet factory. Name the puppy Norbu, Tibetan for "precious gem."
10:30 am:	Pick up biscuits (cookies) for weavers' children.
10:35 am:	Tour carpet factory.
11:00 am:	Have one of the most authentic conversations of my life, drink the best cup of tea ever.
1:00 pm:	Meeting with a lovely entrepreneur to discuss future business ventures, drink a cup of tea.
3:30 pm:	Pick up visa from the Embassy. Breathe a sigh of relief.
5:00 pm:	Go back to vet and have puppy's leg cleaned and redressed. Drink a cup of tea.
6:00 pm:	Dinner with the kids, *dhal bhat*, of course!
6:30 pm:	Meet up with Thangka painter.

	Drink a cup of tea.
7:00 pm:	Take my first sidesaddle motor bike ride through Patan.
7:15 pm:	Arrive home intact.
8:00 pm:	Sing Devi to sleep.
8:10 pm:	Rescue tomcat from (now) 3 legged (but still) spunky puppy.
8:30 pm:	Read to Jackie, still my little boy.
9:00 pm:	Watch bad American TV, or maybe Bollywood, drink a cup of tea

I love Nepal.

The next few days fly by in a whirlwind of last-minute errands and shopping trips. Most of the friends we met along the way are gone, back to their respective homes or away on holiday. We are the last ones standing. Too soon, we are settling into our room at Summit and the countdown is officially on. Jack preps Devi on all things America, looking at pictures of our house in the woods, quizzing her on the names of our dogs and cat, pointing to the sky every time we hear an airplane passing overhead, telling her, "You and me and *Ama* are all going on the airplane to America in just a few more days!" This is Devi's cue to exuberantly hop up and down, clapping her hands and squealing, "Mer-ca!" All I can think about is how much I'm going to miss our concrete block home, the parade of street dogs, the fruit-heavy garden, the sanctuary of Summit, and most of all, our Nepali family.

After the men from the shipping company pick up our crate, the landlord stops in and I reluctantly hand over our skeleton keys.

"Thank you so much for such a lovely home. I appreciate you keeping us safe during the troubles," I offer, referring to the time of political turmoil.

"Yes, Madam," he smiles with the customary elusive bobbling of his head, and I hope we haven't been too much trouble.

Good Dog rubs his stinky head on the back of my leg, wishing to be let in for dinner, and I feel a pang of guilt, leaving him as his original owner did before us. "If the dog needs anything, Dr. Devkota will take care of him," I softly suggest.

"Okay, okay," and again his head bobbles. I force myself to believe that this time it means "yes."

Next on my list is a stop by the orphanage to say goodbye to Rajkumar and show off Devi's visa. Walking down the alley I remember the little girl who fell asleep on my shoulder during our ride home on the school bus so many months ago, synchronously named Devi, and I try to imagine a very different life for her. I'm amazed by all the ways I've been guided during our time in Nepal, and give thanks with every crunchy gravel step.

Ducking through the gate at the orphanage, I bow to the guard, *namasté*, and step inside to the sounds of raucous laughter. Before climbing the steps to the office, I peek into the big community room downstairs and see the older girls sitting together, singing and laughing, playing big girl pat-a-cake games and doing each other's hair. My heart softens as I think of them here together. They have lost their homes and families, but now they have each other, and their laughter dances through the air like butterflies.

Upstairs, Rajkumar is planted behind his desk. Once a fearsome force, he has become a dear friend and confidant. I tap on the door, and he looks up from his paperwork.

"Kate! Come in," he welcomes me, calling a *didi* to bring tea.

"Look!" I pull out Devi's US-issued visa, "Everything at the Embassy was fine, no questions asked," I say triumphantly. "Thank you for your patience, I know my circumstances didn't make this easy. I really appreciate you letting Devi stay with us."

"Congratulations!" He smiles, genuinely happy our process has concluded successfully. Then it's time for his surprise for me. "Madam, I know you have wanted to learn more about Devi and how she came to be here, but until you had her visa secure, I could not give you any information. I did not want you to have any troubles like your friends." He then tells me the story of how Devi's father left when she was born, disgusted that her mother dishonored him by giving birth to a daughter. (In Nepal, many men still believe a woman can control the sex of her unborn child). Her mother was destitute, but another man came along who was willing to marry her, but he, too, would not accept a female child, especially not one from another man. Having little choice, her mother took Devi to an auntie, who then brought her to the police station with the story that she was abandoned in her village. It was then that the officer brought her to the orphanage.

"Madam, I must ask you to keep this information to yourself. I would not want it to bring harm to anyone working for the children of Nepal. The only reason I have shared it with you is because you are now my friend, and I can trust you. I know how much you love your little girl."

My head spins trying to take in the story.

"Would you like to meet her mother?" Rajkumar asks thoughtfully.

"Well, of course . . ." I stutter, shocked by the offer as well as Rajkumar's willingness to help me in this very unconventional way. "When?"

"Oh, I do not know, but I will try to find her. When you leave?" Rajkumar continues, strong and steady.

"In just a few days," I sigh, hoping he can find her in time. Now that we've moved out of our flat, even if I could change our tickets, I wasn't sure Summit would have room for us to stay.

"I will try to locate her. Call me and I see what I find."

I'm flooded with questions, but before I can get past the first one—if "Devi" is, in fact, her birth name and Rajkumar attesting that it is—the office fills with *didis* busily tending to one task or another, and I know the information gathering session is over.

I slowly walk down the alley from the orphanage, my mind buzzing with the secrets to Devi's past. I desperately wish for Rajkumar to find her mother, clinging to the hope that she will not be lost from Devi forever. It's ironic that Devi was given up by a woman unable to care for her because she was single, only to be entrusted to another single woman with opportunities for independence unknown to the women of this country. As I stumble across the busy road in a daze, I stop off at the mini *stupa* near our neighborhood to walk mindful circles and send out prayers as I spin the wheels, wishing for Devi's mother to be found.

Our last days are a blur consumed by final errands and time in the swimming pool as I try to make the end of our stay a fun-filled vacation in spite of my anxiety about leaving our Nepali home. Jack is increasingly resistant to our departure, and I find myself trying to convince him it will be wonderful to go back to school and see his friends, but he isn't buying it. Nepal has been an exciting playground filled with adventure, and he doesn't want to give it up any more than I do. A final trip to Boudha helps, but he cries all the way home, insisting he is ready to live in the monastery in spite of my reminders about what Rinpoche instructed.

"Don't worry," I whisper, holding him tight. "We'll be back."

"But when?" he wails.

I don't have an answer for him. It's the answer I'm searching for myself.

Unfortunately, Rajkumar isn't able to find Devi's mother, and while I am initially devastated, I trust there is a reason, and I try to stay positive, allowing the missed opportunity to float away in the summer breeze. I can't imagine meeting her without Devi along, but I am sure that if Devi sees her, she will recognize her, and then I will be the one taking her away and destroying whatever delicate relationship is growing between us. I wonder if maybe it just isn't the right time. I struggle to find peace in not knowing, so I put together a small package for Devi's mother with pictures of the kids, the last of our wildflower seeds, and a pink rose quartz necklace Jack's godmother made for me when I decided to adopt. I tuck everything inside a card, thanking her for trusting me with her beautiful daughter, and hope someone will translate for her. I want her to know how much Devi is loved, not just by me, but by her big brother as well. Dinesh agrees to take the package to Rajkumar in case Devi's mother is ever found.

I planned to take the kids back to Fire and Ice for our final dinner in Kathmandu, but when Dinesh invites us to his house, I can't refuse. He prepares a lovely traditional meal, nothing fancy, but, as always, delicious, and it feels perfect to be with our Nepali family for one last evening. While the kids play in the courtyard late into the summer night, Dinesh, Leena and I sit drinking cup after cup of tea, laughing about all the stray puppies, as well as humans, I'd brought home. We reminisce about Jack's antics setting fires on the roof and Devi's epic tantrums. I'm so thankful for all they have done for us. I can't imagine how I would've have gotten through this time without them and their unwavering kindness and support. It's heartbreaking to say goodbye at the end of the night, and Dinesh insists on walking us to the gates of Summit one last time.

Back in the room, the same room Jack and I stayed in when we first arrived, I hustle both kids into a last chance bath then finish packing while Norbu dashes around, dragging clothes out of open suitcases and nipping at the kids' feet as they jump from bed to bed. Eventually everyone settles down and falls asleep, but I'm so wired, I don't even try and tiptoe out to the gardens. I slip off my sandals to feel the cool grass under my feet as I bathe in the memories. I think back to the day we arrived, when I saw Devi for the first time, meeting Christina, then Nora, then Tessa, then Dave, and how each of them enriched our time here and the quality of our lives. I feel blessed to such a great degree, not just with this child I first saw on a computer screen, but by the culture, the land, and most important, the people. And now the time has come to go "home."

The next morning, I do my best to keep things as low key as possible, hoping to prolong Devi's steady emotional state, knowing the day ahead will be full of overstimulation and triggers. Taking the kids up to the bountiful breakfast buffet to fill their bellies before beginning our journey, I try to choke down an omelet, but

I feel the time ticking, and am nauseated by the thought of actually leaving. Jack's disinterest in going back to the States makes it worse.

"Just one more day?" he begs, unable to grasp the intricacies of scheduling international travel. I flash back to when we first arrived, when those same puppy dog eyes pleaded with me to take him back to our little mountain town.

With our luggage loaded into the Summit van, it's time to go. I check under the beds and in drawers one last time, not daring to think of when we would be back to collect anything we might leave behind.

"Jack, Devi," I call the kids in from the garden, handing Devi her turtle backpack, filled with her most treasured board books and her bear, Babu. Then Jack, no longer my little boy, looking so much bigger in comparison to his pack with the giant pink bunny once again strapped on, takes responsibility for Norbu in her carrier as well. I forlornly glance around the garden one last time, then climb the moss-covered steps to see Dinesh and Leena waiting by the van, smiling bright. "Madam, we could not let you go without saying one last goodbye," Dinesh confesses, kindness spilling from his heart.

"Yes, Madam, we miss you," Leena chirps, holding a hand forward to shake. I reach out to take it, then hug her close, overcome by their kindness, coming to see us off. Dinesh, too, steps forward for a brief embrace, and then they each hug Jack and Devi, telling them, "Be good to Mommy!" We snap a few pictures and climb aboard the van, no longer pausing to look for seatbelts.

As we pull down the Summit drive, I look out the back window to see Dinesh and Leena watching us go and burst into tears. Jack notices them too and hangs out his window, arms waving frantically, tears streaming down his face. Then it's Devi's turn, standing on the seat next to me, blowing kisses out the back window, bangles jingling as her chubby arms fly from lips to sky. As we turn onto our little lane, I say one last thank you to our steadfast neighbor, Ganesh, for keeping us safe and aiding me in overcoming the seemingly endless obstacles. Then, looking to the other side of the lane, I watch our little house on the hill grow small and eventually disappear as we wind around curves and turn onto the main road to cross the bridge toward the airport.

Once our bags are unloaded and entrusted to porters, we accept our fate and pass through security to be greeted by a kind Thai Airways hostess who invites us to pre-board. We settle right in, Devi between Jack and me, tiny Norbu tucked under her seat. As fellow travelers slowly file by, I try to relax with whispers of *Om Mani Peme Hum* trickling from my lips. Jack explains all things airplane to wide-eyed Devi, showing her how to take out her tray table, turn on the overhead light and change the channels on the mini TV screen she is thrilled to find on the seatback in front of her.

Then, hearing the engines fire up, we all hold hands as we taxi along, heading down the runway, faster, faster, faster, and lift off.

As I look down on the vibrant patchwork city below, surrounded by emerald green hills with cotton ball clouds huddling nearby, all I feel is gratitude. Thank you, Kingdom of Nepal, for helping me see the beauty of another world. Thank you for cultivating patience in my mind and heart in the midst of chaos. Thank you for teaching my son compassion. And thank you for my sweet Devi, the most precious gift of all.

Om Mani Peme Hum.

I bow to the God within you.

There are so many who brought this story to life, but without my amazing son, Jack, we never would've found Devi. Jack, you knew your little brother or sister was out there waiting for us to find them; I am so thankful for your guidance and sweet persistence! And to Devi, you are the bravest person I know. Thank you for allowing us into your world and letting us love you, and loving us right back. A heartfelt thank you to Dinesh and Leena; we never would have made it though our time in Nepal without you. Thank you for welcoming us into your family, a kinder and more selfless love, I have never known. To our Nepal crew, all those mentioned, as well as those who were not, our memories are some of my most cherished. I give great thanks for lessons learned from each and every one of you, Namaste. Deep gratitude to Mimi, my grandmother, who never gave up on me, and saw her adopted great granddaughter no differently than her blood. A kind thank you to my mother, who gave not only her blessing and financial support, but also her expert editory eye in helping to straighten up this manuscript and make it publishable.

I wouldn't be where I am without many amazing teachers, notably, my high school creative writing teacher, Michael J. Mariani, who taught me to show my story, rather than tell it. William Shealy, my first religious studies professor at Virginia Wesleyan College, who opened the world of spirituality for me, introducing my American mind to the idea of collective consciousness. Bill Boyer, anthropology professor at James Madison University who leveled the cultural playing field and taught me to think critically, even when it was uncomfortable. And finally, Lama Shenpen Drolma. Thank you for lighting the path.

Many thanks to my first editor, Janel James, who firmly believed this was a story worth telling. She patiently fished through hundreds of journal entries to help me find what glowed, and she gave me the framework to keep moving forward. I was blessed by the late Mary Jean Wiggins, who loved to listen to me read, and motivated me with her sweet, but honest feedback. Much appreciation to Robin Craig, Deborah Long, Dawn Gordon, Dave Larson, Jean Meyers, and Catherine Tweel Katona for reading early drafts and cheering me on. Special kudos to my bubba, Dennis Harris, for reading one incarnation after another and still offering endless, genuine encouragement. Huge thanks to our mountain town for giving us a loving community to come home to. Much appreciation to Kathy Newhouse for helping make our dream of adoption a reality. Sincere thanks to Janean Quigly for being an inspiration and always "getting it" like no one else did. Jennifer Hicks, thank you for helping hold the vision of my little girl in the lotus blossom. Your steadfast love and support mean more than words. Cathy Uno, we wouldn't be the family we are without your wise and compassionate guidance over all of these years. You helped us unravel the past, and offered tools to build our future. I am incredibly thankful to Kim Davis and Madville Publishing for taking a chance on an unknown author. Your patience and support has been gold. A special shout out to Jacqui Davis for her unique ability to see inside my head and create the fabulous cover art I'd dreamt of. The most humble of thanks to the Kingdom of Nepal, for granting me the privledge of raising one of your children, I have never been bestowed a greater gift. And finally, thanks Dad. Thank you for always believing in me, for giving me the space to make my own mistakes, and for never turning your back. Thank you for giving me the mental strength to persevere, for instilling a moral compass and passion to use my gifts for the benefit of others, and finally, for teaching me there is a world beyond our backyard. Thank you for your soft heart, biting wit, and unconditional love. You are greatly missed.

www.ingramcontent.com/pod-product-compliance
Lightning Source LLC
Chambersburg PA
CBHW030101170426
43198CB00009B/451